FOREWORD

TO THE HAYWOOD TRIAL CENTENNIAL EDITION

David Grover was my debate coach when I was a senior at Boise High School in 1954-55. That was the same year I first became aware of the Haywood trial. In 1965, I first read Debaters and Dynamiters and found it well written and compelling. Over the years since then, I have returned to its pages to enhance my understanding of the trial, its precedents, and the personalities who made it the "Trial of the Century." Now, I have the privilege of introducing a new edition published jointly by the Idaho Legal History Society and Caxton Press in preparation for the centennial anniversary of the trial.

For those of you into whose hands this book comes for the first time, read it carefully. It will serve you well in grasping the significance of the rich story it tells. In my view, it is the best description we have of the Haywood trial.

Byron J. Johnson
Retired Justice of the
Idaho Supreme Court
May, 2006

Debaters and Dynamiters

Debaters
and

Dynamiters

The Story of the HAYWOOD TRIAL

by David H. Grover

Caxton Press
Caldwell, Idaho
2006
Published in cooperation with the
Idaho Legal History Society

Originally published as part of the Oregon State University
Press Studies in History series,

ISBN-10: 0-87004-394-3
ISBN-13: 978-0-87004-394-9

Lithographed and bound in the United States of America by
CAXTON PRESS
Caldwell, Idaho
173748

CONTENTS

ILLUSTRATIONS

1

AN INTRODUCTION to the HAYWOOD TRIAL

IN THE SUMMER of 1907 the eyes of the world focused briefly on Boise, the tiny capital city of Idaho, where a man was on trial for his life. The charge was murder. It was not an ordinary run-of-the-mill slaying nor even a particularly bizarre or atrocious crime of passion that attracted such worldwide attention to this trial. Instead, it was a cold and deliberate killing that had deep and complex social and economic roots. It was, as many murders are, a crime of great human interest, but it was also, as few murders are, a crime of considerable consequence to society.

The defendant was William D. Haywood, secretary-treasurer of a large American labor union, the Western Federation of Miners. Haywood was charged with conspiring to assassinate ex-Governor Frank Steunenberg of Idaho, who had been killed in a bomb explosion at his home in Caldwell on December 30, 1905. Charged with Haywood were two other men, Charles H. Moyer, president of the Western Federation of Miners, and George Pettibone, one-time member of the union and now an adviser to its officers. A fourth defendant, Jack Simpkins, a member of the union's executive committee, was also under indictment for the crime but could not be found. The defendants had elected to be tried separately, with Haywood's trial occurring first.

Political assassinations have been rare enough in 20th-century America to be newsworthy in themselves. But the circumstances of this case were particularly interesting. Governor Steunenberg had held office during a time of violent labor troubles in the Coeur d'Alene mining district of North Idaho. He had declared the area in a state of insurrection and asked for federal troops to suppress the riots. After a lengthy military occupation, quiet returned to the Coeur d'Alenes, and the union responsible for the trouble, the Western Federation of Miners, lost not only the strike but its influence within the state as well.

To those people searching for a reason why anyone would want to kill the likable Frank Steunenberg, the events of 1899 provided an answer. An entirely plausible explanation of Steunenberg's death could be built around his role in the Coeur d'Alene troubles. The enmity incurred at that time might well have resulted in retaliation six years later and three hundred miles away. To many people his death looked like the work of the Western Federation of Miners.

Shortly after Steunenberg's death, a Federation miner named Harry Orchard had been arrested in Caldwell for the actual bombing of the governor, and had been taken to the penitentiary in Boise for safe-keeping. During the next few weeks Orchard was visited regularly by James McParland, a master detective of the Pinkerton Agency. Late in January, 1906, Orchard confessed to McParland that he had killed Steunenberg, and had also committed a number of crimes of violence during the Colorado "labor war" of 1903-04. According to this confession, all of these crimes, including the Steunenberg murder, were committed with the blessing of the top officials of the Western Federation of Miners for whom Orchard operated as a paid professional dynamiter.

The fact that a labor union and its leaders had been involved in a criminal plot was further reason for public interest in the trial. The position of the American labor movement was none too secure in 1907. Millions of people were ready to prejudge the labor leaders guilty; other millions were equally ready to acquit them without a trial. The Socialists screamed loudly that Haywood, a laboring man, had no chance in the capitalistic courts of this country.

The circumstances surrounding the arrest of Haywood, Moyer, and Pettibone gave ammunition to the Socialists and labor critics of the trial. Since the three men were in Denver at the time of Steunenberg's death and had not fled from Idaho, they could not be extradited as fugitives from Idaho. In a quasi-legal move that looked more like kidnapping than extradition to many people, Idaho sent men to Denver to make hurried arrests of the union leaders, bundled them aboard a special train, and rushed them back to Idaho—on a Saturday and Sunday when the normal legal channels for habeas corpus were closed. When various state and federal court appeals subsequently upheld Idaho's methods, it seemed to many observers that the scales of justice were out of balance in the Haywood case.

Another unusual series of events had occurred during this pre-trial period. President Theodore Roosevelt in a letter to a friend had referred to Haywood as an "undesirable citizen." The Socialist press asserted that this comment was prejudical to a fair trial. Demonstrations were organized in various American cities with parade marchers wearing buttons reading, "I am an undesirable citizen." Eugene Debs was particularly active in this campaign, giving hundreds of speeches from coast to coast and writing vitriolic criticism in the *Appeal to Reason,* the widely read Socialist journal published in Girard, Kansas. In one unusually bitter attack entitled "Arouse, Ye Slaves" Debs even threatened armed revolution if Haywood were convicted.

The principal attorneys of the trial were colorful men who added interest and prestige to their respective sides. The prosecution was headed nominally by the Canyon County prosecutor, Owen M. Van Duyn. But the real head of the prosecution forces was the state's special prosecutor, James H. Hawley. Hawley was the prototype of the "Sagebrush Lawyer," a frontier circuit-riding advocate who had participated in hundreds of criminal cases throughout the state of Idaho, a man destined to be governor in a few short years. Another special prosecutor was William E. Borah, newly elected to the United States Senate, the man who had delivered the eulogy at the funeral of Frank Steunenberg. The other member of the prosecution staff was W. A. Stone who represented the Steunenberg family.

The legal talent for the defense was equally impressive. Heading the defense was the regular Western Federation attorney, Edmund F. Richardson of Denver, a veteran of the legal battles of the Colorado labor wars and a particularly devastating cross-examiner. The other key man of the defense was Clarence Darrow of Chicago; he had defended Eugene Debs in the Pullman strike case and had campaigned for amnesty in the Haymarket bombing affair, but he was not yet a national celebrity. The lesser lights of the defense staff included John Nugent of Boise, Edgar Wilson of Boise, Fred Miller of Spokane, Leon Whitsell of Wallace, and Peter Breen of Butte. Wilson was an ex-Congressman and a former law partner of the judge who was trying the Haywood case. Nugent a few years later was elected United States Senator from Idaho. Together, the two legal staffs produced three members of Congress and one governor.

The case was tried in Boise in Ada County on a change of venue from Caldwell in Canyon County. The trial judge, Fremont Wood, a highly regarded jurist, found himself in a rather embarrassing position when his former law partner joined the defense staff, but he refused to disqualify himself. In the end it was Fremont Wood who, more than any other personality of the trial, suffered the ironies of fate that lie in such a complex situation.

The jury for the Haywood trial was made up largely of farmers who had little interest in labor-management relations or in mining. Initially the defense attorneys were openly critical of this jury, but later they were to be quite happy with their verdict. The trial lasted over ten weeks, and cost the state of Idaho some $95,000.

Boise for the moment became the news capital of the world. Fifty correspondents of newspapers, wire services, and "muckraking" magazines gathered for the trial, and 50,000 words a day went through the local telegraph office describing the trial for readers everywhere. To those newspapermen who expected the trial to be conducted with all the violence and bitterness of the events leading up to it, Boise must have been a disappointment. It was a calm and orderly community, and it conducted an orderly and eminently fair trial.

Because it was a fair trial the prosecution had a difficult job connecting Haywood with the murder of Steunenberg. In Idaho the testimony of an accomplice—in this case, Orchard—is not sufficient for conviction. Other independent evidence which tends to connect the defendant to the crime without the testimony of the accomplice is needed for conviction. The prosecution wove a net of circumstances around Haywood, but without Harry Orchard's testimony it had some thin spots. What might have been the clinching prosecution evidence was a confession by Steve Adams, another Federation miner who had admitted participating in many of Harry Orchard's acts of violence for the "Inner Circle" of the union. But the defense reached Steve Adams and persuaded him to repudiate his confession. The hopes of the prosecution faded.

Haywood was acquitted. All sorts of reasons have been offered in explanation of the jury's decision. It would seem that the American legal concepts of *presumption of innocence, burden of proof, reasonable doubt,* and *unanimity of jury vote* made the task of prosecutor in this case too Herculean for even Hawley and Borah.

The verdict was a surprise to both sides. The prosecution, trying hard for a murder conviction, had successfully identified Haywood and the Western Federation of Miners with violence before a jury that was inclined toward law and order. But the jury decided that connecting a man with a series of violent acts and hanging that man for murder were two different things. The defense had tried to make Haywood look like a badly outnumbered fighter in the class struggle, a struggle that at times had admittedly become violent because the capitalistic class had denied the normal political and judical channels of social change to the laboring class. But here was Haywood, freed by the very judge, jury, and state which the Socialists had been so loudly denouncing.

What did the trial mean? Was it really an episode in the class struggle, or was it purely a case of murder? What effect did it have on the American scene? Unfortunately, most of the people who have attempted to answer these questions have had a special bias which has made them blind to even the facts of the case, much less to the conclusions to be drawn from them. In book after book, writers have so completely idealized an individual or a point of view that the interested reader or student can hardly get a balanced account of the trial. This imbalance is particularly noticeable in the books which deal with Clarence Darrow and the radical point of view.

The trial has been variously described as "one of the most famous cases in labor history,"[1] "the most significant incident between the have-nots and the haves in the first decade of the twentieth century,"[2] "the greatest legal battle in American history,"[3] and "one of the most interesting and dramatic chapters in the annals of the labor movement."[4] And yet, at this writing, no author has examined the transcript of the trial to determine what actually took place. Hence, ample justification exists for singling out this particular trial for an examination of forensic persuasion in America.

This book seeks to establish the significance of the Haywood trial. It seeks to analyze the communication between lawyer and jury and between the courtroom and the general public during the trial. It attempts to find out how the jury made its decision, and what effect that decision has had on American society.

The basic source material for this book is the transcript of the trial, a 5,722-page document now a part of the Hawley collection of the Idaho Historical Society in Boise. Contemporary newspaper and magazine accounts of the trial are also utilized extensively. Some use is made of the Pinkerton Detective Agency files in the Hawley and Borah collections of the Historical Society, as well as correspondence in the same collections. A few eyewitnesses to the trial remain, and their observations are included wherever pertinent.

---

[1] Nathan Fine, *Labor and Farmer Parties in the United States 1828-1928* (New York: Rand School of Social Science, 1928), p. 276.

[2] Louis Adamic, *Dynamite* (New York: The Viking Press, 1931), p. 143.

[3] Eugene Debs, quoted in Ray Ginger, *The Bending Cross* (New Brunswick: Rutgers University Press, 1949), p. 254.

[4] Paul F. Brissenden, *The I. W. W. A Study of American Syndicalism* (New York: Columbia University, 1920), p. 170.

In establishing the facts of the case the most impartial accounts available are used, but at some points it is necessary to depend upon sources not universally held in high regard. A good example is the testimony of Harry Orchard that connects many of the events between 1899 and the time of the trial. How should such accounts be regarded? Some authors, e. g., Stewart Holbrook in *Rocky Mountain Revolution,*[5] depend heavily on Orchard's version. Others, particularly Irving Stone in *Clarence Darrow for the Defense,*[6] give it no credence at all. Considering the opinion expressed by Judge Wood in 1908 (see p. 280), the statement of Hugo Munsterberg, the Harvard psychologist who examined Orchard in 1907 (see p. 281), the opinions expressed by the newsmen who heard Orchard testifying in the three trials of 1907-08, plus Orchard's subsequent 47-year imprisonment without changing his story—a strong case can be made for the veracity of Harry Orchard. Nevertheless, Orchard's testimony is not used exclusively in establishing historical facts in this study, except when no other account exists, e. g., in establishing that Orchard lit the fuse under the Bunker Hill and Sullivan Company concentrator.

The historical background of the trial may seem overly detailed in the pages that follow. This documentation is included for one reason only—to enable the reader to understand how the great protagonists in this drama, the Western Federation of Miners and the mine operators of the West, could feel as they did toward each other in 1907. Unquestionably, Harry Orchard's acts in 1904 and 1905 were motivated by a legacy of union lawlessness that had its origin in the "Troubles of 1892." By the same token, corporate and governmental hostility toward the Western Federation became more intense and violent with each new crisis in Idaho and Colorado. With few exceptions, all the principals and witnesses in the Haywood trial had been through one or more of these struggles. Thus, there are ideas, attitudes, devices, places, and people that seem to recur in the telling of this story, an indication of the deep and complex roots of the Haywood affair.

---

[5] Stewart Holbrook, *The Rocky Mountain Revolution* (New York: Henry Holt & Co., 1956).

[6] Irving Stone, *Clarence Darrow for the Defense* (Garden City, N. Y.: Doubleday & Company, Inc., 1941).

PART ONE

*The violent industrial struggle in the mining regions of the West during the quarter century after 1890 show a picture of class war as conceived by Marx. Yet this development, apparently confirming Marx's analysis of the basic antagonisms in capitalism, came, surprisingly enough, not in the citadel of American industrial and financial capitalism but on the Western frontier. In reality it was a class war without a class war ideology. . . . . The extremes of violence in these labor struggles proceeded from no theory of revolution but from the general characteristics of the frontier.**

* Selig Perlman and Philip Taft, *History of Labor in the United States*, Vol. IV (New York: The Macmillan Co., 1935), p. 169.

2

THE COEUR D'ALENE "TROUBLES of 1892"

TO EVALUATE THE HAYWOOD TRIAL of 1907 without some knowledge of the long chain of events which preceded it would be unwise. Particularly, it is necessary to know something of the colorful history of the Western Federation of Miners, the organization which was tacitly on trial in the Boise courtroom along with Bill Haywood. During its early days this union earned a reputation as the "most militant union of the United States"[1] and "the most notorious, the most revolutionary labor organization in the country."[2] To appreciate this reputation and to understand the personalities and issues of the Haywood trial, one must look backward from 1907 some fifteen years.

The Western Federation of Miners came into being as a result of the "Troubles of 1892" in the Coeur d'Alene country of North Idaho. At that time a series of events and circumstances combined to unleash the bitterness and frustration of a mining camp that had passed the first bloom of universal prosperity and had settled down to hard economic realities.

---

[1] Selig Perlman and Philip Taft, *History of Labor in the United States*, Vol. IV. (New York: The Macmillan Co., 1935), p. 172.

[2] Louis Adamic, *Dynamite* (New York: The Viking Press, 1931), p. 143.

The 1880's in the Coeur d'Alenes, as elsewhere in the West, marked the end of the era of the independent prospector and the small miner. Corporation mining now appeared on the scene, ready to supply the larger amounts of capital needed for efficient large-scale operations, and ready also to hire large numbers of wage-earning miners. Social classes were developing in mining communities which had been the epitome of classlessness just a few years earlier. The economic issues were drawn clearly for the Coeur d'Alene miners in 1887 when the mineowners reduced the pay of underground muckers from the prevailing Butte wage scale of $3.50 to $3.00 a day. As a result, the miners turned to unionization as a means of solving their problems.

The first hard-rock miners' union had been formed at Virginia City, Nevada, in 1867, and local unions had existed in the Coeur d'Alenes in the 1880's. But these unions had only limited strength, and were sometimes no more than fraternal organizations. In 1891 a number of the local Coeur d'Alene unions banded together to form the Coeur d'Alene Executive Miners Union, a federation of small locals. This union was fairly effective, its chief accomplishment being the construction of a $30,000 union hospital in Wardner. Prior to this time the mining companies had been deducting one dollar a month from each miner's pay for medical care. This money was now channeled to the miners' hospital instead of to company physicians who were sometimes inclined to be hasty or disinterested. The lone exception to this policy was the Bunker Hill and Sullivan Company which continued to employ its own doctors. This independent attitude of the Bunker Hill and Sullivan management was to prevail throughout the turbulent decade ahead.

In the winter of 1890-91 the miners witnessed a technological change which added to their insecurity under the capitalistic wage system. Compressed air drills were introduced in the mines; this new equipment enabled one miner to do the drilling formerly done by several. The displaced miners were forced to join the ranks of the less skilled muckers who were paid fifty cents a day less for their labor than were the drillmen. This loss of pay intensified the demand for the return to the uniform Butte wage scale of $3.50 a day which had existed prior to 1887. After a short strike the wage demand was met by the employers.

The year 1891 marked the turning point in the economic struggle between the miners and the mineowners. William T. Stoll, a pioneer mining lawyer of the Coeur d'Alenes, said later:

> Prior to 1891 all mines had worked to capacity; prior to 1891 all mines had paid good dividends, powder-and-drill men drawing three dollars and fifty cents a day for their labor, and muckers fifty cents less. Everyone was satisfied, everyone was happy; there were no unions, there was no need for unions—a matter, doubtless, entirely of opinion.[3]

It was, indeed, a matter of opinion. Stoll was the secretary of the Mine Owners' Association and had a managerial point of view. He maintained that unionization ultimately came about through outside "agitators" from Butte. A similar view was expressed by one of the original organizers of the mineowners' group, John Hays Hammond. Hammond asserted that his own Bunker Hill and Sullivan miners were not discontented in 1891; he further implied that the Butte mine operators steered the agitators into the Coeur d'Alenes in order to reduce their own labor problems.[4]

The formation of the Mine Owners' Association in 1891 was the beginning of a series of events that challenged the aroused miners. John Hays Hammond and Fred Bradley figured prominently in the organization of this protective association whose first move was to seek the services of a Pinkerton detective. James McParland, head of the Western division of the Pinkerton Agency, later to play a key role in the 1907 cases against the Western Federation of Miners, recommended the services of an ex-cowboy named Charles A. Siringo.

The story of Siringo is one of the most fantastic tales of the West. He immediately went to the Coeur d'Alenes as a Pinkerton agent in the employ of the Mine Owners' Association. Under the assumed name of Allison he became a miner and eventually an official of the Gem miners' union. The story of how he escaped

---

[3] William T. Stoll, as told to H. W. Whicker, *Silver Strike* (Boston: Little, Brown, and Co., 1932), p. 179.

[4] John Hays Hammond, *Autobiography* (New York: Farrar & Rinehart, Inc., 1935), p. 189.

detection in a community of pro-miner sympathies forms an almost incredible narrative. The story is told, obviously with great admiration, in the autobiographies of William T. Stoll and John Hays Hammond.[5] Siringo, himself, wrote two books describing the events of 1892,[6] in addition to compiling a scrapbook of his exploits which was later widely used by newsmen at the Haywood trial in writing background stories on the Coeur d'Alene troubles.

The laboring men of the Coeur d'Alenes came eventually to hate Siringo, the Pinkerton spy whom Haywood once described as a "swarthy weasel-faced stool pigeon,"[7] but the detective continued to live among them for several days after his identity was finally revealed, a tribute to his raw nerve and the miners' fear of his ability as a gunman.

On the first day of 1892 the mineowners closed their mines; the miners were told that higher freight rates announced by the railroads made operation of the mines unprofitable. On April 1, 1892, the mines were reopened after the owners had successfully negotiated lower freight rates. However, the owners maintained that low silver and lead prices would prevent them from returning to the previous uniform wage scale. They proposed the differential rates of $3.50 and $3.00 which had prevailed from 1887 until 1891. After enduring a long winter without pay the union miners were in no mood to see their previous wage gains taken away. They rejected the owners' original offer, together with a compromise differential rate of $3.50-$3.25, and went on strike.

The owners were equally adamant. Within a month they had recruited strikebreakers and had begun to bring them into the district. But the unions were able to impede this importation, if not through official channels, at least through unofficial ones. For

---

[5] Stoll, *op. cit.*, p. 182 ff.; Hammond, *op. cit.*, p. 190 ff.

[6] Charles A. Siringo, *A Cowboy Detective* (New York: J. S. Ogilvie Publishing Company, 1912); Charles A. Siringo, *Riata and Spurs* (Boston: Houghton Mifflin Co., 1927). Only the first edition of *Riata and Spurs* contains Siringo's Coeur d'Alene adventures; later editions have accounts of western bad men instead. Pressure from the Pinkerton Agency is responsible for the change.

[7] William D. Haywood, *Bill Haywood's Book* (New York: International Publishers, 1929), p. 62.

example, local pro-miner railroad men shunted off a special train arriving with strikebreakers; the "scabs" found themselves the next day in Pendleton, Oregon, some 200 miles away. Union miners also boarded incoming passenger trains in the Coeur d'Alenes to insure that no strikebreakers got off.

The mine managers countered by seeking and getting an injunction which ordered the miners to stop interfering with the procurement of nonunion employees for the mines. This injunction increased tensions. The miners were in control of the communities through which it was necessary to bring the newly arriving strikebreakers. Since many of the mining towns were one-street affairs in the bottom of steep canyons, there was no way to detour around crowds of hostile union miners. The situation was explosive.

On June 4 Governor N. B. Willey issued a proclamation calling on the miners to disperse. But this ultimatum was no more effective in heading off the impending trouble than was the previous injunction. The two opposing forces began to prepare for the battle they knew was coming. The mineowners and their nonunion men were badly outnumbered. In addition, the unions controlled the local civil government (e.g., George Pettibone, one of the defendants in the 1907 trial, was a justice of the peace at Gem). But the mineowners had one advantage: their spy in the enemy camp, Siringo. Through him they were aware of the moves of the union, including the approaching violence at Gem, July 11, 1892, which Siringo later asserted was premeditated.[8]

Even though the inflammatory news of the Homestead riots in the East had reached the miners, tensions were actually easing somewhat in the Coeur d'Alenes when another incident touched off a new and stronger union reaction. On July 10 a union miner and a strikebreaker, after some preliminary name calling, had a fist fight on the streets of Gem. A rumor spread around the mining towns that "scabs" had killed two union men. This rumor triggered the events of the following day, July 11, a day that was to be commemorated for many years to come in the Coeur d'Alenes.

---

[8] Siringo, *A Cowboy Detective,* p. 144.

There are a number of conflicting accounts of the fighting on July 11, 1892, but most accounts agree on the following sequence of key events: a union miner was fired upon, an ineffective rifle battle took place at the Frisco mill, an abortive attempt was made by the miners to dynamite this mill, the mill was then successfully dynamited with explosives which came sliding down a flume, and a deadly rifle battle developed at Gem. Before the day was over several men were killed and a number wounded, including George Pettibone who had devised the flume dynamiting technique.[9]

The Gem mill had been an armed fortress against the union during this battle. After a daring escape from his quarters in Gem, Siringo took refuge in the mill until it was forced to capitulate. He then headed for the hills above the town where he remained until troops entered the area several days later.

At this point, with the unions in control of the area and a large group of nonunion miners in the hands of the rioters, the union's victory seemed complete. But it was only a matter of time until the state and federal governments reacted to the events. On July 12 Governor Willey asked President Benjamin Harrison for federal troops to suppress the uprising, and on July 13 the governor declared martial law in the area. Federal troops were dispatched immediately from Ft. Sherman on Lake Coeur d'Alene.

Meanwhile, the victorious union miners ordered the nonunion men of the Bunker Hill and Sullivan mine to leave the area, and threatened to blow up the mine's concentrator if the men did not do so. On July 12 the Bunker Hill management complied and ordered its nonunion men to get out of town. At the same time, the Bunker Hill management sought to delay the arrival of the troops for fear that the union miners would harm any hostages still in their possession when the soldiers arrived.

These nonunion men of the Bunker Hill mine were then deported by railroad to the Old Mission on the Coeur d'Alene

---

[9] *Portland Oregonian,* July 12, 1892, p. 1; Vernon H. Jensen, *Heritage of Conflict* (Ithaca: Cornell University Press, 1950), p. 33 ff.; Holbrook, *op. cit.,* p. 38 ff.; C. P. Connolly, "Moyer-Haywood Case," *Collier's,* May 11, 1907, p. 13.

River. On the evening of July 12, an armed party, presumably of rioters, attacked these men as they were waiting for the steamer to pick them up. A number of men were driven into the river, shot, and robbed.

On July 14, 1892, federal troops and the minuscule state militia entered the mining communities. The delay in the arrival of the troops permitted many of the miners to flee across the state line into Montana. Nevertheless, many men remained in the mining camps, and the troops arrested almost every union miner they found. Since local jails were inadequate for the hundreds of arrested miners, stockades or "bull pens" were set up to accommodate the prisoners. Conditions in these enclosures were primitive at best.

Martial law and the military occupation of the Coeur d'Alenes lasted until November 18, 1892. During the early part of this period indictments were issued by the hundreds against the miners, but eventually as quiet returned to the area most of the indictments were quashed and the men were released. Originally, the miners had to sign a parole disavowing union participation as a condition of release, but this provision was relaxed as tensions eased. The mines soon resumed operation, and newly released union miners were gradually re-employed.

The few miners remaining in custody were charged with contempt in violating the court injunction, or with criminal conspiracy, a federal charge. James H. Hawley and Pat Reddy represented the miners in these cases, with Fremont Wood, U. S. Attorney for Idaho, serving as the prosecutor of the federal cases. In both the state and federal cases Charles Siringo was a key witness.

Pettibone was convicted on a criminal charge, and was sentenced to serve two years at a federal correctional institution in Detroit where he eventually served several months before being freed by a U. S. Supreme Court decision which ruled the indictment defective. Edward Boyce, later to be president of the Western Federation of Miners, was one of thirteen defendants found guilty of contempt and sentenced to several months in the Ada County jail in Boise.

This Ada County jail was perhaps the true birthplace of the Western Federation of Miners. Ed Boyce told Bill Haywood later that the Western Federation was conceived in this jail by the thirteen prisoners, and that Jim Hawley, attorney for the imprisoned men, had suggested that all the miners of the West should come together in one organization.[10] This is somewhat ironic, for fifteen years later Hawley was to lead the prosecution against the Western Federation of Miners in the Haywood case. Clarence Darrow, in the Haywood trial, called Hawley the "god-father of the Western Federation."

The Western Federation idea which was but a seed in Boise in 1892 blossomed in the spring of 1893. During the previous year the miners' unions of Montana had formed the Montana Miners State Association. They had scheduled a convention in Butte on May 15, 1893. As a result of their reflections in the Ada County jail, some of the displaced Coeur d'Alene miners sent out a call for a simultaneous convention in Butte of delegates from all of the western mining camps.

About fifty delegates answered the call, and the Western Federation of Miners came into being. The union which was set up in Butte in 1893 was remarkably conservative and economically oriented, considering the bitter treatment which many of the men had recently experienced. Essentially it was a craft union of underground miners and muckers. A number of its goals, as stated in the preamble to its constitution, were the goals of the Coeur d'Alene struggle: pay commensurate with job dangers, freedom from the company stores, no Pinkerton men, repeal of conspiracy laws against unions, preferential employment of union men. It was a mild, not a radical program. The goals were to be secured through "education, organization and legislation."[11]

Various writers have been certain of the events of the "Troubles of 1892" as more significant than others in the formation of the union. French observed two basic causes: the reduction of wages, and the company store and boardinghouse policy.[12]

---

[10] Haywood, *op. cit.*, p. 63.

[11] Jensen, *op. cit.*, p. 55.

[12] George E. French, "The Coeur d'Alene Riots, 1892," *Overland Monthly*, July, 1895, p. 32.

Connolly, in his excellent series of articles in *Collier's,* saw the hospital question as the basic issue which gave rise to many other disputes,[13] and support for this position can be found in Smith's description of the Bunker Hill and Sullivan Company attitude of belligerency toward the hospital.[14] Smith says that the real issue in June of 1892 was the existence of the union as a bargaining agent for the miners, and not the wage differential.[15] Jensen suggests that the miners united regionally because they had been ineffective locally, and because they felt a growing sense of insecurity as mining became more capitalistic.[16] Thus, economic security was the overall *raison d'etre* for the new union, whether concerned with medical facilities, wages, mechanization, or the right to organize and bargain collectively.

There may have been important quasi-economic issues, also, which were responsible for the events of 1892 and ultimately for the Western Federation of Miners. Certainly the Pinkerton men were hated by union men in general, and Siringo by the Coeur d'Alene miners in particular. It is possible that the unions might have been less violent if the labor spy had not been used against them. Smith reports a conversation years later with Fremont Wood, the federal prosecutor during the Coeur d'Alene troubles, in which Wood attributed the uprising of July 11, 1892, to the disclosure of Siringo's identity on July 9.[17]

In spite of their attempt to bargain on purely an economic basis, the miners may have been caught up in the rising tide of the class struggle. Even in their new Western Federation of Miners in 1893 they were still trying to be a craft union and to act accordingly. But they had been exposed to enough absentee corporate mine ownership to realize that some of the slogans of the Socialists were true—that management could be a cold, impersonal exploiter of human labor. When John Hays Hammond left the Coeur d'Alenes following the denouement of his Bunker Hill and Sullivan policies, and went off to Africa in pursuit of a new fortune in

---

13 Connolly, *op. cit.,* p. 13.

14 Robert Wayne Smith, *The Coeur d'Alene Mining War of 1892* (Corvallis, Oregon: Oregon State University Press, 1961), pp. 25-27.

15 Smith, *ibid.,* p. 56.

16 Jensen, *op. cit.,* p. 54.

17 Smith, *op. cit.,* p. 63.

gold and diamonds, the Coeur d'Alene miners must have sensed his greater social distance from them, as well as the geographical distance. Their respect for his kind of capitalism could not have increased when they read later how he became involved in the plot to overthrow the Boer government of the Transvaal in the Jameson raid on Johannesburg in 1895. When Hammond was fined $125,000 for his part in the raid, some of his old employees in Idaho must have calculated how many hospitals that money would build, or how many years it would take to use up that much money by paying several hundred underground laborers $3.50 a day instead of $3.00.

It is difficult to know how the men who formed the Western Federation of Miners in 1893 felt about the future of their union. The new union seemingly espoused an economic program similar to that of the American Federation of Labor with which it was to affiliate briefly in 1896. But the methods of 1892, political domination, intimidation, and force, continued to be used by the local unions in the Coeur d'Alenes during the next seven years, a period which was later to be described by a congressional committee as "the most flagrant lawlessness that stains the pages of American history."[18]

The lawlessness of 1892 resumed after the withdrawal of troops from the Coeur d'Alenes, and is clearly a matter of record, in spite of union assertions that quiet returned to the district. Bu what is not so clear is the feeling of the men who belonged to the unions and worked in the mines during this period. Were they really the anarchists and terrorists they have sometimes been described to be? Unfortunately, completely impartial answers are not available, for those people who have undertaken to describe life in this area during these times have generally sided with either the mineowners or with the miners. But we do have the opinions of some observers who *tried* to see both sides of the controversy.

Charley Siringo, the Pinkerton detective, had been reluctant to accept his assignment as a labor spy because he was sympathetic

---

[18] House Report 1999, "Coeur d'Alene Labor Troubles," 56th Congress, 1st Session, p. 25.

with the labor movement in general. But afterwards he reflected, "My mind had taken a regular 'flop' on the labor union question, since telling Superintendent [McParland] that my sympathies were with the unions. I had found the leaders of the Coeur d'Alene unions to be, as a rule, a vicious, heartless gang of anarchists. Many of them had been rocked in the cradle of anarchy at Butte City, Montana, while others were escaped outlaws and toughs from other States."[19]

Smith scoffs at this assertion of Siringo's. But Smith in quoting it, omits Siringo's first sentence in his citation,[20] thus taking the statement out of its qualifying context. Further proof of Siringo's middle-of-the-road position is contained in one of his lesser known books with the interesting title *Two Evil Isms: Pinkertonism and Anarchism*[21] in which he deplored the extremes to which both labor and capital had gone in fighting each other.

Siringo spoke only of union leaders. John A. Finch, a mine-owner and secretary of the Mine Owners' Association which had hired Siringo, spoke of the rank and file of the mine unions in testifying before the U. S. Industrial Commission investigating labor relations in the mining industries. He said,

> I verily believe the majority of the men belonging to the unions of the Coeur d'Alenes were good men. Many are men of more than ordinary education and intelligence and as good men as you can find among that class of people anywhere, but they were thoroughly in dread and fear of the union itself. They never tried to criticize even moderately any of its acts or orders.[22]

A similar conclusion was drawn independently by the congressional committee which visited the Coeur d'Alenes shortly after the Industrial Commission had been there. The concept of an "inner circle" of union officers, striking terror into the hearts of enemies and reluctant friends, seems to have been recorded early in the history of the union in Idaho.

---

[19] Siringo, *A Cowboy Detective,* p. 140.

[20] Smith, *op. cit.,* p. 63.

[21] Charles A. Siringo, *Two Evil Isms: Pinkertonism and Anarchism* (Chicago: Charles A. Siringo, Publisher, 1916).

[22] *Report of the Industrial Commission,* (Washington: Government Printing Office, 1901), p. 493.

In all fairness to the miners' union it should be noted that large numbers of Idaho citizens sympathized with their struggles in the Coeur d'Alenes. In the fall of 1892 a coalition of Democrats and Populists won control of the legislature. One of their first acts was to cut off all appropriations to the state militia, rendering it, for all practical purposes, completely impotent. Subsequently, it was necessary to appropriate some money for the National Guard, but the organization remained weak and unorganized through the rest of the 1890's. During this time some of its guns stored in a hotel in Mullan were stolen by a group of masked men, presumably union miners.

The law-and-order element (this expression, denoting townspeople not in sympathy with the Western Federation of Miners, was used widely by Bill Haywood) urged Congress to establish army posts closer to the mining district than Ft. Sherman at Coeur d'Alene City. Not only did the army ignore the requests, but at the time of the 1899 troubles the War Department was in the process of closing Ft. Sherman. The absence of military power in Idaho led to criticism of the state by prominent people outside its borders, and the wisdom of adding unstable "frontier" states to the United States was questioned.

Citizens of other states had watched with interest the events in Idaho. Perhaps some measure of state pride was involved a few years later when the state of Colorado had its first encounter with the Western Federation of Miners. On this occasion, described in the next chapter, the Colorado National Guard needed no outside help from federal troops to keep the peace. The prestige of the Colorado militia was tarnished, however, by the fact that the whole affair seemed a little like a comic opera.

3

THE CRIPPLE CREEK STRIKE *of 1894*

IN 1894 THE WESTERN FEDERATION OF MINERS won its first important victory in its struggle with the mineowners. But the price of victory was more violence and bitterness, this time in a new geographical setting far from the stormy Coeur d'Alenes, the Cripple Creek area of Colorado.

Gold had been discovered in the Cripple Creek district in 1891 and the area soon developed into a thriving mining camp. But in 1893 financial panic hit the United States; the freewheeling silver purchase program of the federal government under the Sherman Act was largely responsible for the crisis. The price of silver fell sharply, and many silver mines in Colorado and Idaho were shut down. Hundreds of unemployed miners drifted into Cripple Creek to seek work or to prospect. In 1894 several hundred of these men left the district to join Coxey's Army, rather than to chance the uncertainties of the mining situation.

At the same time Colorado was experiencing a rather unsettled political situation. The Populists, with the backing of Silver Democrats, had elected Davis H. Waite as governor. Governor Waite had a turbulent administration characterized by a nickname that has stuck to him—"Bloody Bridles." He acquired it as a result of a remark made in defense of his Populist program, "It is infinitely better that blood should flow to our horses' bridles rather than our liberty should be destroyed."

By the beginning of 1894 wages were uniformly established in the Cripple Creek district at $3.00 a day. The working shifts varied from eight to nine hours, but one prominent mine had gone back to a ten-hour day for the same $3.00 wage. The new Western Federation locals in the district decided to make a stand, even though their bargaining position was weak; they struck for the eight-hour day. The mineowners were in no great hurry to reopen. Their mines were dry and would not suffer in the interim. Futhermore, railroads were being built into the area; the completion of these lines a few months hence would mean cheaper ore shipping for the owners.

However, some of the small mines did reopen with nonunion men, and several others were preparing to do so when trouble began. It was the familiar story of intimidation of strikebreakers by union men. On March 14 the district court enjoined the union miners from interfering with the mines. Two days later a mine superintendent at Victor called for protection against a group of men gathering around the mine. A small group of deputies was dispatched from Cripple Creek, but these men were confronted by union miners and taken before a local police magistrate. As in the Coeur d'Alenes, the local peace officers in the Cripple Creek district were largely union men.

Sheriff M. F. Bowers was concerned for the fate of his deputies. At Colorado Springs (the county seat of El Paso County which included the Cripple Creek district until Teller County was established in 1899) a large crowd of men was deputized to rescue the sheriff's men. Many of these men were ex-Denver firemen and policemen who had been fired by Governor Waite in a political struggle called the "City Hall War."[1] The sheriff also appealed to Governor Waite for troops to preserve order, and Waite promptly but somewhat prematurely sent three companies under Brigadier General E. J. Brooks and Adjutant General Thomas J. Tarsney.

---

[1] Marshall Sprague, *Money Mountain: The Story of Cripple Creek Gold* (Boston: Little, Brown and Co., 1953), p. 141.

The troops were brought into the area on March 18, 1894, but it was soon apparent that no real need for them existed. When Waite learned the facts he ordered the troops withdrawn immediately. Waite seems to have been one of the few Populists who saw value in the National Guard; he also appears to have been one of the few in those turbulent days of mining strife to have had equal regard for the preservation of law and order and the supremacy of civil authority.

Quiet returned to the district for a period of two months. Most of the smaller mines resumed operations under union conditions, specifically, the eight-hour day. But the larger mines remained closed. An offer was made to open these mines on an eight-hour day for $2.75 daily, but the union men rejected this proposal.

The mineowners then organized a protective plan under which an assessment was made to collect money to arm a large body of deputies. When news of this plan leaked out, the miners began organizing a military camp on Bull Hill at Victor under the direction of J. J. Johnson, an ex-West Point cadet. By the latter part of May 1894, two rival "armies" had been created, Sheriff Bowers' "deputies" with around 1,200 men, and the Bull Hill army of about 700 miners.

On the 25th of May several skirmishes took place between advance units of these two armies. On the next day Governor Waite issued a proclamation calling for the strikers to lay down their arms and cease resistance to law, and also calling on the illegal army of deputies to disperse. But both groups stood their ground. It was potentially a more explosive situation than the Coeur d'Alenes had seen in 1892.

Serious attempts at arbitration were being made in the meantime by President Slocum of Colorado College. He went through the union "lines" at Bull Hill to talk to John Calderwood, president of one of the Western Federation locals involved in the strike. Calderwood indicated a willingness to meet with the mineowners to settle the dispute, but the conditions he proposed were unacceptable to the mineowners and the meeting never took place. One unusual occurrence did result from Slocum's attempt at mediation, however: a full scale exchange of prisoners between the two sides, complete with all the formality of military protocol.

After the miners agreed to let Waite represent their interests, a settlement was finally reached at Colorado Springs between Waite and Calderwood for the miners and J. J. Hagerman for the mineowners. But other mine operators refused to accept the agreement. Then it was discovered that the building in which the meeting took place, Palmer Hall at Colorado College, was surrounded by armed men who were intent on lynching Calderwood and Waite. Judge Horace Lunt stepped out on the porch of the building and began an impassioned plea to the crowd to consider the terrible deed they were proposing. During this speech Calderwood and Waite slipped out a back door and hurried across the campus to a waiting carriage. They were driven to the depot where the governor's private train took them to Denver.

Two days later in Denver the agreement reached in Colorado Springs was ratified by the mineowners and the crisis had been passed. The miners had an eight-hour day for a $3.00 wage. The only problem now was in demobilizing the two armies still facing each other at Bull Hill. On June 5 Governor Waite again sent the militia into the district, this time primarily for the purpose of dispersing the deputies and getting the union men off the private property they had occupied.

There was considerable confusion over the relative roles of the military and civil authorities at this stage. Finally, after the miners had agreed to surrender to the militia, a conference was held between mineowners and military officers at which a workable agreement was reached. The deputies left the district, the miners surrendered their arms and the property they had commandeered, and the mines resumed operating under the contract which had miraculously been worked out under such difficult conditions at Colorado Springs.

Whether the events of 1894 contributed to the subsequent ill feeling which dominated the Cripple Creek district ten years later is a matter of some disagreement. Vernon H. Jensen, in a thorough study of labor relations in the western mining camps with the suggestive title of *Heritage of Conflict,* concludes:

> There is every reason to believe that no fundamental heritage of conflict carried over from this dispute to those that were to engulf this same mining district in a bitter siege less than a decade later. The truth of the matter is that both miners and operators carried a wholesome respect for each other and working conditions in these mines were good, the hours standard, and the wages fair.[2]

At the time of the 1904 troubles Bill Haywood observed, however, that the mineowners had never been satisfied with the 1894 agreement.[3] Another 1904 observer, Ray Stannard Baker, a famous writer of the muckraking tradition, detected some "heritage of conflict" on the part of the unions as well. From the strife-ridden hills of Teller County he wrote in *McClure's Magazine:*

> The strike at Cripple Creek in 1894, and that of Telluride in 1901, were called great victories for unionism. They were not. They were defeats. Victories obtained by such violence and bloodshed are always defeats. They laid the foundation for other violence. They encouraged the unions, once successful with rifles and fists, to use rifles and fists again.[4]

Speaking of rifles and fists, it might be wise to point out that Jensen's book, scholarly and authoritative as it is, generally minimizes the violence committed in the name of labor and stresses the lawlessness of the mineowners' groups. On the other hand, Baker, in the best tradition of objective journalism, was neither anti-labor nor anti-capital. He was pro-citizen, pro-America in a Rooseveltian sense. He was equally critical of labor, capital, government, and the public for letting the Colorado situation get out of hand. According to Louis Filler, Baker's intellectual middle-of-the-road writing was responsible for the success of *McClure's Magazine* during the Progressive Era and made it the unofficial organ of the Square Deal.[5] The history of the Western Federation of Miners might be much easier to understand today if a few of the latter-day historians and writers had approached the subject

---

[2] Vernon H. Jensen, *Heritage of Conflict* (Ithaca: Cornell University Press, 1950), p. 53.

[3] Letter, William D. Haywood to New York *World*, June 17, 1904, quoted in Senate Document 122, "Labor Disturbances in the State of Colorado from 1880 to 1904, inclusive," 58th Congress, 3d session, p. 273.

[4] Ray Stannard Baker, "The Reign of Lawlessness," *McClure's Magazine*, May, 1904, p. 51.

[5] Louis Filler, *Crusaders for American Liberalism* (New York: Harcourt, Brace and Company, 1939), p. 88.

with a middle-of-the-road philosophy, as well as the zeal for reform and passion for justice characteristic of the old Square Deal Progressives.

But regardless of the influence the events of 1894 may have had on the future, and regardless of how the histories have been written, the Western Federation had successfully survived its first real test. As Sprague says:

> Though rarely mentioned by labor historians among the great strikes of history, the Cripple Creek strike was tremendously important. It brought enormous prestige to the Western Federation of Miners. By winning Calderwood's demand for a three-dollar, eight-hour day at Cripple this pioneer industrial union was started well on its way to becoming the most powerful labor organization in the United States.[6]

Nevertheless, the miners had seen that the determination of the mineowners could be as great as their own, and that the methods of the mineowners could be as coercive as those of the union. Perhaps most important in the light of later events, the Western Federation men may have misinterpreted the fair treatment given them by Governor Waite as presaging future support from *any* public official elected with labor help in any labor-management dispute regardless of circumstances. The events of 1899 in the Coeur d'Alenes were to come as a staggering surprise to the union on this score.

---

[6] Sprague, *op. cit.*, pp. 154-155.

4

THE COEUR D'ALENE "TROUBLES of 1899"

SEVEN YEARS HAD PASSED since the "Troubles of 1892" in the Coeur d'Alenes. The most tangible product of that earlier day, the Western Federation of Miners, had survived and grown strong in Shoshone County. Less tangible products of 1892, intimidation and fear, had also been kept alive.

Between 1892 and 1899 a tense truce existed in the area. When the federal troops were withdrawn in November of 1892 a number of fugitive radical union men returned to the area, bringing with them a reign of terror. Retaliations took place against those citizens who had identified themselves with the state in the prosecution of court cases. A number of people were driven from the area, an occurrence which was known locally as "kneeboning."[1]

John Kneebone, a key witness for the prosecution in 1892, was one of the first to feel the retaliation of the union. After his initial deportation he returned to the Coeur d'Alenes where he continued to work in the face of numerous threats. In July of 1894 Kneebone was murdered. On this occasion forty masked men took him from a mine shop along with four other mine em-

---

[1] *Portland Oregonian,* July 9, 1899, p. 10.

ployees. Kneebone was shot, but the four others escaped and fled from the district. The grand jury which investigated the crime deplored the condition of terror existing in the area which prevented anyone coming forth with clues to the identity of the killers.

Violence to men and property, particularly Bunker Hill and Sullivan Company property, continued throughout this period. In the words of the report of the U. S. House of Representatives investigating committee which visited the area in 1900:

> A secret organization controlled the civil authorities in Shoshone County. The mandate of the "dark lantern" order was more powerful than the law of the State. Whatever was the desire of the secret clan became the law of the community. Sheriffs connived at the actions of criminals. Newspapers succumbed to the baleful influence and became willing organs to justify damnable conspiracy and inflame prejudice against men who would not become slaves to the lawless element. Men suddenly disappeared, leaving no trace behind.[2]

The committee put it more succinctly when it observed, "The proof shows that anarchy and insurrection have, in fact, existed in that county since 1892."[3]

Although the union politically dominated the Coeur d'Alenes, it had not been able to improve its economic position beyond the wage scale which had been paid even before unions existed in the district. The depressed silver market of 1893-94 hurt the area and slowed the return to normal conditions after the 1892 troubles. But by the middle of 1894 several important mines agreed to pay the old uniform rate of $3.50 a day for all underground work. By 1899 this was considered the standard rate for the district and was paid by all mines except the Bunker Hill and Sullivan.

This company paid a differential rate of $2.50 and $3.00 at the time. The management justified this rate on the fact that the mine was dry, which eliminated the expensive rubber clothing purchases necessarily made by the employees of the other Coeur d'Alene mines, an outlay that might run as high as $12.00 or $15.00 a month. The cost of board at the Bunker Hill boarding house

[2] House Report 1999, *op. cit.*, pp. 24-25. This document is the primary source for the following account.

[3] House Report 1999, *ibid.*, p. 28.

was also one dollar a week cheaper. Managers of other Coeur d'Alene mines actually testified before the U. S. Industrial Commission that a miner was better off under the lower wage scale of the Bunker Hill and Sullivan mine than in the higher paying mines.[4]

But the union did not see it that way. It looked upon this nonunion mine as a threat to the wage scale and the union shop in the district. It had secretly organized some of the employees of this mine, but the company had spotters and detectives busy ferreting out these union men and dismissing them. On April 23, 1899, a committee from the Wardner union met with the mine manager and demanded a $3.50 uniform wage scale and recognition of the union. A strike against the company for these goals was announced.

Even though the company had been busy discharging union employees during the previous several days, the mine management acceded to pressure and agreed to a wage increase of fifty cents a day, bringing its rates to a new differential of $3.00 and $3.50. However, the company made it clear that its employees would have to choose between employment under these rates or union membership; they could not have both. As a result, within a day about fifty men quit.

On April 26 a crowd of armed union men prevented nonunion men from working in a nearby concentrator; they also seized the aerial tramway belonging to the Bunker Hill and Sullivan Company. The nonunion men were told that they could not work the mines any longer unless they worked under soldiers. It was a strangely prophetic threat, for three days later, on April 29, 1899, occurred the event that brought soldiers to the Coeur d'Alenes once again, and a major disaster to the Western Federation of Miners.

On this day the miners' unions at Mullan, Burke, and Gem—the mining communities well up in the canyons—held early morning meetings. The men were told that they were going to Wardner to make a show of force against the nonunion Bunker Hill and Sullivan mine. Paul Corcoran, the financial secretary of

[4] Report of the Industrial Commission, *op. cit.*, p. 2.

the Burke local, was the key man in the day's activity. His union had to make the first move in a series of strong-armed acts which even the union newspaper admitted were preplanned.[5] At ten o'clock several hundred Burke miners, some armed and masked, commandeered the regular Northern Pacific mixed train waiting to make the return trip down Canyon Creek to Wallace. The engineer was ordered first to stop at the Black Bear mine powderhouse above Gem where powder was loaded onto the train. At Gem another stop was made. Several hundred more miners climbed aboard, and several freight cars were added to the train to accommodate them.

The miners apparently decided they did not have enough powder for the day's activities, since they ordered the train backed up from Gem to the Frisco mine powderhouse. The Frisco mill had been the scene of the spectacular flume dynamiting during the "Troubles of 1892." Here, in 1899, the miners stole the dynamite they needed, 80 boxes or a total of 400 pounds. The train then resumed its journey down the canyon to Wallace.

At Wallace the train stopped briefly. The train crew was concerned about the rest of the trip to Wardner which would have to be made over the tracks of another railroad, the Oregon Railway and Navigation Company's line. While the conductor was trying to get train orders from the O. R. and N. station agent, the miners forced the engineer to leave without him.

Meanwhile, another large group of miners several hundred strong had marched down another canyon from Mullan to Wallace where they boarded the train. On the way these men had picked up rifles which had been cached beside the road. When the train left Wallace for Wardner it carried nearly one thousand men, some masked, a number well armed.

Sheriff Young of Shoshone County rode the train from Wallace to Wardner. The train moved slowly; it was necessary to send flagmen ahead of the engine inasmuch as no one had any

[5] Wallace *Idaho State Tribune,* May 3, 1899, quoted in House Report 1999, *ibid.,* p. 6-7.

knowledge of the train schedule on the O. R. and N. tracks. During this trip the sheriff talked to the miners, many of whom he knew by name, but he made no real effort to avert trouble or to notify the Bunker Hill and Sullivan officials.

The train arrived in Wardner about one o'clock in the afternoon. One of the best descriptions of what happened next is contained in the account published by the official Western Federation paper, the *Idaho State Tribune* of Wallace, May 3, 1899. The editor, James Sovereign, onetime Grand Master of the Knights of Labor, was an enthusiastic eyewitness to the events:

> A detachment of union miners armed with Winchester rifles was dispatched to the mountain side beyond the mill, and the work of placing under the mill the 3,000 pounds[6] of dynamite, taken from the magazine of the Frisco mine at Gem, was commenced. At no time did the demonstration assume the appearance or the attitude of a disorganized mob. All the details were managed with the discipline and precision of a perfectly trained military organization. Each miner participating in the affair either wore a strip of white handkerchief in the buttonhole of his coat or a strip of white cloth tied on his right arm. Sixty armed scabs in the employ of the Bunker Hill company offered the only resistence, [*sic*] and they gave expression to the most pitiable and lamentable cowardice. Only a few desultory shots from the miners were necessary to send them fleeing over the mountains . . . .
>
> At 2:30 the arrangements were complete, the dynamite was placed under the mill in three departments, the fuse attached, and all was in readiness for the destruction of one of the largest concentrators in the world, costing the company the enormous sum of $250,000. All miners and friends of the miners were warned to take a safe distance from the work of destruction about to begin. The fuses were lighted, and at 2:26 [*sic*] there was an awful crash, and broken machinery and fragments of the building were hurled high into the air. Fifteen seconds later another followed, and in about the same time a third. From the force of the third shot debris was hurled in every direction, and a huge canopy was formed in the heavens. Fragments of machinery and broken timbers rained down upon the ruins for several seconds. The shock of each explosion was terrific and was heard 20 miles away. The work of destruction was complete. The great concentrator was as completely demolished as it could have been if months had been spent in preparing the giant explosives for that purpose. The work was planned and executed by men who have received the training of a lifetime in the handling of dynamite.[7]

---

[6] Other accounts speak in terms of 400 pounds.

[7] *Idaho State Tribune, loc. cit.*

The "desultory shots" mentioned by Sovereign produced at least one death. A union miner named John Smythe was killed as he advanced toward the mill during the skirmish. There is some evidence to indicate that Smythe may have been killed deliberately by the dynamiters.[8]

Most of the Bunker Hill employees escaped, but three of them were captured by the mob and forced to run a gauntlet of rifle fire. William Huff escaped unharmed, but James Cheyne was fatally wounded and R. R. Rogers slightly wounded. During the rifle battle at the mill, the dynamiting, and the roughing-up of the prisoners, Sheriff Young walked back and forth doing nothing. At one point he reportedly asked a newspaper reporter to "Give the miners the best of it."[9]

Although numerous accounts exist of the 1892 dynamiting, surprisingly little has been written which describes accurately the events of April 29, 1899. Harry Orchard's version is about the only reasonably complete account. He would have had no particular reason to stretch the truth in any of it. Even though he had been in the union only for a month, he rode the train to Wardner and personally lit the fuse on one of the three powder charges under the Bunker Hill and Sullivan concentrator. Orchard identified W. F. Davis of Gem as the man in charge of the Wardner operations.[10]

Late that afternoon Davis herded the miners aboard the train for the return trip up the canyon. As boisterous as the miners were, they must have realized it would be only a matter of hours until the inevitable reaction to such a major act of violence would come.

Even before some of the miners had gone to bed that night, the governor of Idaho had telegraphed President McKinley:

> In pursuance of the statute in such cases made and provided, I, Frank Steunenberg, governor of Idaho, the legislature not being in

---

[8] Testimony of Dr. I. S. Collins and Sophia Moffit in Paul Corcoran case, abstracted in House Report 1999, *op. cit.*, p. 41 and p. 50.

[9] House Report 1999, *ibid.*, p. 12.

[10] Testimony of Harry Orchard, transcript, pp. 125-126.

session and it not being possible to convene it, do hereby apply to the President of the United States to call forth the military forces of the United States to suppress insurrection in Shoshone County, State of Idaho. This action is sustained in the fact that all of the available Idaho National Guard volunteered for service in the Philippines, and said county is in a state of insurrection. I am of the opinion that at least 500 troops in the aggregate will be necessary, but smaller detachments should be ordered in as rapidly as possible.

Frank Steunenberg, Governor[11]

Frank Steunenberg was in his second term as Idaho's governor when the Coeur d'Alene riots of 1899 occurred. He had been born in Iowa in 1861. After working his way through the agricultural college at Ames, he married and headed west. Upon coming to Idaho he had first worked as a printer, and he maintained his membership in the typographical union even after he went into newspaper publishing and sheep ranching. He had located at Caldwell, an agricultural community about thirty miles west of Boise where his father and several brothers and sisters lived.

He early became interested in politics. He served in the territorial legislature, and in the constitutional convention in 1889. Although the rest of his family were Republicans, Frank Steunenberg was a Democrat. In 1896 with Populist and labor support he was elected as Idaho's fourth governor.

He was a man of temperate habits who neither smoked, drank, nor swore, and a man of strong family devotion. He transacted no personal business on Saturdays which he observed as the Sabbath. His most noted idiosyncracy was the fact that throughout his lifetime he never wore a necktie, and would never offer an explanation of this quirk.

On April 29, 1899, Steunenberg was sick and confined briefly to a Boise hospital. Being unable to visit the Coeur d'Alenes to view the situation personally, he delegated Bartlett Sinclair, the state auditor, as his "personal representative" in the area. By May 1 Sinclair was in Wardner reporting to the governor on the situation, particularly with respect to the inability of Sheriff Young

[11] Quoted in House Report 1999, *op. cit.*, p. 7.

to maintain law and order. On Sinclair's recommendation Governor Steunenberg on May 3 declared martial law, proclaiming Shoshone County to be in a state of insurrection and rebellion.

The military had moved promptly upon receipt of President McKinley's order granting Steunenberg's request for troops. General H. C. Merriam was ordered on April 30 from Denver to Boise to consult with the governor. From his train on May 1 Merriam ordered troops from Walla Walla and Spokane; on the following day additional troops were ordered from army posts at Helena and Havre, Montana; Salt Lake City; Boise; Cheyenne; and Vancouver, Washington.

Governor Steunenberg met Merriam's train at Glenn's Ferry, some 70 miles east of Boise, and briefed him on the events in the Coeur d'Alenes. Merriam continued on to Wardner, arriving on May 4. The first troops had arrived in the area on May 2, and a number of arrests had already been made prior to Merriam's arrival.

The army had been specifically ordered to aid the Idaho civil authorities in maintaining law and order, but not to take charge of either the arrest or detention of prisoners. The state had deputized a number of special assistants to Sinclair, and these agents were to make the actual arrests and to supervise the large number of prisoners soon to be confined. As in 1892, a number of union miners—including Harry Orchard—fled before the troops arrived; all those remaining were arrested and detained once again in a "bull pen" without charges filed against them.

It is not necessary to discuss the detailed administration of the martial law here. In many respects it was 1892 all over again. As might be expected, there was a great deal of criticism of the military intervention. But the congressional investigating committee generally upheld both the military authorities and the state authorities; however, a dissenting minority report called the conduct of the army "reprehensible."[12]

---

[12] House Report 1999, *op. cit.*, p. 132.

One of the most widely criticized aspects of the martial law was the limitation placed on the right of habeas corpus. In a famous court case which was to serve as a precedent for the state of Colorado a few years later, William Boyle, a "bull pen" prisoner, was denied a writ of habeas corpus by the state supreme court. Two features of this decision were quoted in later decisions: first, that in such insurrections the governor may suspend or disregard the writ of habeas corpus, and second, that the truth of the facts set forth in a proclamation of insurrection will not be inquired into by the courts.[13]

William Boyle had been a county commissioner of Shoshone County along with William R. Stimson and Moses S. Simmons. These three men were subsequently removed from office in an impeachment proceeding before Judge Mayhew who said, ". . . they have disregarded and neglected their official duties and by their acts demonstrated their incompetency and unfitness for the public trust imposed in them by the people of this county."

Sheriff Young was removed in the same impeachment hearing. In passing judgment upon this case the court concluded, "The highest peace officer of the county, conducting himself as he states in his own evidence, has disgraced the office to which he has been elected and has shown himself to be incompetent and unfit as a public servant."[14] Young was replaced, incidentally, by Dr. Hugh France, the Bunker Hill and Sullivan Company doctor who was also the coroner of Shoshone County.

Of course, the most famous—or infamous—part of the "Troubles of 1899" was the military prison or "bull pen." It has been suggested that this institution, originating in the Coeur d'Alenes, was the forerunner of the modern concentration camp. In any event, it was admittedly a harsh measure of military necessity. More than 700 men were housed during the busiest period of apprehension and confinement; these represented about three quarters of the 950 miners reported not at work on April 29. Initially the prisoners were confined in a barn and a number of boxcars,

---

[13] *In re Boyle,* 57 Pacific 706.
[14] House Report 1999, *op. cit.,* p. 77.

but construction of a prison stockade was undertaken immediately. This structure was ready just sixteen days after the first arrests were made. Conditions in it were generally satisfactory in the opinion of the congressional committee which investigated the charges against the army.

The new stockade, however, served as a challenge to some of the confined miners. Several attempts were made to tunnel out of the prison, but none was successful. On August 28, seven men who were about to be tried made an escape assisted by an army non-commissioned officer who had been bribed. Peter Breen, the Western Federation attorney from Butte and a veteran of the 1892 "bull pen," was suspected of having something to do with this escape and henceforth was not allowed to represent men in the prison.[15]

Another widely criticized feature of the military occupation was the work permit system instituted by Bartlett Sinclair. Over the opposition of the mineowners Sinclair required miners who wanted to start working again to sign a statement denying participation in the crimes of April 29 and denying membership in any society which incited or approved those crimes. The congressional report observed, "This 'permit system' can only be defended on the ground of the extreme necessity of martial law, and whether it should be continued after martial law ceases is a question which only the State of Idaho can decide. It has proved a most effective means toward accomplishing the end for which it was devised."[16] Colorado officials must have noted this endorsement, for in a few years they adopted the permit system under similar circumstances.

The most important legal battle taking place during 1899 was the Paul Corcoran case. Corcoran, the financial secretary of the Burke miners' union, was charged with the death of James Cheyne, the Bunker Hill and Sullivan employee who had been killed at the time of the dynamiting. The state made this case its key prosecution of the dynamiters, using its best legal talent in the prosecution. James H. Hawley and William E. Borah acted as special

[15] House Report 1999, *ibid,* pp. 92-93.
[16] House Report 1999, *ibid.,* p. 115.

prosecutors, a role they were to repeat in the Haywood trial eight years later. Judge George A. Stewart of Boise was sent by the governor to Wallace to try the case, and a special jury list was drawn up from the more agrarian parts of the county to insure a better chance of getting a conviction in the mining community, an act which was subsequently ruled legal by the Idaho Supreme Court.

Colonel Pat Reddy, onetime colleague of James Hawley in the 1892 defense of the miners and now attorney for the entire "bull pen," undertook the defense of Corcoran. Associated with him were F. C. Robertson of Spokane and Peter Breen of Butte. One of the most spectacular events of the trial occurred when Borah took the jury out to the canyon to prove a point. Several witnesses had testified to seeing Paul Corcoran riding on top of a boxcar on the dynamite train in the canyon on April 29. Defense witnesses testified that no man could ride on a swaying boxcar in such a position at the speed of that particular train. Borah, before the eyes of the assembled jurors, rode on top of a boxcar moving at the same speed through the canyon to prove that it could be done and that a man could be recognized under such conditions.[17]

Borah and Hawley won their case. Paul Corcoran was convicted of murder in the second degree and sentenced to seventeen years in the state prison. Two years later he was pardoned by the state board of pardons. In an interesting observation on the Paul Corcoran case some years later, James Hawley said:

> The object of the state officers who were behind the prosecution and of the attorneys conducting it, was not so much to impose punishment upon those who had been connected with the crimes committed, as it was to show to the members of the unions and those who had used their influence to carry out their own selfish design that the law would reach anyone connected with such illegal acts, no matter how high his standing in the community and although it might be proved that he had not personally participated in any of the unlawful acts. The men whose guilt could easily be proven were comparitively [sic] unknown members of the unions and their conviction meant but little, so far as the future of the Coeur d'Alenes was concerned. It became a question with those in charge as to who would be the proper man, by reason of his high standing as a citizen

[17] *Portland Oregonian,* July 22, 1899, p. 8.

> and good reputation in the community, united with the fact that he was a man of family and possessed of abundant means, and it was determined that Paul Corcoran, the secretary of the Burke union, fully met these requirements and that if convicted upon the charge of murder . . . it would mean more for the future orderly conduct of affairs . . . than that of any other man against whom an indictment was found.[18]

Hawley's statement notwithstanding, he and Borah had made a good case against Paul Corcoran. It was generally an attempt to show a conspiracy to kill, rather than to pin the actual killing on Corcoran. But one witness, a woman who had helped the badly wounded Cheyne down the hill into town, had testified to seeing Paul Corcoran in the group of men who had shot Cheyne.

There was much conflicting testimony, as might be expected. A number of witnesses swore that Corcoran remained in Burke that day, although others who had been on the train and in Wardner identified him as one of the masked and armed rioters. Jensen, using as a primary source the report of the congressional committee which includes abstracts of testimony in the Paul Corcoran case, chooses to ignore that testimony which embarrasses the union, and makes the flat assertion that Corcoran was "not at Wardner at the time of the dynamiting . . ."[19]

Jensen makes another interesting observation. Relying heavily on an account published in the *Miner's Magazine,* the Western Federation of Miners journal, he develops at some length the theory that other mine managers in the district, particularly Joseph McDonald of the Frisco, were behind the dynamiting of the Bunker Hill and Sullivan property.[20] Credence is given to this theory by a similar statement of Connolly who spoke of a mine manager who addressed meetings of his miners, "counseling extreme measures against the Bunker Hill Company if it did not accede to the demands."[21] But no allusion to this alleged counter-

---

[18] James H. Hawley, *History of Idaho* (Chicago: S. J. Clarke Publishing Co., 1920), p. 254.

[19] Vernon H. Jensen, *Heritage of Conflict* (Ithaca: Cornell University Press, 1950), p. 85.

[20] Jensen, *ibid.,* pp. 77-79.

[21] C. P. Connolly, "Moyer-Haywood Case," *Collier's,* May 11, 1907, p. 14.

conspiracy occurs in the testimony of the Corcoran trial where the defense might well have attempted to use this theory.

Only a few of the miners confined in the "bull pen" were ever brought to trial. Thirteen were convicted on a federal charge of interfering with United States mail, mail that had been carried by the Northern Pacific mixed train commandeered by the dynamiters. Most of the "bull pen" occupants were released in a few weeks, but the permit system of Bartlett Sinclair prevented many of them from working again in the Coeur d'Alenes. A number of miners left the area for Cripple Creek and other mining camps throughout the West where they rejoined those who had fled earlier from the federal troops.

The 1899 actions of Governor Steunenberg had the net effect of destroying the power of the Western Federation of Miners in Idaho, and exporting from the state a number of bitter and violent men. Steunenberg was criticized severely by the contemporary labor press, which is understandable, but, less understandably, he continues to be vilified by modern liberal writers. Vernon Jensen calls his conduct calloused and vindictive.[22] Yet his critics, then and now, have offered no real alternative course of action that Steunenberg might have taken in the face of such provocation.

In the long run, Steunenberg's actions gave the Western Federation of Miners far less justification for bitterness than the actions of the Colorado state government produced a few years later. And, if the miners had made a mistake in their show of power in the Coeur d'Alenes in 1899, they acted like the proverbial "damn fool" in making the same mistake twice when they tried a similar policy in Cripple Creek in 1903-04.

---

[22] Jensen, *op. cit.*, p. 197.

5

THE COLORADO LABOR WAR of 1903-04

DURING THE OPENING YEARS of the 20th century the Western Federation of Miners had reason to be both frustrated and pleased with its ten-year record. The Coeur d'Alene strike had been lost, the union broken in Idaho, and its men scattered to the winds. But in Colorado, on a broader front, the union had done well since 1894 in winning its demands for wages, hours, and union recognition. The economic goals of the union were being attained; it was time to test the social and political power of the union.

After a brief affiliation with the American Federation of Labor in 1896-97, the Western Federation had turned toward industrial unionism and toward the political left. The union leadership was now in the hands of two new officers, President Charles H. Moyer and Secretary-Treasurer William D. Haywood. Both men were active Socialists. As one contemporary writer described them, "They not only want socialism but they want it this morning."[1]

Moyer had come up from the mining camps of the Black Hills, after a brief stay in Joliet penitentiary on a Chicago

[1] Ray Stannard Baker, "The Reign of Lawlessness," *McClure's Magazine,* May 1904, p. 52.

burglary conviction.[2] Haywood had come to the union headquarters from Silver City in southwest Idaho. Neither man had been involved directly in the previous Cripple Creek or Coeur d'Alene troubles, but both of them were tough, seasoned fighters in labor-management conflict.

To the credit of the Western Federation of Miners, that union organized the eight-hour day movement in Colorado. On this issue it had wide public support. The eight-hour fight was common to most of the mining strikes in Colorado at the time. The legislature had flaunted the will of the people on this question, and there was strong feeling against the corporations and trusts which stood to gain from the postponement of such legislation. Had the Western Federation acted with more restraint in 1903-04, it might have emerged from the Colorado labor wars the shining hero rather than the villain of the piece.

In 1895 an eight-hour bill for the mining industry had been presented in the Colorado House of Representatives. The legality of the proposal was immediately questioned, and the state supreme court was asked for an advisory ruling. The court replied that such a bill would be class legislation, and would therefore be clearly unconstitutional. The bill failed to carry for this reason.[3]

In 1899 the legislature enacted an eight-hour bill which was duly signed by the governor. This bill was a verbatim copy, except with respect to penalties, of a WFM-sponsored Utah statute of 1896 which had been upheld by the United States Supreme Court in 1897. However, the Colorado Supreme Court unanimously found this new statute unconstitutional. A movement then began to secure the adoption of a constitutional amendment which would provide for the enactment of eight-hour legislation. In 1900 the platforms of the Republicans, Democrats, and Populists each called for such an amendment.

The legislature in 1901 complied by drawing up an amendment to be submitted by referendum to the voters in 1902. Again,

[2] *Portland Oregonian,* May 12, 1907, p. 1.

[3] Senate Document 122, *op. cit.,* pp. 51-52. The following account of the eight-hour fight and the strikes of 1903-04 is largely from this source.

all political parties endorsed the measure, and the issue was put to the voters at the general elections of November 1902. The measure carried 72,980 to 26,266, indicating a strong mandate for the legislature to enact promptly the necessary legislation.

Unfortunately, the new legislature which met in 1903 was split, with Democrats controlling the senate and Republicans the house. Each chamber wrote its own bill, but conference committees were unable to iron out the differences. Corporation lobbyists, particularly those of the Colorado Fuel and Iron Company, brought strong pressures to bear on the legislators. The Western Federation of Miners tried as best it could to offset the corporation pressure, but at the end of the session, the legislature adjourned without having passed an eight-hour bill.

Governor Peabody called a special session of the legislature in July to consider another matter, and the lawmakers had an opportunity to pass the eight-hour legislation if they so desired. But each chamber contented itself with resolutions blaming the other chamber for the failure of the eight-hour legislation in the regular session. Before the people of Colorado were ever to get their eight-hour day amendment the issue was to be a part of labor struggles which brought violence to Idaho Springs, Telluride, and particularly to Cripple Creek.

Conditions for the miners were generally quite advantageous in Cripple Creek in 1903. Even before the eight-hour-day fight had begun in Colorado, the miners in Cripple Creek had a well-established eight-hour day as a result of their 1894 strike. Furthermore, the mines were generally dry, the wages good, and the communities far more urbanized than the average western mining camp. But the union found it necessary to call a strike in the district in support of an organizing effort being conducted at four reduction mills in Colorado City, an industrial suburb of Colorado Springs.

These reduction mills depended upon Cripple Creek for their ore. The management of each mill was decidedly anti-union, and the wage scale was well below that for comparable work in other mining areas of the West. The Western Federation struck these mills, even though it was not the bargaining agent for the mill employees. Some of the mills were able to keep operating with nonunion men and imported strikebreakers. Since the only way to make the strike effective was to shut off the supply of ore, the union then called a strike of Cripple Creek miners in those mines which shipped ore to the Colorado City mills. About 700 men were idled for two weeks. The strike was then called off when the reduction mills agreed not to discriminate against union men. Improvements in the wage scale were also announced by all mills except the Standard mill.

As a result of the Standard mill's refusal to re-employ union men and to improve its wage scale, the Cripple Creek strike was resumed within a matter of several months. The secondary boycott was extended to additional mines in the Cripple Creek district, inasmuch as during the earlier strike some mines had sent ore out of the district to other places, to be transshipped to the struck reduction mills at Colorado City. In this second strike some 3,500 miners were idled.

It has frequently been said that the high officials of the Western Federation of Miners called these two strikes. The 1903 convention of the union had amended the constitution to provide for the executive board calling other local unions out on strike in support of an existing strike. There *was* an existing strike at Colorado City in 1903, so it is possible that Haywood and Moyer ordered the miners out in support of the mill workers. However, in 1904 Haywood denied that this had happened:

> So much has been said and written about the strikes in Colorado that it seems unnecessary to review them at this time. There is one point, however, which is worthy of consideration here, and that is the assertion of the mine owners that the strikes were called by the executive board of the organization. Nothing could be further from the truth. The strikes of 1903 were not declared in the Cripple Creek district until every union in the district had voted on the proposition and referred the entire matter to the district union for consideration and settlement. The action of the district union was indorsed by the executive board. At the annual convention held in May-June, 1903, additional power was vested in the executive board, but as all constitutional amendments and legislation must be passed by referendum, this amendment adopted by the convention was voted on later by the members of all local unions, and it did not become

> part of the constitutional law until January, 1904, nearly five months after the second strike of 1903 in the Cripple Creek district had been declared through the action of the local unions and district unions. At the time of the strike called on March 17, 1903, and at the time of the strike called on August 8, 1903, the executive board was in no way empowered to initiate a strike, and I take this opportunity of correcting the impression that has been made by nearly every writer of note that has reviewed the Colorado situation.[4]

The report of the Commissioner of Labor to Congress accepts the Haywood version of the calling of the strike. But it makes an observation which still leaves the issue in doubt when it says, "Although the members of the Federation loyally obeyed the strike order, there is no doubt that this second sympathetic strike was very unpopular with the miners, however [popular] the first one may have been. Indeed, many well-informed, disinterested persons assert that 90 percent of the miners were opposed to the second sympathetic strike, and this has been admitted even by some prominent members of the Federation."[5] It is difficult to believe this implication that even though 90% of a group of 3,500 miners did not favor the strike, the strike was still called through democratic action at the local union level.

Harry Orchard had a plausible explanation of this discrepancy. He asserted that the local unions did call the strike, but on the orders of Haywood and Moyer. The most radical local, the Free Coinage union at Altman, was fairly small yet had two pro-Haywood men on the three-man district strike committee; the largest local, a conservative union at Victor, had none. This situation permitted the small radical element in the Federation to determine policy for all, a situation that seemed to prevail in several Western Federation camps.[6]

During the first few weeks of the second sympathetic strike there was no unusual violence in the Cripple Creek district. One mine, the El Paso, resumed operating, but no other mines were opened. Then a pattern of intimidation began to develop. On

---

[4] William D. Haywood, Statement, November 7, 1904, quoted in Senate Document 122, *op. cit.*, p. 44.

[5] Senate Document 122, *op. cit.*, p. 161.

[6] Harry Orchard, "The Confession and Autobiography of Harry Orchard," *McClure's Magazine*, August, 1907, p. 371.

August 29, 1903, the shaft house of the Sunset-Eclipse mine was destroyed by fire. The fire was thought to be of incendiary origin; the Mine Owners' Association offered a reward of $2,500 for information leading to the arrest of the person or persons responsible. Violence erupted as an elderly nonunion carpenter who had been employed to build a fence around a mine was severely beaten, and a crippled justice of the peace, who had fined a miner for carrying a gun, was slugged on a public street.

On the 2nd of September a guard at a mine saw several men crawling along one of the levels of the mine. When he challenged them, a shot was fired at him. He returned the shot, and the men fled. This reportedly happened at the El Paso mine,[7] but it may have been the same incident which took place in the Vindicator mine. The intruders at the Vindicator were apparently Harry Orchard and Joe Schultz, reconnoitering the mine to determine where to place the bomb that was later to explode there.

On the same day a flow of messages took place between the interested parties to the dispute. The Mine Owners' Association asked the sheriff, H. M. Robertson, to call on the governor for troops. When the sheriff, a union man, declined, the mineowners then wired directly to the governor. A similar request for troops was sent by the mayor of Victor. The union issued a statement deploring the violence, followed by a petition to the governor pointing out that troops were not needed in Cripple Creek.

Governor Peabody appointed a three-man commission to visit the area to determine the facts. The commission was composed of a lawyer who was also advocate general of the militia, a high-ranking militia officer, and the attorney general of the state. On the night of September 3 these three men arrived in Cripple Creek. They met with the mayor of Cripple Creek, Sheriff Robertson, members of the Mine Owners' Association, and members of the Citizens' Alliance, a newly formed merchant's association opposed to the strike. No representatives of the union were interviewed by the commission. On the following day at four o'clock in the morning the commission left the area, having

[7] Senate Document 122, *op. cit.*, p. 171.

spent less than eight hours of darkness in their investigation. On their way back to Denver the commission sent two telegrams to Governor Peabody setting forth the gravity of the situation.

When the commission reported orally to Governor Peabody on September 4, the governor called out the National Guard. By the next day 1,000 troops had been rushed into the mining camps under the command of Adjutant General Sherman Bell who announced upon arrival, "I'm here to do up this damned anarchistic Western Federation."[8]

The relationship between the Mine Owners' Association and the state of Colorado with respect to this military action was a questionable arrangement. In order to finance the campaign the state issued certificates of indebtedness bearing 4% interest which were subscribed to by the mineowners. The agreements provided funds for the guardsmen, plus cooks, laborers, detectives, secret service men, and any other civilians necessary to carry out the campaign successfully. There is evidence which indicates that such agreements existed prior to any appeal for troops in Cripple Creek.[9]

Mass meetings were held in Victor and Cripple Creek protesting the arrival of the soldiers. In Cripple Creek the meeting was addressed by Frank Hangs and Eugene Engley, two attorneys who represented the union in that area. After these meetings, protest resolutions signed at each gathering by over 1,000 people were forwarded to Governor Peabody.

Some of the mines resumed operating on September 8, 1903, but the mineowners made it clear that they would not negotiate with the union for re-employment of men. Men who wanted work were required to renounce the Western Federation of Miners. This announcement marked the point of no return for both sides. From this point the mineowners were committed to breaking the union, and the union was committed to whatever techniques of survival it could muster.

---

[8] Marshall Sprague, *Money Mountain: The Story of Cripple Creek Gold* (Boston: Little, Brown and Co., 1953), p. 141.

[9] C. P. Connolly, "Moyer-Haywood Case," *Collier's*, June 29, 1907, p. 29.

September and October of 1903 were marked by a number of jurisdictional disputes between the military and the civil authorities. A military "bull pen" was set up, in which miners and townspeople who were too critical of the military occupation were confined briefly. The entire staff of the Victor *Record,* a pro-Federation morning paper, was confined at one time, but the wife of a linotype operator managed to publish the paper on schedule.

Local civil authorities were unsuccessful in serving processes against militiamen who, while carrying out their orders, had been charged with violations of various statutes. A Colorado law exempted the militia while on duty from the service of any civil process. To prevent any off-duty service, the military commanders in Cripple Creek closed their military areas to civil authorities.

The writ of habeas corpus was not suspended during the occupation, but it was flaunted and abused by the military. On several occasions when required to produce "bull pen" prisoners in court, the troops marched the men to the courthouse, deployed in military picket line around the building, and detailed sharpshooters to adjacent buildings. Gatling guns were set up around the building, and soldiers with fixed bayonets guarded the prisoners until court was called to order. The militia was represented by the advocate general, the same officer who served on the commission which recommended military intervention in the area. As a gesture of compliance with civil authority, the soldiers in the courtroom removed their hats during the proceedings. But at the end of one hearing when the court ordered the release of the prisoners, the National Guard general in the courtroom arose, saluted the court, and respectfully declined to obey the order. Later that day, however, under instructions from Governor Peabody the militia released the prisoners.

In spite of the presence of the troops, tensions eased. By mid-October about 2,900 men were back at work in the Cripple Creek mines. The number of soldiers on duty had been reduced to about 700, and by the end of the month only about 200 remained in the district.

In November an attempt was made to wreck a train on the Florence and Cripple Creek Railroad. An ex-miner named

McKinney was arrested for the crime. He told two stories, one that he had made the attempt in the company of three prominent union men, and the other that he was in collusion with detectives of the Mine Owners' Association, who had promised him immunity if he would go through with the scheme to throw suspicion on the union. The state tried the three union men first, with McKinney as state's evidence reverting to his original story, but the men were acquitted. The case against McKinney was finally dropped by the district attorney. It is interesting to note that the bonds put up for McKinney were furnished by the mineowners.

During this train-wrecking episode Harry Orchard, disgruntled over not being asked to participate in a venture that seemed much safer than planting bombs in mines, had tipped off the railroad detectives that an attempt at derailment would be made. He even made a trip to Denver with one of the detectives to get "inside" information at union headquarters, but he appears to have been just playing the detective along for the few dollars in it for himself. At union headquarters Orchard met Haywood for the first time. According to Orchard, Haywood knew of his work in Cripple Creek and praised him for the Vindicator mine explosion which had just occurred.[10]

On November 21, 1903, Charles H. McCormick, superintendent of the Vindicator mine, and Melvin Beck, a shift boss, were killed by an explosion at the 600-foot level of the mine where no work was being done. This was Harry Orchard's first success in the Cripple Creek area, and it was only a qualified success. He had unknowingly set the bomb on the wrong level where it killed Beck and McCormick, men whom Orchard had known and liked, instead of the intended victims, a cage full of "scabs." The coroner's jury at the time, including both union and nonunion men, concluded, ". . . this jury is unable to determine the exact cause of said explosion." But the state commissioner of mines in his official report said that the death of the two men "was caused by deliberate intent on the part of some one unknown."[11]

---

[10] Orchard, *op. cit.*, p. 379; also, second installment, September, 1907, p. 507 ff.

[11] Quoted in Senate Document 122, *op. cit.*, p. 192.

On December 4, 1903, Governor Peabody proclaimed Teller County to be in a state of insurrection and rebellion. This proclamation was responsible for further suppression of inflammatory criticism, the surrender of arms to the military, the suspension of habeas corpus, and the beginning of the policy of deportation. It was a drastic move, but apparently it produced the desired results. For on the 28th of January 1904, noting that "peace and good order in said county are being fully restored," Peabody revoked the proclamation. Early in February the number of soldiers in the district was cut to 50, and on April 12, 1904, they were completely withdrawn.

During this period of apparent calm the Mine Owners' Association and the Citizens' Alliance consolidated their positions. In March the mineowners instituted a permit system whereby any miner seeking work would have to be cleared by an employment office. Western Federation men were blacklisted. Others, after satisfying the Mine Owners' Association secretary, were given an employment card which was carried until employment was found. The new employer picked up the card and returned it to the Association. If the man left the job, he could obtain his card again provided his services had been satisfactory. If he was considered an agitator, or if his services had not been satisfactory, his card was not returned and the man could not get work again in the Cripple Creek mines.

In the Coeur d'Alenes it had been possible for townspeople to remain quietly neutral in the labor disputes. But in Cripple Creek the Citizens' Alliance made such neutrality impossible. One of the declared objects of the Alliance was to discourage strikes and boycotts, and yet the Alliance was behind an agreement of businessmen in Cripple Creek and Victor not to employ anyone connected with the Western Federation of Miners, the local trades assembly, or the American Labor Union. Any businessman not signing could expect to be boycotted by the Alliance. The unions, to be sure, also used intimidation to maintain the solidarity of their membership. Both sides asserted, "You are either with us, or you are against us."

It is remarkable that under these conditions there was not more violence than there was, particularly after the repressive measures of January had been proclaimed. Perhaps the union leadership had gotten too involved in the situation at Telluride where another violent clash with the militia was taking place. Or perhaps the entire district was wearying of the year-old strike. In any event, the district was quiet during the first part of 1904.

The Western Federation of Miners held its annual convention in Denver during May and June of 1904. A great deal of dissatisfaction was expressed by delegates concerning the handling of the Cripple Creek strike. The situation looked hopeless; President Moyer was in custody as a result of the Telluride trouble, and there seemed to be no chance of victory for the union. Haywood wanted something done. He turned to Harry Orchard for a show of violence that would impress the delegates.

Orchard, with the aid of Steve Adams, arranged to blow up the Independence depot of the Florence and Cripple Creek Railroad. This station was used by a number of nonunion miners who commuted to the Findley mine. On June 6, 1904, as the train pulled into the station at 2:15 a.m., Harry Orchard and Steve Adams yanked on a long wire that triggered an enormous dynamite bomb. In the explosion thirteen men were killed and a number badly wounded. The dynamiters made their getaway; Adams fled, and Orchard resumed a prearranged camping trip with John Neville and his son. But the aroused citizens of the area were determined to avenge the terrible killing.

Feeling ran high throughout the district as news of the explosion spread. A state of insurrection was again proclaimed, and the local militia was immediately mobilized. Shortly after noon that day a meeting of mineowners was held. Sheriff Robertson was brought to the meeting and asked to resign. When he refused, guns were produced and a coiled rope was dangled before him. He then signed a resignation prepared by the mineowners. The county commissioners were then forced to appoint Edward Bell as sheriff. Significantly, the new sheriff was a member of the Mine Owners' Association and the new undersheriff was the secretary of the Citizens' Alliance.

Soon a crowd of several thousand persons assembled in Victor. C. C. Hamlin, secretary of the Mine Owners' Association, went before the crowd, along with Sheriff Bell and S. D. Crump, attorney for the Association. Standing on a wagon, Hamlin began an inflammatory speech denouncing the dynamiting of the depot and demanding that the district be purged of the influence of the Western Federation of Miners, whose badge he called "a badge of murder."

At this moment two men in the audience wrestled over a gun. The crowd broke for cover. Several dozen shots were fired; seven men were hit, two of them fatally. Sheriff Bell then had the soldiers of the local militia surround the miners' union hall and take positions on the roof of the building across the street. A pitched battle, lasting nearly an hour, developed between the soldiers and an equal number of miners inside the hall. Finally the miners surrendered, the wounded being taken to the hospital and the others to the local armory.

Squads of soldiers, deputy sheriffs, and armed citizens scattered over the entire district, arresting union members. The union stores were closed and looted, and the prounion Victor newspaper was again closed. Local civil authorities friendly to the unions were forced to resign, and the offices were filled with men chosen by the Mine Owners' Association or the Citizens' Alliance.

Deportations of men from the area started almost immediately. On June 7, 28 union men were escorted to Denver on the train. On June 8 a deportation commission was established to determine which men were to be taken out of the area. On June 10 the first list was published, and 79 men were sent out of the district by special train under military escort. The next morning the men were released at the Kansas-Colorado state line near Holly, Colorado, and told never to return to Cripple Creek. On June 14 another group of 33 men was deported to the New Mexico-Colorado border. A final deportation train was run on June 28 with 39 men being taken to Palmer Lake, Colorado.

Other persons were driven out of the district by armed men, or fled in order to avoid deportation. Individual and small group deportations continued to be made throughout 1904. Eugene Engley, the Federation lawyer who had once been Colorado's attorney general under "Bloody Bridles" Waite, and Frank Hangs, another Federation attorney, were both driven out. During this time numerous acts of retaliation were carried out by "white-cappers" against union sympathizers.

Soon the Western Federation of Miners had been completely expelled from the Cripple Creek district. The blow to the union was particularly severe, inasmuch as it had been losing another strike at Telluride in San Miguel County at the same time. This Telluride strike was in itself long and violent, but it has been overshadowed in labor history by the Cripple Creek strike.

The Telluride strike had many parallels with the Cripple Creek strike. It began in September 1903, as a mill strike, later becoming a miners' strike. The militia intervened with the same repressive measures. The Mine Owners' Association and the Citizens' Alliance arbitrarily judged who was a good citizen, and deportations awaited those who were not.

Even some of the personalities of the Telluride troubles were the same as those of Cripple Creek. Adjutant General Sherman Bell spent considerable time in Telluride. So did Eugene Engley who managed to get himself arrested and deported in Telluride in January as well as in Cripple Creek in June. But the most interesting personality of the San Miguels was Bulkeley Wells who doubled as mine manager and captain of the militia. Wells had come out from Boston in 1902 to succeed Arthur Collins, the assassinated manager of the Smuggler mine. He was instrumental in the defeat of the union in the Telluride strike. By the time of the Haywood trial in 1907 Wells was adjutant general of Colorado.

The most unusual event of the Telluride troubles was the habeas corpus fight of Charles H. Moyer. Moyer had been arrested originally in March 1904 in Ouray, Colorado, while Harry Orchard was acting as his bodyguard. The charge was flag-desecration, growing out of a Western Federation poster on which thirteen strong—but generally true—accusations concerning the state of Colorado had been printed on the stripes of an American flag. In a long battle between the Western Federation attorneys, E. F. Richardson and John Murphy, and the militia officials, Sherman Bell and Bulkeley Wells, Moyer finally in June obtained a writ of habeas corpus from the United States Circuit Court of Appeals in St. Louis. By this time, the Telluride strike was lost and Cripple Creek was soon to be the Waterloo of the Western Federation.

An account of the Colorado labor wars would be incomplete without some reference to the Idaho Springs strike. This strike in 1903 was on the eight-hour question and involved only about 250 men. But it had most of the elements of the larger strikes, including bombings, deportations, a Citizens' Alliance, and "whitecappers." Only the militia was missing. The legal battles for the union were fought and won by E. F. Richardson, but to no avail. The strike was lost, and the union blacklisted here, too.

Although the Western Federation of Miners was considered the loser in the Colorado labor war of 1903-04 in reality there was no clear victory for anyone. The combined expense of only the National Guard operations in the state during this period amounted to over $600,000.[12] Not only did the state get deeply involved financially in these difficulties, but it undertook activities that were clearly not the function of state government. The militia was corporation financed, and its participation in arrests, prosecutions, and deportations went far beyond the role of the federal troops in the Coeur d'Alenes. The Citizens' Alliances, too, were an above-the-law innovation with no precedent in previous labor disputes. The citizens of Colorado had no reason to be proud of the way the union had been defeated in that state by the militia, the courts, and the mobs.

By the same token, the Western Federation of Miners could not hope for much popular support in the future. Through its record of violence in Telluride and Cripple Creek it had shown itself to be a two-faced organization, one face to the public expressing the legitimate aspirations of the labor movement in the western mining camps, and another face to mine operators and reluctant miners threatening the violent consequences to those who thwarted the union.

---

[12] Senate Document 122, *op. cit.*, p. 360.

At the time, only a handful of writers recognized the wrongs committed by both sides in this great economic struggle, as well as the essential righteousness of the goals of both sides. It was too easy for the general public to close its eyes to such unpleasantness. It remained for the Haywood trial to startle the public with the eye-opening realities of the methods used in the struggle between labor and capital in the mines of the West.

6

"The CRIME of the CENTURY"

On December 30, 1905, Harry Orchard killed Frank Steunenberg. On that day Steunenberg had walked downtown from his home in Caldwell after dark to complete a business transaction which he had postponed until his Sabbath ended at sunset. As he hurried home through the falling snow he passed a short stocky figure going in the opposite direction. This was Harry Orchard who had minutes before rigged a dynamite bomb on the side gate of the Steunenberg residence. At about 6:45 the former governor reached the gate and opened it. A string tied to the gate pulled the stopper from a vial of sulphuric acid. The acid spilled over some blasting caps and the bomb exploded. Steunenberg's right side was blown away, and he fell mortally wounded.

Neighbors helped Steunenberg into his house and called a doctor, but within twenty minutes the man was dead. The news spread quickly throughout the small community. At seven o'clock Governor Frank R. Gooding in Boise was notified by telephone. Quickly he ordered a special train to take him the thirty miles to Caldwell. He also authorized a large reward for the capture of the assassin.

The Caldwell authorities, realizing that the criminal must still be in their community, sealed off all avenues of escape. Conversation centered on the assassination and speculation as to the identity of the killer. The police checked the registers of all hotels and boarding houses, and the names of strangers were placed on the list of suspects.

Harry Orchard was scarcely a stranger. He had been around Caldwell for several months posing as a sheep buyer named Tom Hogan. He had frequented the Saratoga Hotel where the bar was the favorite spot for local businessmen to pass the time of day. In the hotel coffee shop he had met a waitress with whom he soon struck up a friendship.

During this time he had also made a number of inquiries concerning Steunenberg and his personal habits. This action did not arouse suspicion, however, since his role as a sheepman looking for a good business deal made this kind of behavior quite natural. On several occasions Jack Simpkins came to Caldwell and helped him look over the town. Orchard-Hogan met Steunenberg only once during this period of "casing" the situation, but he did follow the ex-governor about considerably. On at least two occasions, once in the Idanha Hotel in Boise and again on a Boise-Nampa train, Orchard had bombs set for Steunenberg but did not use them.

When he finally disposed of Steunenberg in the Caldwell bombing Harry Orchard remained as calm as an innocent man would have been. Returning to the hotel minutes after the bombing, he helped the bartender tie a package by holding a steady finger on the knot. The next day, although noticeably quiet and untalkative to his waitress friend, Orchard was the picture of unconcern in a town that was buzzing with talk about the murder. Perhaps he was too unconcerned; when he called a prominent rancher out of a group of men discussing the murder to inquire about the possibility of buying a good bunch of wethers cheap, it must have been too much. Harry Orchard became a suspect. His room at the hotel was searched. Several bits of damning evidence were found including traces of dynamite and fishline which matched the string on the Steunenberg gate.

By chance, Sheriff Harvey K. Brown of Baker County, Oregon, was in Caldwell at the time. He recognized Thomas Hogan as Harry Orchard, a miner he had known in the Cracker Creek district of eastern Oregon. This identification prompted further investigation which included the opening of Orchard's trunk which had been left in the baggage room of the depot since his arrival in town. Records showed that Orchard had opened the trunk on the day of the murder. Now, when the authorities opened the trunk, they found a revolver, a pair of brass knuckles, and a pair of nippers of the kind used in setting caps in powder. It was enough to convince the local police that they were on the right track. Orchard, still under the name of Hogan, was formally charged with murder on January 1, 1906.

At his preliminary hearing before Judge Church on January 2 Orchard told the court that he would have legal counsel as soon as news of his arrest appeared in the newspapers. True to Orchard's prediction, on the following day a telegram arrived from Robertson, Miller & Rosenhaupt, the Spokane law firm which had represented the Western Federation of Miners in the Coeur d'Alene troubles. It announced that Fred Miller would start the next day for Caldwell.

On January 3, 1906, Sheriff Edward Bell of Teller County, Colorado, arrived in Caldwell and positively identified the prisoner as Harry Orchard, the Western Federation man wanted in Cripple Creek for the Independence depot bombing. On January 8 Fred Miller finally arrived in Caldwell after mysteriously leaving his original train at Walla Walla. Miller later attributed this delay to illness, but it may have been caused by the lawyer's reluctance to get involved in the case. Jack Simpkins was in Spokane, and probably was responsible for arranging Miller's trip to defend Orchard. Miller may have changed his mind after leaving Spokane, particularly if he read in the morning papers on the train of Sheriff Bell's identification of the prisoner in Caldwell. It is a matter of record that later that day Miller left the train, and that Simpkins sent a cryptic message to union headquarters in Denver. The telegram said, "Cannot get a lawyer to defend Hogan. Answer."[1] Thus, it appears that Jack Simpkins, a member of the

---

[1] Testimony of Charles H. Moyer, Transcript p. 3878 ff. Copies of the telegram and cipher code appear in the transcript at this point.

union's executive committee, had acted for the union in arranging legal aid for Orchard even before news dispatches were carrying the correct identification of the assassin. Months later in the Haywood trial the prosecution tried to determine exactly what had taken place between Simpkins, the law firm, and the union by calling Fred Miller as a witness. But Miller had joined the defense staff and was kept out of the state during most of the trial, taking depositions in San Francisco.

In the meantime President Charles H. Moyer of the Western Federation of Miners had given out a statement announcing a Federation inquiry to prepare for any charges that might be brought against the organization. In a telegram to the financial secretary of the Silver City local, Bill Haywood ordered the employment of attorney John Nugent to represent the interests of the union in the Orchard affair. The Silver City miners complied, but rather reluctantly, as they considered the position of the WFM in Idaho quite delicate.

The state of Idaho was also taking steps to solve the crime. Inasmuch as the criminal investigation function of government in Idaho was as impotent as the militia, it was necessary for the state to employ a detective agency to conduct investigations. Originally the Thiele Agency of Spokane was employed, but by mid-January of 1906 the famous Pinkerton Agency entered the case. At the same time the suspect, Harry Orchard, was moved from the Canyon County jail in Caldwell to the Idaho state penitentiary in Boise.

At the penitentiary Orchard was kept in solitary confinement for a period of ten days. At the end of this time he was confronted by the man who became the most controversial and yet little-known figure of the entire case, James McParland of the Pinkerton Agency. McParland was the manager of the Western division of the detective agency. He was a mild looking, rather elderly man, the sort of person who could easily be taken for a retired business or professional man. But McParland had acquired a reputation as one of the most successful and ruthless men ever to serve as a detective in the United States, largely as a result of his work among the Molly Maguires, a secret terrorist organization in the anthracite coal fields of Pennsylvania some thirty years earlier.

In many respects it was McParland who was responsible for the strategy of the prosecution during the next year and a half, in lining up witnesses and conducting the "leg work" so essential to a successful prosecution. James H. Hawley entered the case as the state's special prosecutor within a few days after the crime, and during the early stages of investigation he and McParland met frequently with Governor Gooding to lay plans for the arrests and investigations which were to follow. But, since most of the events and principals of the case were related to Western Federation activities in Colorado, James McParland, who was familiar with those activities, assumed a certain degree of leadership within the prosecution forces.

When McParland met Harry Orchard in the penitentiary in Boise, Orchard was still maintaining his innocence through his lawyer, Fred Miller, who had gone to Denver to collect a $1,500 retainer from the WFM. In a series of long conversations with Orchard (during which Orchard guessed McParland's identity, a tribute to the detective's reputation among mining men), McParland convinced Orchard that he had been "used" by the "Inner Circle" of the Western Federation who would now abandon him. According to Orchard's version of what happened during these visits as well as McParland's daily reports, the detective cited examples of how members of the Molly Maguires had gone free after turning state's evidence against their co-conspirators.[2] Although he was careful not to promise immunity, McParland implied that the state of Idaho would look with great favor upon a similar confession from Orchard.

Although it has been asserted that a religious motive caused Orchard's decision at this time, the evidence indicates that Orchard was as yet motivated purely by instincts of self preservation. In any event, during a three-day period at the end of January 1906 in the warden's office at the prison Orchard gave McParland the

---

[2] Harry Orchard, "Confession . . .," November, 1907, pp. 125-126. Also in McParland Pinkerton reports, *circa* January 30, 1906.

information the dectective wanted, while a stenographer recorded it. This was the famous confession of Harry Orchard. Oddly enough, there seems to be no copy of this original document extant today. Understandably, the detective agency did not immediately make the confession available to the press since this would have tipped off those people implicated by the confession before steps could be taken to assure their arrest.

Sketchy versions of the confession later found their way to the press, but from these it was impossible to know exactly what was contained in the original version. Harry Orchard by the time of the Haywood trial had expanded the confession into a magazine serial version in *McClure's* and further into a book,[3] with the religious influence of Dean Hinks of the Episcopal cathedral in Boise being apparent by this time. But initially Orchard seems to have been trying to save his skin, rather than his soul, in confessing to his crimes.

The Haywood trial offered the first authoritative version of the Orchard confession to the public as Harry Orchard recited his crimes on direct examination and admitted a few more on cross-examination. Virtually all of this information must have been given to McParland in the original confession in the penitentiary, however, since the state proceeded early in 1906 to build its strategy around Orchard's avowed criminal acts. Among these crimes were the blowing up of the Bunker Hill and Sullivan concentrator at Wardner in 1899, the bombing of the Vindicator mine in Cripple Creek in 1903, the Independence depot explosion in 1904, the murder of Lyte Gregory (a detective who had worked for the Mine Owners' Association in Idaho Springs) in Denver in 1905, assassination attempts in Denver on Governor Peabody, Supreme Court Justices Gabbert and Goddard, Adjutant General Sherman Bell, and certain corporation officials, the bombing of Fred Bradley (Bunker Hill and Sullivan manager in the second Coeur d'Alene troubles) in San Francisco in 1904, and the assassination of ex-Governor Steunenberg. In several of these crimes Steve Adams had served as Orchard's accomplice. All of the

---

[3] Harry Orchard (Albert E. Horsley), *The Confession and Autobiography of Harry Orchard* (New York: McClure Co., 1907).

crimes, said Orchard, were encouraged and abetted by the "Inner Circle" of the Western Federation of Miners, particularly Charles H. Moyer, William D. Haywood, George Pettibone, and Jack Simpkins.

With the information contained in this confession James McParland could now begin planning the arrest of the men implicated by Orchard. The whereabouts of Jack Simpkins was unknown, but Moyer, Haywood, and Pettibone were known to be in Denver. The Pinkerton Western Division office was also in Denver, so the union officials could be kept under close scrutiny. It would be necessary to extradite the three men to Idaho, but conventional extradition procedures were slow and subject to habeas corpus writs. In order to insure a fast and foolproof extradition a daring plan was worked out by McParland and Hawley.

Essentially the plan called for the secret signing of extradition papers between the two governors involved, Gooding of Idaho and McDonald of Colorado. This action would be followed by a secret expedition of Idaho officials to Denver, where, on a prearranged Sunday morning, the union leaders would be arrested by Colorado officials, put aboard a special train, and rushed to Boise under guard of both Idaho and Colorado officials as well as Pinkerton detectives.[4] Elaborate planning and communications were necessary to carry out such a scheme, and for this purpose the Pinkerton Agency developed a code for the names of dozens of men who were involved in the coming arrests and investigations, not only the key men of the defense but the prosecution as well. The names of animals were used in the code, and the assignment of names clearly reflected the prosecution's opinion of the man. The "Inner Circle" men got such names as Viper (Bill Haywood) and Rattler (George Pettibone), while the prosecution leaders became Tiger (James Hawley) and Owl (James McParland). Those men who conceivably could be of great value to the state through confessions or cooperation were given ambivalent names such as Fox (Steve Adams) or Possum (Harry Orchard).

[4] Letter, James McParland to Governor Gooding, February 8, 1906. Much of the description of the special train trip is taken from this and subsequent Pinkerton reports.

McParland's complex plan was presented to Governor Gooding on February 8, 1906. Four days later the Canyon County attorney, Owen M. Van Duyn, filed a sworn complaint against Moyer, Haywood, and Pettibone. This document has been widely referred to as the "perjured affidavit" because it charges the three men with having been present at Caldwell on December 30, 1905, and having committed the act of murder, although it was known that the men were in Denver. This affidavit may appear to be perjury to the critic unfamiliar with Idaho law, but there was a statutory provision in Idaho which permitted Van Duyn to swear legally as he did.

> The distinction between an accessory before the fact and a principal and between principals in the first and second degree, in cases of felony, is abrogated; and all persons concerned in the commission of a felony, whether they directly commit the act constituting the offense, or aid and abet in its commission, though not present, shall hereafter be prosecuted, tried, and punished as principals, and no other facts need be alleged in any indictment against such an accessory than are required in an indictment against his principal.[5]

In other words, Van Duyn could legally swear that Haywood as an accessory was physically present at the commission of the crime by the principal, Harry Orchard. Citing this affidavit, Governor Gooding of Idaho then prepared extradition papers for the three men.

In mid-February James H. Hawley, Owen M. Van Duyn, and James McParland went to Denver where they presented the extradition papers to Governor McDonald. McDonald signed the papers, an act which he could legally justify by citing the "full faith" clause of the United States Constitution, even though he might have been aware that the men were not extraditable fugitives in the ordinary sense.

The Idaho officials met Governor McDonald in Denver on Thursday, February 15. The lightning extradition was planned for early Sunday morning. The tightest secrecy prevailed. McParland had devised ways of preventing any possible interference and had

[5] Fremont Wood, Instruction No. 21 to the jury, Transcript, p. 5669 ff. Also in Charles F. Koelsch, *The Haywood Case* (Boise: Idaho Mining Assoc., 1946), p. 20.

tried to throw any potential pursuers off the trail. For example, the Pinkerton man who was to buy sandwiches and provisions for the special train had been instructed to obtain them at a specific cafe in West Denver. As he waited for the order to be made up, the agent was supposed to talk about a train trip he was starting on shortly, a trip to the south. In reality the special train would be going north from Denver toward Cheyenne, but McParland apparently thought the union officers and attorneys might be confused by the southbound tip if they tried to check on the disappearance of Moyer, Haywood, and Pettibone.

On Saturday night all was in readiness. Denver deputies had been assigned the actual job of arresting the three men inasmuch as Idaho had no authority at this point. Pinkerton agents accompanied the local officers. The arrests were to be made early in the morning, but Moyer inadvertently disrupted the timetable when he went to the railroad depot and got aboard a train which was soon to leave for the Black Hills. This forced the Pinkertons to move ahead and arrest the three men immediately before Moyer's train left or before a warning was spread to the other men.

Moyer was arrested on board his train at the Union Depot at about 8 o'clock in the evening. Bill Haywood was arrested at about 9:30 in company with a woman—reportedly his sister-in-law—in what was then referred to as a "house of assignation."[6] George Pettibone was picked up at home about 11:30. The three men were held for part of the night in separate cells of the Denver County jail, but at about three o'clock on Sunday morning they were moved to a hotel just a block from the Union Station. This shuttling about of the prisoners was designed to prevent the service of any legal writs.

Originally the train had been scheduled to leave from the 40th Street yards, but now it was brought to the Union Station on the north side of the city in order to make a faster departure. The three prisoners were put aboard the train at six o'clock Sunday morning, guarded by three Pinkerton detectives, two Colorado militia officers, and one Idaho official. The handcuffed prisoners already knew one of their guards well: Bulkeley Wells, now the

[6] Letter, William E. Borah to "Grier," June 20, 1907. Also in Pinkerton reports of the arrests.

adjutant general of the Colorado National Guard. They were soon to get acquainted with another of their guards, Deputy Warden J. C. Mills of the Idaho state penitentiary.

The race for the Idaho border began on Sunday morning, February 18, 1906. Railroad officials had agreed with the Pinkerton Agency that the train would not stop in any town, and would make its crew changes and fuel and water stops at isolated sidings. McParland was particularly concerned about going through Cheyenne which was a state capital with a U. S. marshal who could serve federal writs. Therefore, the engineer maintained a 30 m.p.h. speed through the Cheyenne yards, too fast for any man to board the train.

The train raced along through Wyoming all day Sunday. No attempt was made to serve any writs at the few lonely sidings at which the train stopped. Judging from McParland's reports on the whole affair, such attempts would not have been honored. It was about 530 miles from Denver to the Idaho state line on the Union Pacific (Oregon Short Line) railroad. The train reached the line Sunday night, and McParland's plan had worked. The prisoners were within the state of Idaho where no habeas corpus writs could be expected from local officials. One anxious moment for the guards occurred in the middle of the night when a hot box forced the train to stop at Pocatello, a strong labor town. No trouble developed, however, and the train resumed its mission when the journal box had been cooled and lubricated. At 9:15 on Monday morning, February 19, the train reached Boise and the prisoners were taken immediately to the state penitentiary.

On the following day Steve Adams was arrested at Haines, Oregon. With Adams accounted for, McParland gave the news of Orchard's confession to the press, although the details were intentionally vague and inaccurate. In fact, so little was known concerning the actual details of the confession that C. P. Connolly, in an excellent and authoritative series of articles at the beginning of the Haywood trial in 1907, attributed to Orchard six crimes not mentioned in the confession.[7]

---

[7] C. P. Connolly, "The Moyer-Haywood Case," *Collier's,* May 18, 1907, p. 22.

Some of these crimes, however, turned out to be the work of Steve Adams. In late February 1906, Adams was placed in the Idaho penitentiary and confined with Harry Orchard. Orchard had apparently agreed with McParland to try to get Adams to confess. Without revealing his own confession, Orchard persuaded Adams to lay the blame for his acts on the "Inner Circle." At the same time McParland was plying Adams with favors, particularly good cigars. On or about March 1 Steve Adams confessed to McParland a series of crimes, some of which he committed with Harry Orchard and some in which other WFM men, particularly Vincent St. John and Jack Simpkins, were involved.

Vincent St. John had been apprehended several weeks earlier at Burke, Idaho. This fact suggests that the state had known what to expect in the Steve Adams confession. Simpkins, however, was never found and he remains to this day one of the great mysteries of this case. During 1906-07 he was reportedly seen in such widely scattered places as Oakley, Idaho; North Park, Colorado; Cananea, Mexico; and La Grande, Oregon. The Thiele Detective Agency asserted that Simpkins met Clarence Darrow in October 1906 at Spokane.[8] Smith reports an interview with John Wourms, a prominent labor lawyer of North Idaho, in which Wourms professed to know accurately the movements of Simpkins during this period. Wourms asserted that Simpkins made his way to British Columbia, but returned to the San Juan Islands of Washington during the Haywood and Pettibone trials of 1907.[9] Holbrook also mentions Puget Sound as the reported hideout of the fugitive.[10] Jensen suggests, and the idea is within the realm of possibility, that Jack Simpkins may have been a Pinkerton detective who simply disappeared rather than have his true identity revealed.[11] However, it does not seem reasonable for the Pinkerton Agency to risk the loss of the case—and it was eventually lost—by preventing a star detective witness from testifying in order to insure that his real identity would not be revealed. In 1892 they

---

[8] *Idaho Statesman,* April 23, 1907, p. 5.

[9] Unpublished notes of R. W. Smith. The interview with Wourms took place in Wallace, Idaho, January 3, 1935.

[10] Stewart Holbrook, *The Rocky Mountain Revolution* (New York: Henry Holt & Co., 1956), p. 298.

[11] Vernon H. Jensen, *Heritage of Conflict* (Ithaca: Cornell University Press, 1950), p. 201.

had no such qualms about disclosing the identity of Charley Siringo, one of the most valuable men they ever had. Thus, Simpkins must remain a riddle in this case.

At this point the prosecution seemingly had done a masterful job of implicating and arresting the men they were after. But the Western Federation of Miners was not idle in the meantime. On the day after Moyer, Haywood, and Pettibone arrived in Boise by special train, the regular train brought in E. F. Richardson, the Denver attorney for the union. Within 48 hours Richardson had begun habeas corpus proceedings in the Idaho Supreme Court. This action was the opening shot of a long and colorful legal battle which was to be waged for the next fifteen months before the first of the three men would finally be tried in May of 1907.

7

THE PRE-TRIAL EVENTS

FROM MARCH OF 1906 until May of 1907 a number of interesting events occurred which served to heighten national interest in Idaho's prosecution of the Western Federation of Miners' officials. Chief among these were the habeas corpus cases which went to the U. S. Supreme Court, the labor demonstrations in support of Haywood, President Roosevelt's famous "undesirable citizens" remark, the trial of Steve Adams, the political campaign of 1906, and the indictment of William E. Borah for land fraud.

Immediately upon arriving in Boise on February 20, 1906, in pursuit of the special train, E. F. Richardson instituted habeas corpus proceedings in the Idaho Supreme Court in behalf of Moyer, Haywood, and Pettibone. Early in March, Moyer's petition was argued before this court. Richardson based the petition on what he alleged was the illegality of the extradition procedure and on defects in the arrest warrants. Moyer denied being in Caldwell at the time described in the warrants, and asserted that the Idaho officials knew he had not been present at the crime when they went to Colorado and brought him to Idaho in violation of the U. S. Constitution. Moyer insisted that he was not a fugitive from justice and thus not extraditable, citing the 4th, 5th, and 14th amendments to the U. S. Constitution and sections 8, 13, and 17 of the Idaho constitution.

The state answered by moving to strike out all references to the removal of the three men from Colorado to Idaho and any conspiracy on the part of officials in the two states. The state supreme court upheld this motion and ruled on March 12, 1906, that the manner of removal of the defendants was not subject to the review of the court after the prisoners were within the custody of Idaho officials. The habeas corpus writ was denied, and the prisoners were remanded to the Canyon County sheriff.

Richardson then prepared a bill of exceptions which was signed by the Idaho Supreme Court, thus permitting an appeal to the federal courts. On March 15, Richardson filed petitions for habeas corpus writs with Judge Beatty of the U. S. Circuit Court in Boise. Four days later the case was argued before this court, with the arguments being largely the same as those used before the state supreme court. The verdict, too, was similar. Judge Beatty ruled that his court had no power to inquire into the methods of extradition once the prisoners were legally in Idaho's custody.

Richardson's next move was an appeal to the U. S. Supreme Court, based on writs of error in the Idaho Supreme Court and the United States Circuit Court. The test case, that of *Pettibone* vs. *Nichols* (Jasper Nichols, the Canyon County sheriff), was accepted by the court and docketed for the session of October 1906.

Each side assembled its legal talent, the men who were soon to be pleading before the Supreme Court as a prelude to the trials of Steve Adams and Bill Haywood. For the prosecution stood James H. Hawley, the dean of Idaho attorneys. With him was the young Boise attorney, William E. Borah, who had joined the prosecution staff although busily engaged in seeking election to the United States Senate. Borah and Hawley were thoroughly familiar with the circumstances of the Western Federation of Miners and the Steunenberg murder. In 1892, shortly after hanging out his shingle in Idaho, Borah had been a spectator at the Boise trials during which James Hawley defended the Coeur d'Alene miners including George Pettibone. In 1889 the two lawyers teamed up in a successful prosecution of Paul Corcoran as the aftermath of the "Troubles of 1899." They had opposed each other on occasion as well, notably in the famous Diamondfield Jack case of 1897 in which Borah represented the state and the sheepmen while Hawley represented the cattle interests behind the defendant. In a sense both men won this case; Diamondfield Jack was found guilty of murder, but was saved from hanging by a dramatic eleventh-hour reprieve engineered by Hawley and ultimately was pardoned.[1]

Although the two men differed politically on many issues and were never law partners, they were good friends as well as an effective legal team. MacLane describes their relationship this way:

> Hawley . . . was the acknowledged leader of the Idaho Bar and was at the height of his powers and reputation . . . Borah as his associate, while a much younger man, had attained a great reputation throughout the west, and was Hawley's rival in popular estimation for the leadership of the Bar, but while associated with him in many cases Borah always acquiesced in Hawley's leadership and made no pretense of competing with him for that position.[2]

The defense, too, had become a team, albeit not one that was ever to be noted for its harmony and mutual respect. Richardson had been joined by Clarence Darrow, the Chicago labor lawyer who had been hired by the defense committee of the Western Federation of Miners. Darrow, like most labor lawyers at this point in American history, could not point to a long list of cases he had won, for the legal rights of the labor movement were not well enough established to provide the necessary precedents in law with which to win such cases. But simply having participated in these important, and sometimes notorious, trials was a mark of prestige among such attorneys, regardless of outcome. Darrow had once been a corporation lawyer, but had been drawn into the labor disputes around Chicago in such famous cases as the Haymarket bombing and the Pullman strike. Most recently he had represented the coal miners in the arbitration of 1902. Richardson had been kept busy in the legal battles of the Colorado labor war of 1903-04, particularly in the Telluride and Idaho Springs strikes.

---

[1] Charles S. Walgamott, *Six Decades Back* (Caldwell, Idaho: The Caxton Printers, 1936), pp. 176-177.

[2] John F. MacLane, *A Sagebrush Lawyer* (New York: Pandick Press, 1953), pp. 156-157.

In the sense of prestige and reputation he had been successful, although he had lost the war while winning the battles.

These four men, Hawley and Borah for the State of Idaho and Richardson and Darrow for the miners, met for the first time in a courtroom when on October 10-11, 1906, they argued the Pettibone habeas corpus case before the United States Supreme Court. The arguments were necessarily restatements of the issues considered in the lower courts, the appellant asserting the illegality of the extradition and the existence of conspiracy and fraud in the removal of the prisoners, while the respondent maintained that the method of removal was not subject to inquiry by the courts but was nevertheless perfectly legal. On December 3, 1906, the Supreme Court affirmed the decision of the lower court in a 7-1 vote (a vacancy existed on the court.) There were three salient points of the circuit court ruling which were sustained. First was a delineation of responsibility for state governors with respect to fugitives. The circuit court had said that in extradition proceedings independent proof, apart from the requisition papers, that the accused was a fugitive from justice need not be demanded by the governor of the surrendering state before issuing an arrest warrant.[3] In the Supreme Court decision, written by Justice John M. Harlan, the court noted that any consideration of the motives of the governor of Colorado would be immaterial and inappropriate. The governor

> . . . would not have violated his duty if it had been made a condition of surrendering the petitioner that evidence be furnished that he was a fugitive from justice within the meaning of the Constitution of the United States. Upon the governor of Colorado rested the responsibility of determining in some proper mode, what the fact was. But he was not obliged to demand proof of such fact by evidence apart from the requisition papers. . . . His failure to require independent proof of the fact that petitioner was a fugitive from justice cannot be regarded as an infringement of any right of the petitioner under the Constitution or laws of the United States.[4]

The second feature of the circuit court decision had been the statement that arranging and carrying out the arrest and deportation of the accused so as to leave him no opportunity to

---

[3] *Pettibone v. Nichols,* 203 U. S., p. 111.
[4] *Ibid.,* p. 114.

prove before the governor of the surrendering state that he was not a fugitive from justice, or to appeal to some court of that state to prevent his illegal deportation, did not violate provisions of the United States Constitution or the federal statutes relating to extradition proceedings.[5] The question here was the speed at which Moyer, Haywood, and Pettibone had been arrested and removed from Colorado. Said the Supreme Court:

> That he had no reasonable opportunity to present these facts before being taken from Colorado constitutes no legal reason why he should be discharged from the custody of the Idaho authorities. No obligation was imposed *by the Constitution or laws of the United States* upon the agent of Idaho to so time the arrest of the petitioner, and so conduct his deportation from Colorado, as to afford him a convenient opportunity, before some judicial tribunal sitting in Colorado, to test the question whether he was a fugitive from justice, and, as such, liable, under the act of Congress, to be conveyed to Idaho for trial there. (Italics are in decision.)[6]

The final point of the circuit court ruling had announced that a person held in actual custody by a state for trial in one of its courts under an indictment for crime against its laws would not be released on habeas corpus by a federal circuit court because the methods by which his personal presence in the state was secured may have violated constitutional or statutory provisions.[7] In affirming this position the Supreme Court said in effect that the legality of the extradition was not an issue when the present custody of the prisoner was otherwise legal. The final paragraph of the high court's decision included this comment:

> Even were it conceded, for the purposes of this case, that the governor of Idaho wrongfully issued his requisition, and that the governor of Colorado erred in honoring it and in issuing his warrant of arrest, the vital fact remains that Pettibone is held by Idaho in actual custody for trial under an indictment charging him with crime against its laws, and he seeks the aid of the circuit court to relieve him from custody, so that he may leave that state and thereby defeat the prosecution against him without trial. In the present case it is not necessary to go behind the indictment and inquire as to how it happened that he came within reach of the process of the Idaho court in which the indictment is pending.[8]

---

[5] *Ibid.*, p. 111.
[6] *Ibid.*, p. 115.
[7] *Ibid.*, p. 111.
[8] *Ibid.*, p. 119.

It is this part of the Supreme Court decision which provided ammunition for the contemporary Socialist critics who attacked the whole United States judicial system as well as the legality of the Idaho trials. It also embarrassed the prosecution forces. Hawley had argued along two main lines: first, that inquiry into the methods of extradition was not a proper subject of judicial review—the point under discussion here—and second, that the extradition was legal nonetheless, particularly with respect to Idaho's laws which permit accessories to be described in indictments in the same terms which apply to principals. The first two points of the Supreme Court decision tend to bear out Hawley's assertion of legality, but the third point—that the legality of the extradition is immaterial—overshadowed the other points, particularly since it appeared in the conclusion of the decision. Even though the Supreme Court had ruled on many previous occasions, and has since ruled on many occasions, that the methods of extradition are not to be inquired into, that was not the whole issue in the Moyer-Haywood-Pettibone cases. But, unfortunately for the prosecution, many people thought it was.

Justice McKenna wrote the dissenting opinion in this case. It was widely quoted by the Socialists at the time, and has been cited in numerous accounts since. Its most famous phrase is, "Kidnapping is a crime, pure and simple."[9] But McKenna built his opinion on the premise that what the Idaho governor did was to "falsely represent" that the men were present at the commission of the crime, and that the Colorado governor knew of the "false" accusation. McKenna thus seems to have overlooked the fact that the Idaho statute, peculiar as it might have been (". . . no other facts need be alleged in any indictment against such an accessory than are required in an indictment against his principal"), permitted the Idaho governor to proceed as he did.

Labor's reaction to the Supreme Court decision was understandably strong. Many labor and Socialist groups passed resolutions condemning the court. One of the most violent came from the Western Federation of Miners stronghold in Goldfield, Nevada. It read in part:

---

[9] *Ibid.*, p. 120.

> Whereas, a man is presumed to be innocent until proven guilty, and these three citizens have protested their innocence, have ever been ready and willing to go to trial and have appealed to the highest court in vain for justice and have been denied justice by that court, and
>
> Whereas, the action of the supreme court of the U. S. is a disgrace to this country, that vaingloriously boasts of its freedom, causing us to doubt the integrity of the court because of the creation in our minds of the suspicion that they do not and cannot dispense impartial justice; that they are men, mortals, controlled by environment, hypnotized by the God Mammon, and have become the tools to the corporate greed and avarice that is oppressing this country and which is slowly throttling the liberty of the United States people; creating in our mind the suspicion that they are mental prostitutes to respectability and gold; that by their decision they have trailed the robes of justice into the mud of materialism and have weakened the belief of the people that the courts are the bulwarks of liberty. . . .
>
> Therefore, We, in mass meeting assembled on this, the 20th day of January, 1907, do condemn them in unmeasured terms, and we, as liberty-loving, peace-desiring and good citizens of Goldfield, Nevada, call upon all thoughtful citizens of this republic to assemble and protest against this outrage, this travesty of justice, and we do desire to impress upon all citizens that in this mad worship of the dollar that our liberties have become null and void and this country is facing a crisis which must be met with prudence, wisdom and courage; therefore, be it
>
> Resolved, that we demand that the judges of the U. S. supreme court be elected by popular vote. . . .[10]

The author of this interesting document was reported to have been Vincent St. John who had been extradited from Idaho to Colorado on a murder charge growing out of the Telluride troubles, a charge that had later been dropped for lack of evidence.

Labor unions and Socialist groups had not waited for the Supreme Court decision to begin criticizing the imprisonment of Moyer, Haywood, and Pettibone. As early as March 1906, demonstrations and meetings were held to pledge support to the labor officials. Early in that month at Socialist gatherings in Chicago this rhyme was composed:

---

[10] *Idaho Statesman,* January 21, 1907, p. 1.

Will Moyer and Haywood die?
If they die,
Here's our cry:
There are twenty million workmen who will know the reason why![11]

Socialist paraders, a year later, were still chanting this rhyme.

Other mass meetings were held early in 1906 in such widely scattered points as New York and San Francisco. In the latter city after an orderly fund-raising meeting a parade proceeded down Market Street carrying red banners. At Market and Kearney there was violent speaking, and disorder turned to riot when the police tried to disperse the crowd. Similar red flag incidents occurred in a number of Socialist demonstrations; there was even an anti-American attitude in some, characterized by the singing of the "Marseillaise" and the carrying of banners proclaiming slogans of the Socialist International.

The Socialist press was quick to press the attack. Eugene Debs went to Girard, Kansas, the publication center for the *Appeal to Reason.* Soon the normally gentle Debs was writing bitter denunciations of capitalistic justice on the front pages of the paper. On March 10, 1906, he wrote his famous "Arouse, Ye Slaves" article in which he hinted at armed revolution if the miners' leaders were railroaded to the gallows. This issue was followed by the "rescue edition" of April 28, which claimed a distribution of 4,000,000 copies compared to the normal circulation of several hundred thousand. Not only did the *Appeal to Reason* hammer away with the traditional slogans of class warfare, but it used all the sentimental devices of yellow journalism. On February 16, 1907, it ran a picture of a smiling, dimpled child captioned "Henrietta Haywood." Beneath the picture were the words of a song entitled, "Will Papa Die?" identified as having been written by one Col. Dick Maple, editor of *The National Rip-Saw,* to be sung to the tune of "Hold the Fort." The first verse said,

Ho! my comrades, see the signal flaunting in the West:
  See the hateful scaffold building—all at Greed's behest.
See those boys of Colorado: hear their martyr's cry:
  Hear "Bill" Haywood's little baby ask, "Will Papa die?"

---

[11] *Portland Oregonian,* March 5, 1906, p. 2.

And the chorus:

Oh! ye lads of Fair Columbia, listen to the cry:
  Hear that fairhaired babe of Haywood's ask,
"Will Papa die?"[12]

In *The Socialist,* a paper which moved from Ohio to Idaho during 1906 to be nearer the scene of the trials, a full-page cartoon was printed showing a vicious character labelled "Capitalism, alias Mine Owners Association," sitting on a heap of skulls at the base of a gibbet. On the gibbet an empty noose hangs while three vultures perch on the top beam—Gooding, Borah, and Smith (the Canyon County judge who was slated to try the cases.)[13]

Speakers were equally intemperate. At a mass meeting of coal miners in Pittsburg, Kansas, a man named Rolfe urged workers to arm themselves and prepare for a bloody struggle. "The Dred Scott decision," said Rolfe, "was followed by the Civil War. The Moyer-Haywood decision will be followed by a rebellion of the working class."[14]

At Goldfield, Nevada, the Western Federation of Miners and the newly founded Industrial Workers of the World closed up the town on January 20, 1907, in an enormous demonstration which coincided with the second anniversary of the St. Petersburg "Red Sunday" massacre of Russian workers. The Goldfield marchers wore ribbons which said: "Bloody Sunday. Moyer Haywood and Pettibone." At a mass meeting in the miners union hall Vincent St. John was the principal speaker, beneath banners that proclaimed "If they pack a jury to hang our men, we will pack Hell full of them," and "A capitalist for every hair of our brothers' head."[15]

As violent and full of threats as these demonstrations and writings were, it remained for another event to trigger even greater demonstrations and more scathing denunciations by Socialists and labor sympathizers. For some time President Theodore

---

[12] Quoted in Bulletin No. 25, Tamiment Institute Library, January-February, 1960, p. 1.

[13] Reproduced in *Idaho Statesman,* October 5, 1906, p. 5.

[14] *Idaho Statesman,* January 21, 1907, p. 1.

[15] *Idaho Statesman,* January 21, 1907, p. 1.

Roosevelt had been engaged in a running argument with E. H. Harriman, the railway magnate. In a letter to James S. Sherman, a Congressman from New York, Roosevelt late in 1906 had referred to Harriman as an "undesirable citizen" comparable to Debs, Moyer, or Haywood.[16] For some reason Roosevelt released this statement to the press early in 1907. The reaction of the Socialists was intense. Roosevelt was accused of trying to prejudice the upcoming trials in Idaho. Enormous parades and demonstrations took place in many cities, with marchers wearing buttons proclaiming "I am an undesirable citizen." A number of labor and Socialist groups passed resolutions condemning Roosevelt's interference, and a number of newspapers commented editorially that it was, at best, an indiscretion on his part.

Among many others, the chairman of the Cook County Moyer-Haywood Conference, Honore Jaxon of Chicago, wrote to Roosevelt in April of 1907 protesting the "undesirable citizen" reference. In answering Jaxon, Roosevelt made his own position clear, and endorsed the kind of objectivity pursued by such writers as Ray Stannard Baker and C. P. Connolly:

> I have received your letter of the 19th instant, in which you enclose the draft of a formal letter which is to follow. I have been notified that several delegations bearing similar requests are on the way hither. In the letter you, on behalf of the Cook County Moyer-Haywood Conference, protest against certain language I used in a recent letter, which you assert to be designed to influence the course of justice in the case of the trial for murder of Messrs. Moyer and Haywood. I entirely agree with you that it is improper to endeavor to influence the course of justice, whether by threats or in any similar manner. For this reason I have regretted most deeply the actions of such organizations as your own in undertaking to accomplish this very result in the very case of which you speak. For instance, your letter is headed "Cook County Moyer-Haywood-Pettibone Conference" with the headlines: "Death cannot, will not and shall not claim our brothers." This shows that you and your associates are not demanding a fair trial, but are announcing in advance that the verdict shall only be one way, and that you will not tolerate any other verdict. Such action is flagrant in its impropriety, and I join heartily in condemning it.

---

[16] Letter, Theodore Roosevelt to James S. Sherman, October 8, 1906, in Elting E. Morison, editor, *The Letters of Theodore Roosevelt,* Vol. V (Cambridge: Harvard University Press, 1952) pp. 447-452.

But it is a simple absurdity to suppose that because any man is on trial for a given offense he is therefore to be freed from all criticisms upon his general conduct and manner in life. In my letter to which you object I referred to a certain prominent financier, Mr. Harriman, on the one hand, and to Messrs. Moyer, Haywood and Debs on the other, as being equally undesirable citizens. It is foolish to assert that this was designed to influence the trial of Moyer and Haywood and to assert that it was designed to influence the suits that have been brought against Mr. Harriman. I neither expressed nor indicated any opinion as to whether Messrs. Moyer and Haywood were guilty of the murder of Governor Steunenberg. If they are guilty they certainly ought to be punished. But no possible outcome either of the trial or the suits can affect my judgement as to the desirability of the type of citizenship of those whom I mentioned. Messrs. Moyer, Haywood and Debs stand as representatives of those men who have done as much to discredit the labor movement as the worst speculative financiers or the most unscrupulous employers of labor and debauchers of legislatures have done to discredit honest capitalists and fair dealing business men. They stand as the representatives of men who by their public utterances and manifestos; by the utterances of the papers they control and inspire, and by the words and deeds associated with or subordinated to them, habitually appear, as guilty of incitement to or apology for bloodshed and violence.

If this does not constitute undesirable citizenship, then there can never be any undesirable citizens. . . . they represent as thoroughly undesirable a type of citizenship as can be found in this country; a type which, in the letter to which you so unreasonably take exceptions, I showed not to be confined to any one class, but to exist among some representatives of great capitalists as well as among some representatives of wage earners.

In that letter I condemned both types. Certain representatives of the great capitalists in turn condemn me for including Mr. Harriman in my condemnation of Messrs. Moyer and Haywood. Certain of the representatives of labor in their turn condemned me because I included Messrs. Moyer and Haywood as undesirable citizens together with Mr. Harriman. I am as profoundly indifferent to the condemnation in one case as in the other. . . .

You say you ask for a "square deal" for Messrs. Moyer and Haywood. So do I. When I say "square deal," I mean a square deal to everyone; it is equally a violation of the policy of the square deal for the capitalist to protest against denunciation of a capitalist who is guilty of wrong doing and for a labor leader to protest against the denunciation of a labor leader who has been guilty of wrong doing. I stand for equal justice to both and so far as in my power lies I shall uphold justice whether the man accused of guilt has behind him the wealthiest corporations, the greatest aggregation of

> riches in the country, or whether he has behind him the most influential labor organization in the country.[17]

Roosevelt's position apparently placated some union members. A delegation from the Central Federated Union of New York visited the president to discuss his attitude on Moyer and Haywood, and reported that their visit had been "pleasant and satisfactory."[18] Roosevelt released to these union men the text of a letter he had written to the United States Attorney General a year earlier. In that letter Roosevelt had directed the Attorney General to report any miscarriages of justice in the Haywood case on the part of the states of Idaho or Colorado and on the part of the friends of the prisoners.[19] This information tended to vindicate Roosevelt from the allegations made against him by his critics, but by no means were his critics silenced.

Conservative labor leaders, such as Samuel Gompers and John Mitchell, were in a somewhat ambivalent position during this time. They extended the moral and financial support of their unions to the Haywood defense, but they could not go too far in aligning themselves with the vociferous radical element of the labor movement without jeopardizing their own position. Governor Gooding of Idaho, who had been severely criticized by labor for his role in the extradition, invited Gompers and Mitchell to visit Idaho with a committee of workingmen to investigate the charges of conspiracy for themselves, and to interview Orchard and Adams to determine whether they had made any deals with the state—but not to hear their confessions. It was a shrewd political move for Gooding. Labor pressure on Gompers forced the union leader to decline the invitation and to denounce the illegal and brutal "kidnapping." Gompers telegraphed Gooding, "Surely, if Orchard and Adams cannot give details of confession, what benefit can result from Mr. Mitchell's and my hearing their general statement?"[20] But by declining Gooding's invitation the union leaders put themselves in the awkward position of prejudging the case

[17] *Idaho Statesman,* April 24, 1907, p. 1. Theodore Roosevelt, letter to Honore Jaxon, April 22, 1907, quoted in Morison, *op. cit.,* pp 653-655.

[18] *Idaho Statesman,* May 3, 1907, p. 1.

[19] *Idaho Statesman,* May 6, 1907, p. 1. The letter, Roosevelt to William Henry Moody, March 26, 1906, appears in Morison, *op. cit.,* pp. 196-200.

[20] *Portland Oregonian,* March 31, 1906, p. 2.

and identifying themselves with that part of the labor movement which had criticized Gooding for a similar prejudgment.

The year 1906 was an election year in Idaho, and Gooding was seeking re-election. A readymade issue existed for the governor: law and order. The most influential organ of political opinion in the state, the *Idaho Statesman* of Boise, editorialized that the Steunenberg murder case was the vital question of the campaign. "Our people must come to an understanding of the fact that we cannot afford to repudiate the governor under the existing conditions."[21] Gooding stumped the state, hinting at the evidence to be given in the upcoming trials, and assuring that the defendants would be given a fair trial while managing to imply that they would be convicted.

Borah campaigned for Gooding, while at the same time courting for himself public sentiment which might influence the next legislature's choice for Idaho's available seat in the U. S. Senate. The supremacy of the law and order issue was apparent with Borah, too; he dramatically told one audience that if he were to be named to the Senate "this moment with the condition that I resign my work in this noted case the certificate would instantly be returned and I would pursue the prosecution of this case, which is the basest and most awful in the annals of crime."[22]

The Idaho political situation was watched with interest nationally as well as in the Pacific Northwest. President Roosevelt sent William Howard Taft, his Secretary of War, to Idaho to make "law and order" speeches in support of Gooding's candidacy. In Boise where he was eloquently introduced by William E. Borah, Taft proclaimed, "Should Governor Gooding be defeated, this issue would be heralded the country over as a repudiation by the people of the State of Idaho of the Governor because he stood for law and order."[23]

This challenge must have been seriously considered by the

---

[21] *Idaho Statesman,* October 11, 1906, p. 4.

[22] William E. Borah, speech at Moscow, Idaho, reported in *Idaho Statesman,* October 12, 1906, p. 3.

[23] *Portland Oregonian,* November 4, 1906, p. 4.

Idaho electorate who otherwise had no clear choice between Democrats and Republicans running for office. In the election that November the Republican party was given a clear mandate, winning the governorship, all elective state offices, and both houses of the legislature. Gooding, however, had the smallest plurality of any winning candidate. This might suggest that many voters did not identify Gooding as the only "law and order" candidate. His opponent was Charles O. Stockslager, chief justice of the Idaho Supreme Court—and onetime judge in the Diamondfield Jack case. Stockslager had been instrumental in bringing McParland into the Haywood case. He also qualified as a "law and order" candidate by having ruled adversely on the habeas corpus petitions of Moyer, Haywood, and Pettibone. Incidentally, Stockslager won in Ada County, future site of the trials.

Gooding's biennial message to the new legislature in January 1907 reviewed the Steunenberg affair. It spoke of the state's decision to assume the prosecution instead of Canyon County, it reviewed the appointment of Hawley, Borah, and Stone as prosecutors, and it discussed the deficit financing arrangements which the state had made in order to conduct the trial.[24] Shortly thereafter the legislature elected William E. Borah to the United States Senate. Still later, when the House passed a resolution commending Gooding for his prosecution of the murder trials, the defense attorneys must have viewed with alarm the apparent supremacy of the "law and order" forces in Idaho.

The trials themselves had not been forgotten in the meantime, but had merely been postponed by a series of events, chiefly the U. S. Supreme Court hearings on the habeas corpus petitions. The original grand jury true bills against the three defendants had been returned in Caldwell in March of 1906. Trial had been set for May, but had to be postponed until the Supreme Court decision had been made. During this period of waiting a new district judge, E. L. Bryan, had been elected. When the case was finally ready for trial early in 1907 Judge Bryan found it necessary to disqualify himself inasmuch as he had served briefly as a lawyer for Harry Orchard under an appointment made by his predecessor,

[24] *Idaho Statesman,* January 9, 1907, pp. 9-10.

Judge Frank Smith. Judge Fremont Wood of the adjacent judicial district for Ada County entered the case in place of Judge Bryan. Shortly thereafter a change of venue motion was granted by Judge Wood and the site of the trial was shifted to the Ada County courthouse in Boise.

Still another delay occurred when the two legal staffs became involved in the prosecution of the Steve Adams case in North Idaho. Adams, after his confession to McParland, had been kept under close but comfortable security (he lived with his wife in a cottage at the prison) by the state who wanted to use him as a star witness against the Western Federation of Miners' officials. The defense forces were worried about the effect of Adams' testimony, but they were unable to see the prisoner who was held incommunicado and without charge in the penitentiary.

But the Western Federation attorneys prevailed upon an uncle of Steve Adams, James W. Lillard of Baker County, Oregon, to visit Adams in the penitentiary and persuade him to repudiate his confession. Lillard was also to assure Adams that the union attorneys would then defend him when and if he were brought to trial. Lillard succeeded in seeing Adams in the penitentiary and even managed to get his nephew released on a habeas corpus writ in the district court of Ada County. On September 8, 1906, the state made no effort to restrain the prisoner and he was released from the courtroom. On the same day, however, Shoshone County authorities sent word that they wanted Adams on a murder charge, growing out of the death of two claim jumpers on Jack Simpkins' land in North Idaho in 1904, a crime that Adams had apparently revealed in his confession. Adams was returned to the penitentiary to be held for the Shoshone County officials.

During the time that Adams had been held in the prison, the state had checked several features of his confession to locate any corroborating evidence which could be used in court. Late in March, Adams was taken to Pocatello to locate a buried cache of "Greek fire," a liquid explosive that he had planned to use on a trainload of scabs in 1903. Most of the bottles were found intact. On another expedition later that spring Bulkeley Wells and Deputy Warden Mills took Steve Adams to Telluride, Colorado, to try to find the body of J. W. Barney, the murdered nonunion shift boss of the Smuggler Mine whose body Adams had helped to bury in 1901. On this trip Adams failed to locate the body because of snow on the ground, but eventually on a second trip after the Haywood trial was over he led the officials to the body. During these trips to Colorado with Steve Adams, J. C. Mills got well acquainted with Adams; he believed that Adams was telling the truth in his confession and that Adams lived in deadly fear of the Western Federation of Miners.[25]

Perhaps it was this fear, or perhaps it was his uncle's persuasiveness, but Steve Adams decided to repudiate his confession. When he was arrested on the Shoshone County warrant charging him with murder, Adams announced his repudiation. On September 13, Warden Whitney and several guards took Adams from the penitentiary and started on the long trip to North Idaho. Fearing the habeas corpus writs which might be served in Oregon or Washington, the two states through which the train trip to North Idaho normally would be made, the party made the trip "overland," by way of Weiser and Council by rail, and over the balance of the trip by wagon. This trip took five days, but it permitted the state of Idaho to retain jurisdiction over the prisoner.

After a preliminary hearing in Wallace in September, Adams was bound over for trial for the murder of Fred Tyler, one of the two deceased claimjumpers. Trial was set for the January 1907 term of court under Judge W. W. Woods (not to be confused with Judge Fremont Wood of Ada County, soon to be presiding over the Haywood trial.)

The state's prosecution of Steve Adams on the murder charge was generally considered to be a part of the overall strategy of the Moyer-Haywood-Pettibone prosecution. Since Adams could no longer be counted on as a corroborating witness to strengthen Harry Orchard's testimony, the state needed a lever to force him into testifying against the union leaders. If Adams himself could be convicted of a serious crime the state could then hold out the hope of commutation or pardon to him in return for his service as a witness against Moyer, Haywood, and Pettibone.

---

[25] Conversation with Mrs. J. C. Mills, Boise, Idaho, August 10, 1960.

In a sense the Steve Adams trial was a dress rehearsal for the Haywood trial which followed shortly thereafter. Hawley shared the prosecution duties with the local prosecutor, Henry P. Knight. Darrow and Richardson, with WFM defense fund backing, represented Adams. Each side had the opportunity to feel out the opposing forces while testing its own strength. McParland reported the existence of a rift between Darrow and Richardson even before the Adams trial was underway;[26] later he observed that Darrow was more persuasive than Richardson with juries.[27] Such bits of intelligence enabled each side to plan its grand strategy.

The Adams case was a hard one for a jury to decide. The prosecution had a corpse (a box of bones which was brought into the courtroom) and a repudiated confession which the judge had admitted as evidence subject to the jury's judgment as to its free and voluntary origin. The defense had an alibi, established by a number of Adams' cronies, and Adams' testimony that his confession was extorted from him by threats of hanging or deportation to Colorado. The jury was a well-balanced group representing many social classes and occupational groups. They could not agree, and the case ended with the jury hopelessly deadlocked at 6-6.

With the Adams case out of the way for the time being, the state could move ahead with the prosecution of the Western Federation officials. After Fremont Wood replaced Judge Bryan and Boise replaced Caldwell as the scene of the trial, the trial of William D. Haywood was finally set for May 9, 1907.

Less than a month before the trial was scheduled to begin, the prosecution forces were embarrassed by a startling new development. A federal grand jury, meeting in Boise to investigate land frauds in Idaho, returned indictments against several persons including William E. Borah who was slated to serve as a prosecutor in the Haywood trial. Borah was implicated because of his role as attorney for the Barber Lumber Company in its acquisition of timber claims.

---

26 Pinkerton report, McParland to Gooding, January 2, 1907.

27 Pinkerton report, McParland to Gooding, March 4, 1907.

There has been considerable discussion of the political basis of this indictment. The Western Federation attorneys in general were pleased to see Borah's awkward new position at the start of the trial, but they were hardly capable of having engineered the federal grand jury indictment themselves. The commonly accepted explanation of the motive behind the indictment concerns factional rivalry within the Republican party. Borah had captured the leadership of the party in Idaho with his election to the Senate a few months earlier. The U. S. District Attorney for Idaho, Norman M. Ruick, apparently acting in behalf of certain leaders of the Republican machine within the state, spearheaded the effort to involve Borah in the land frauds.[28]

Land frauds were occurring in a number of western states at this time because of imperfections in the various acts of Congress affecting the public domain. Thus, there was a certain degree of routineness in the Boise grand jury's investigation. The consensus in Idaho, however, seemed to be that Ruick had deliberately timed the investigation to embarrass Borah at the moment when the Senator was preparing to prosecute wrongdoing. Significantly, it was necessary for Ruick to expand his grand jury to nearly double its normal size before he could get a majority (12-10) to vote to include Borah in the indictment.[29]

The indictment hung over Borah's head during the Haywood trial. What effect it had on his performance in the trial is not clear, but Borah was worried enough to consider resigning his new Senate seat. He wrote to Senator Bourne, "Not having [an exoneration from the administration], I have thoroughly made up my mind to go ahead, secure my acquittal and resign my position as senator."[30] His personal correspondence during the summer of 1907 reflects his concern with his own position, rather than his role in the Haywood trial. For a freshman Senator not yet seated, Borah had a remarkable number of friends in high places, and he corresponded with many prominent men who interceded in his behalf in Washington. This intercession helped to swing

---

[28] Claudius Johnson, *Borah of Idaho* (New York: Longmans, Green and Co., 1936), p. 84.

[29] *Portland Oregonian,* April 18, 1907, p. 1.

[30] William E. Borah, letter to Jonathan Bourne, July 6, 1907.

Roosevelt and the Attorney General from an attitude of skepticism over Borah's innocence to one of impatience with Ruick instead.

In the fall of 1907, after the Haywood trial was history, Borah was tried in federal court in Boise. His old friend James H. Hawley represented him. Although the indictment was technically faulty Hawley chose to seek an acquittal rather than to have Borah go free under any stigma of moral guilt. Using bold and imaginative strategy, Hawley waived cross-examination of witnesses and even his own summation argument. In the summation arguments the prosecution had opened with a statement of facts in the case, reserving for the closing argument all of the persuasive appeals normally employed at this point. The prosecution had even "imported" a particularly persuasive lawyer, M. C. Burch of Detroit, to make this final argument. But the judge ruled that since Hawley had waived argument, the prosecution could not reply. Thus the case went to the jury with no defense argument, and only a factual presentation for the prosecution.

Borah was acquitted. That evening in a triumphant speech from the porch of the Idanha Hotel in Boise he promised an enthusiastic audience that he would get rid of his prosecutors when he got to Washington, "these human hyenas who feast on the dead as well as the living"—a reference to the fact that the deceased Frank Steunenberg had been indicted in connection with the land-fraud cases.[31] Within a few months Borah succeeded in carrying out his promise: President Roosevelt, upon the Idaho senator's recommendation, removed and replaced the U. S. District Attorney and the U. S. Marshal for the state.

This discussion of the Borah indictment and trial has been carried to its conclusion here, even though chronologically it ended after the Haywood trial, in order to point out Borah's unique power and influence at this stage of his career. In a sense he had his own press corps, prominent newspaper men who had worked in his behalf during the days prior to his trial. Chief among these would be Calvin Cobb, publisher of the *Idaho Statesman* (who also seemed to be implicated in the Barber Lumber affair), Martin

[31] Conversation with Hawley's son James, Boise, Idaho, August 1, 1960.

Egan of Associated Press, Oscar King Davis of the *New York Times,* William Allen White of the *Emporia Gazette,* and C. P. Connolly of *Collier's.* Borah paid Connolly $300 in August 1907, presumably for the writer's influence in Washington.[32] Each of these men covered the Haywood trial; their friendship and/or financial relationships with Borah must necessarily cast some doubt on their impartiality in covering that trial.

The newsmen who covered the Haywood trial, whether pro-Borah or not, must have sensed the great drama and irony in the events which were soon to be unfolding before them. By a strange twist of fate here was Borah participating in the last trial of his legal career with the suspicion of wrongdoing hanging over his head. Here was James H. Hawley, the godfather of the Western Federation of Miners, now ready to denounce and expose the union as a criminal organization. Here was Clarence Darrow, who had recently written a number of philosophical tracts opposing violence, preparing now to defend the union's acts of brutality because they were committed for a good cause. Even the setting had an irony of its own; this was the same Ada County courthouse in which the Western Federation of Miners had been conceived in 1892, within sight of the Owyhee Mountains where Bill Haywood laid down his pick in 1901 to launch his career as a labor leader.

If the events of the preceding 18 months were any indication, the newspaper men and their readers everywhere could look forward to a trial replete with all the passion and human conflict produced when powerful men play for great stakes.

---

[32] Acknowledged in C. P. Connolly letter to William E. Borah, September 12, 1907.

PART TWO

*A trial at law is simply a competition in persuasion. It is a contest where many influences are brought to bear to persuade a judge or a jury to take certain action. Law is administered through the minds, the consciences, the emotions, and the prejudices of men. It is the task of the attorney to consider all these matters and endeavor to discover and utilize all the various influences that have a bearing on the problem.**

* Albert S. Olson, *The Problem of Proof* (Newark, New Jersey: The Essex Press, 1926), p. 85.

8

TWELVE GOOD MEN and TRUE

ONE OF THE UNIQUE FEATURES of forensic speaking is the choice the speaker is allowed to exercise in determining who will be in his immediate audience, the jury. American lawyers enjoy the right of challenge in the selection of jurors, not only challenges for cause which must be justified before the judge, but peremptory challenges as well, those extralegal and extralogical decisions which permit lawyers to play hunches and to utilize their knowledge of human psychology. In important trials, when social issues or legal consequences may hinge on the verdict of the jury, a great deal of time and effort goes into the examination and selection of the twelve men.

The attorneys in the Haywood case recognized that they were involved in a truly important trial. Fremont Wood, in reflecting on the trial some years later, observed:

> At the time of the selection of the jury it became apparent that the case was being tried before a greater jury than that selected in the courtroom and this fact undoubtedly had its influence upon the Court and also upon the attorneys representing both sides who realized that every movement was being scrutinized by more interested people than had ever before followed the trial of an individual case in the history of the country.[1]

---

[1] Fremont Wood, *The Introductory Chapter to the History of the Trials of Moyer, Haywood, and Pettibone* (Caldwell, Idaho: The Caxton Printers, 1931), p. 33.

Thus, several distinct audiences were recognized by the attorneys planning their strategy: judge and jury, the courtroom, the community, and the national and international audience. But the only one over which the lawyers exercised direct control was the jury itself. By choosing this twelve-man audience well, the attorneys could minimize the need for having the larger audience on their side, too.

By no means did the process of jury selection begin only in the courtroom when this great trial opened on May 9, 1907. For a number of weeks before the trial, agents for the defense and counteragents for the prosecution had been engaged in canvassing Ada County to determine the political and social orientation of potential jurors. Pairs of men, posing as magazine and book salesmen, toured the county, talking about the trial and drawing out reactions from the individuals to whom they talked.

The canvass was not a new device in the history of the Haywood case. Early in 1907 the defense had conducted a canvass in Canyon County to provide documentary proof of the bias of the local citizenry in successfully arguing for a change of venue. Now, several months later, the defense was once again involved in a canvass. The most interesting feature of the Ada Country canvass was the fact that the prosecution had direct access to the information which was obtained. At least one Pinkerton agent, Operative 21, was employed by the defense on the canvass. This detective was able to furnish to the prosecution long lists of names of prospective jurors, together with the defense ratings of each man's usefulness.

Seven of the twelve men who finally were selected for the Haywood jury had been rated earlier after being polled by these defense agents. In White Cross precinct George Powell was listed as "O.K. for defense" while Dan Clark was rated "N. G.," no good. In Green Meadows precinct H. F. Messecar was reported to be a Republican and "N. G." In Union precinct S. D. Gilman was found to be a Democrat and "O. K." while J. A. Robertson and Lee Schrivener were said to be Republicans and "N. G." to the defense. In Maple Grove precinct Finley McBean was listed as a Republican and "N. G."[2]

[2] Pinkerton reports, Operative 21, April 14, 24-25, 26, 28, 1907.

Significantly, every one of these pretrial ratings proved to be wrong when the jurors voted on the first ballot at the conclusion of the trial. Those rated "N. G." all voted for acquittal and those rated "O.K." all favored conviction. It is difficult to say whether this contradiction indicates that the defense forces had faulty information or whether the defense knew of the prosecution detectives and deliberately fed them erroneous information. Considering the fact that the canvassers were largely Socialist drifters paid $3.50 a day for their efforts, it is quite possible that their ratings on the list may have been hasty judgments based on information reluctantly given by the Ada County farmers who were suspicious of strangers talking about the upcoming trials.

These farmers were understandably reluctant to get involved in the Haywood trial. After all, the Western Federation of Miners was a notorious organization whose retaliatory measures were the central issue of the trial. As the *New York Times* reported, "This has been a man-killing country, and under the shadow of a strong suspicion that there may be avenging murders by cranks or others it may prove difficult to get twelve men willing to run the risk."[3] This may have been an Eastern reporter's exaggerated view of the situation, but nevertheless it was clear that prudent Ada County men were not anxious to serve on the jury.

This lack of enthusiasm for jury duty was apparent from the time jury selection began in the courtroom on May 9 until the jury was finally complete on June 3. The regular panel of jurors called for this session of court was made up of 35 men; it was subsequently necessary to call three special venires of 100, 60, and 61 before twelve jurors could be selected. Part of this mortality rate can be attributed to the high incidence of business and personal excuses offered by the jurors, but part of the responsibility must also lie with the lawyers who liberally exercised their right of challenge.

Idaho at that time used what was known as the "California procedure" in selecting a jury. Initially twelve men were called to the jury box. The prosecuting attorney then went through all

[3] *New York Times,* May 3, 1907, p. 2.

twelve, passing or challenging for cause. Any man challenged was replaced immediately if the judge sustained the challenge. When the prosecutor had been through the jury once, the defense began their challenges. Thus the jury box was kept full at all times, but the turnover of jurors was extremely high. Only two of the twelve men who were originally called on May 9 survived to serve on the jury during the trial. These two were Samuel F. Russell and S. D. Gilman. By contrast, Finley McBean who finally occupied chair number two had been the thirty-third man to sit in that seat during the selection of the jury.

Each side, in addition to its challenges for cause, was allowed ten peremptory challenges. Prior to the legislature's meeting in January of 1907 the state had had only five of these challenges, but the legislature altered the law to provide for an equal number for each side. There was some discussion of whether this constituted an *ex post facto* law, but Judge Wood ruled that it did not.

The challenges for cause were exercised in a rather predictable pattern for the most part. The prosecution wanted to know if the potential juror had any opposition to capital punishment, any reluctance to believe circumstantial evidence (on which the state would have to depend), any prior knowledge of the case or bias toward the defendant, any reluctance to believe Harry Orchard, etc. The defense, knowing it had essentially a conservative group of men with whom to deal, had to ask questions about many of the social issues of the day. The jurors were asked about their views of the Coeur d'Alene troubles, the Citizens' Alliances, the Pinkerton Agency, Taft's "law and order" speeches in Idaho, President Roosevelt's "undesirable citizens" letter, the rights of labor, and whether they had had any social or business relationships with the two very popular and well-known prosecution attorneys.

The defense operated as a team in conducting the examination of jurors. Darrow and Richardson did most of the questioning, but Edgar Wilson, Judge Wood's law partner, also examined some jurors. John Nugent was utilized to phrase the challenges of the visiting lawyers, particularly Darrow, in the proper Idaho legal terminology. The defense lawyers consulted the typewritten reports of the canvass and talked among themselves and with Haywood before accepting jurors or exercising challenges.

Most of the jurors who were challenged had opinions or biases. Some were patently anxious to admit their bias in order to get excused, and when this reason became so popular that the judge found it necessary to deny such challenges, some of the inventive reluctant jurors switched to scruples against capital punishment as an effective way of avoiding jury service. When the additional venires were called, many jurors offered business or personal excuses; of the 100 called in the first special venire, 25 were immediately excused for valid reasons. Farmers had the most legitimate reasons in that the irrigated cropland of the Boise Valley needed constant summer attention. But so many men on the first special venire begged off that the judge found it necessary to crack down on excuses, just as on challenges, as the selection process continued.

With jurors fighting so hard to avoid service, the lawyers had to be careful not to lose potentially friendly jurors. Clarence Darrow, who had no theory of persuasion, had a very definite system of jury selection. As Martin Maloney points out, "Darrow was an expert in selecting and influencing juries. He knew, almost instinctively, how to select men to whom his habitual appeals would be effective. . . . Darrow habitually proceeded on the theory that a man's intellectual and emotional habits carry over from his everyday life to his period of jury service."[4] Darrow, twenty-five years afer the Haywood trial, spelled out his formula for jury selection in terms which, with few exceptions, seem to describe his strategy in Boise reasonably accurately:

> Jurymen seldom convict a person they like, or acquit one they dislike. The main work of a trial lawyer is to make a jury like his client, or at least, to feel sympathy for him; facts regarding the crime are relatively unimportant. I try to get a jury with little education but with much human sympathy. The Irish are always the best jurymen for the defense. I don't want a Scotchman, for he has too little human feeling; I don't want a Scandinavian, for he has too

---

[4] Martin Maloney, "Clarence Darrow," in Marie Hochmuth, editor, *A History and Criticism of American Public Address,* Vol. III (New York: Longmans, Green and Co., 1955), p. 295.

> strong a respect for the law as law. In general I don't want a religious person, for he believes in sin and punishment. The defendant should avoid rich men who have a high regard for law, as they make and use it. The smug and ultra-respectable think they are the guardians of society, and they believe the law is for them. The man who is down on his luck, who has trouble, who is more or less a failure, is much kinder to the poor and unfortunate than are the rich and selfish.[5]

The singular exception to this theory of jury selection in the Haywood trial pertains to the "Scotchman." Not only did Darrow permit men of Scottish ancestry to get on the jury, but both of them stood solidly with the defense on all jury ballots.

Darrow's technique with jurors was in keeping with his theory of jury selection. Noting the difference between Darrow's approach and that of E. F. Richardson, the *New York Times* observed:

> His method is very different from that of Richardson. The Denver man keeps his seat and goes at his man in a vigorous, emphatic way, using voice enough to be heard at the furthest extremity of the courtroom. Darrow stands up, walks over directly in front of the talesman, and talks in a quick confidential manner, as if just he and the talesman were discussing a matter in which no one else had any interest.[6]

Even Darrow had troubles with jurors in the Haywood trial, however. On one occasion, toward the end of the jury selection when peremptory challenges were running low for both sides, Darrow had a particularly difficult time getting rid of a juror who was obviously not very intelligent. When the defense attorney challenged for cause and gave as his reason the "manifest incompetence" of the juror, Borah professed indignation at a slur on the quality of Idaho manhood. Three times Darrow challenged for various reasons, but each time the judge warned Darrow that if any challenge were denied the defense would be stuck with the juror and could not re-examine him. Darrow then withdrew his challenges, and spent a very uncomfortable hour trying to draw out some challengeable defect in the juror, at the same time asking

---

[5] At a dinner of the Quadrangle Club in Chicago in 1933, quoted in Edwin H. Sutherland, *Principles of Criminology* (Philadelphia: J. B. Lippincott Co., 1934), p. 258.

[6] *New York Times,* May 18, 1907, p. 3.

Borah repeatedly if he would like to challenge the juror. Borah was enjoying himself immensely watching Darrow squirm and refused, of course, to take the juror off the defense's hands. Eventually Darrow had to use a precious peremptory challenge to get rid of the man.

Much good will and pleasant professional rivalry characterized this part of the trial. It was a battle of wits, and not yet one of tempers and passions. When Richardson asked Daniel Clark what kind of a Democrat he was—referring to the party split in Idaho —James Hawley arose to announce, "I object to that question on the ground that it is a libel on the Democratic Party. There are too few of us left in the State to be split up." The humor was enjoyed by all, including Judge Wood who was a staunch Republican. Another laugh resulted when Richardson tried to find out if Clark's being a "straight Democrat" meant a DuBois or a Steunenberg Democrat. This time Hawley protested that answering either way would make one wing of the party or the other "not straight."

Another enjoyable moment occurred when Finley McBean was being questioned by Borah. It became apparent that McBean had developed an opinion from reading about the trial in the newspapers, but that this opinion had recently changed. When Borah asked why, McBean replied, "Well, the more I read about the case the less I knew about it." This answer was apparently highly satisfactory to both sides, and McBean was promptly accepted for the previously unsettled second chair.

Both sides lost jurors who might have helped them. Richardson, in trying to pursue a line of questioning which seemed to be pointing toward a challenge, stumbled onto the fact that his juror, a man named Wingate, would not believe Harry Orchard's testimony. The attorney immediately went off in another direction as a decoy, and eventually passed the juror. But the damage had been done; Borah opened up on the question of Orchard's testimony and discovered that Wingate would not believe Harry Orchard even if the judge's instructions gave special attention to the witness's credibility. Borah then challenged for cause, and the challenge was sustained. Thus, the defense lost a juror who would have certainly prevented a conviction. Wingate, incidentally, was replaced by A. P. Burns who was accepted for the final jury by both sides. Burns admitted receiving impressions from his newspaper reading, even some opinions from what he had read of Orchard's confession. He had some prejudice against Orchard, but no opinion of Haywood.

Possibly the state lost a favorable juror in the person of J. E. Tourtellotte, although the facts are so unusual as to defy valid conclusions. Tourtellotte, under examination, admitted that he was against capital punishment, except in two specific situations: in time of war, and in the case of people who advocate the destruction of orderly government and social institutions. In examining Tourtellotte, Borah revealed for the first time in the trial the state's intentions of proving that the Western Federation of Miners was an anarchistic conspiracy. It was a calculated risk; if Borah could get a juror who felt so strongly about anarchy that his repugnance toward it overcame his otherwise strong antipathy toward capital punishment, landing such a juror might be worth disclosing the state's plan to the defense. Borah passed Tourtellotte for cause. Unpredictably, Darrow also accepted him, apparently confident that he could prevent the state from proving the kind of anarchy that Tourtellotte considered a capital offense.

But Tourtellotte himself had the last word. After he had been accepted he told the judge he did not believe he could conscientiously take the juror's oath because of his feelings toward capital punishment in general. Inasmuch as Idaho law provided that a man could not be made to serve on a capital case if he had convictions against capital punishment, Judge Wood was forced to accept Tourtellotte's statement at face value and to excuse him.

Toward the end of the jury selection process, several of the defense attorneys seemed to have despaired of getting the kind of jury they wanted. Richardson pointed out in a statement to the press that out of thousands of eligible jurors, including 1,200 men who had marched in the last Labor Day parade, only one union man and two other working men had been called for jury duty, while at the same time out of 60 bankers in the county, nine had been called. Defense attorney John Nugent's views, as reported by Operative 21, were not optimistic:

> Nugent said they consider McBean a safe man but might investigate further. Nugent is not pleased with the jury as it now stands and said the best they could hope for was a hung jury.[7]

Darrow, however, seemed more hopeful at the moment. In a statement to the press he indicated that an impartial jury could be found.[8] This statement contrasted with Darrow's pre-trial position that the minds of the local citizens had been poisoned through inflammatory newspaper articles. Darrow may have realized that he was actually getting the kind of plain, homey jurors so necessary to his kind of pleading. Then, too, he may have been impressed with Boise's sense of fair play when Borah pointed out to the court that the *Idaho Statesman* had never printed the story concerning Moyer's conviction as a burglar while virtually every other paper had given it prominent display. In any event, Darrow seemed reconciled to the kind of jury which was taking shape.

On June 3, 1907, the jury was completed with the acceptance of O. V. Sebern. For the next seven weeks these twelve men were the key to the verdict.

In *seat one* was Thomas B. Gess, one of the few jurors who was a resident of Boise proper. Gess was born in Missouri in about 1842, and had been a resident of Idaho since 1868. He had been a farmer but was now engaged in real estate and insurance. He was a Democrat, and one of the few jurors who professed membership in a church, the Christian Church. Perhaps most significant was the fact that he had known Frank Steunenberg quite well since 1890.[9]

In *seat two* was the red-haired Scotsman, Finley McBean. He was a farmer on the "Bench," close to the Ada County fairgrounds. The newspaper accounts differed on his age, one putting it at 62 while two others called him 52.

---

7 Pinkerton report, Operative 21, May 26, 1907.

8 *Portland Oregonian,* May 23, 1907, p. 2.

9 Most of the details concerning the jurors are from the *Idaho Statesman,* June 4, 1907, pp. 1-2, and the *Portland Oregonian,* June 4, 1907, pp. 1-2.

The *third seat* was occupied by Samuel D. Gilman, a 56-year-old Republican who farmed 80 acres near Star. Gilman had served in the Idaho Volunteers in the Philippines during the Spanish American War, and was thus not personally familiar with Steunenberg's actions in 1899. He told Hawley that he had not been influenced by Roosevelt's letter, Taft's speeches, or the legislature's endorsement of the prosecution.

The youngster of the jury was Daniel Clark in *seat four*. He was only 32 years old in a jury whose average age was near 60. He farmed 80 acres at Eagle, and was a registered Democrat. Once he had been a client of one of Borah's law partners, but Borah had represented the other side in the case, thus eliminating the possibility that Clark could have been challenged for bias toward Borah.

In *seat five* was George Powell, a bearded 60-year-old Democrat who was somewhat deaf. Originally a native of Kansas, he had been in Idaho for 15 years and now farmed 40 acres near Meridian.

Another farmer from Meridian was in *seat six*. This was O. V. Sebern, whose interesting background included 26 years in Wyoming during which he was a juror in the famous Tom Horn trial in Laramie County. Tom Horn was an ex-Pinkerton man who was a hired killer for a group of cattlemen; eventually he was hanged after conviction by the jury on which Sebern served. When Sebern was called for the Haywood jury the defense had used all its peremptory challenges and could not keep him off the panel. Sebern was 52, a native of Iowa, and a Republican. He had been denied a business excuse to get off the jury. He had relatives in Boise, and the Sebern family today appears to be the only one of the twelve families involved which has remained in Ada County.

Seat number seven was occupied by H. F. Messecar, a Republican rancher from Eagle where he operated 240 acres. Messecar had been born in Canada, and was about 56 years old. Physically, he was small and wiry: he was reported to be a stutterer.

In *chair eight* was Lee Schrivener, also from Eagle where he ran a 40-acre farm. Schrivener had once been a sheriff in Kansas. Asked by Darrow if he had ever hanged anyone, Schrivener had replied, "No sir, we didn't do much hanging back in Kansas." He was 57, and a Republican.

Juror number nine was J. A. Robertson, at 72 the oldest man on the Haywood jury. He had been a farmer, but at present was living in Boise. Frank Steunenberg had at one time boarded with him for a period of two years. Robertson had been born in Scotland, and was a Presbyterian. He also was a Republican.

Levi Smith, a 55-year-old native of Kansas, was in *seat ten*. Smith was once a farmer, but was now engaged in building fences for an interurban railway. He lived in Boise, and considered himself a Republican. Under examination he admitted that one of the state attorneys had helped him on a legal matter, but said no fee was involved.

In *seat eleven* was Alfred P. Burns, age 50. Burns had been a farmer, a grocer, and once had belonged to the carpenters' union in Nebraska. He lived in Boise, and was at present not engaged in any work. He was a Republican, but the defense had not been able to get a clear line on what to expect of him. Operative 21 reported:

> I talked with Barber [a defense canvasser?] who said he had learned very little about A. P. Burns, some said he was favorable to the defense while others claimed him equally favorable to the prosecution . . .[10]

Burns did say, however, under examination that he was not prepared to give the same credence to Orchard that he would extend to other witnesses.

Seat twelve was occupied by Samuel F. Russell. Russell had once been a justice of the peace in Ada County, but was at that time farming on the Boise Bench. He had been a Republican but was now a Prohibitionist. He was 68 years old, a six-footer with a long beard. He was born in Pennsylvania, had come to Illinois at 19 where he did some rail splitting, and had then come west after the Civil War. He had read about the Haywood case, and

[10] Pinkerton report, Operative 21, May 21, 1907.

had opinions but not on Haywood or Orchard. He indicated, however, that his opinion could not be changed by the evidence. Although he had remained on the jury from the first day, the defense had given serious thought to using its last peremptory challenge on him[11] even though, seemingly, Russell's inflexible opinion would have justified a challenge for cause.

This, then, was the Haywood jury: 9 farmers, 1 real estate agent, 1 ex-carpenter, and 1 foreman of a fence-building gang. One man had belonged to a union fourteen years prior to the trial. There were 8 Republicans, 3 Democrats, and 1 Prohibitionist on the jury, and 9 native-born citizens, 2 Scotsmen, and 1 Canadian.

Before long, the press and other observers would be saying some very complimentary things about this jury. Ethel Barrymore, who came to Boise that summer in a road show of *Captain Jinks of the Horse Marines,* visited the trial with Gifford Pinchot and Margaret Cobb, daughter of the *Statesman* publisher. Miss Barrymore wrote in her autobiography,

> The jury were the most wonderful looking men I've ever seen. They were all ranchers with the bluest eyes, like sailor's eyes, used to looking at great distances. They made me think of Uncle Sam as Uncle Sam ought to look without the goatee. They were magnificent, all of them . . .[12]

Before the jury had been assembled, special precautions were taken to guard them closely. A house was rented immediately across the street from the courthouse in order that the jurors might be accommodated comfortably and safely within easy reach of the courtroom. A cook was hired for the jury, and four bailiffs were assigned to guard the jurors constantly. A special stairway was built for the jurors from a fire escape landing accessible from the judge's private chambers.

Modifications were also made to the courtroom in order to accommodate all of the legal staffs, reporters, and spectators. The Ada County courthouse was a conventional square brick building with a cupola, standing on an unfenced city block of tree-lined

---

[11] Pinkerton report, Operative 24A, May 25, 1907.

[12] Ethel Barrymore, *Memories, An Autobiography of Ethel Barrymore* (New York: Harper and Brothers, 1955), p. 158.

lawn. The courtroom was about 45 by 70 feet with bare plaster walls. Hard benches resembling church pews provided seating for about twenty persons per row in about twelve rows. Additional space within the rail for newsmen and special guests raised the total seating of the room to about 300. The judge's position was at the east end of the room. Immediately in front of him, with their backs to him, sat the jury. However, the jurors were provided with swivel chairs which could be swung around toward the judge when necessary. The traditional and necessary cuspidors were provided for the jury.

The witness chair was a rather high affair in front of the judge and jury. The witness faced the judge and jury, and had his back to the audience. The attorneys were grouped around two tables, one on each side of the witness chair. At other tables, farther to each side, sat the court stenographers and reporters and the newsmen who were covering the trial.

News coverage of the trial was intensive. Several authors have estimated that 50 magazines and newspapers were represented, and this seems a fair guess. The *Statesman* on May 9 listed the names of 33 writers who were then in town or were due in shortly. As the trial progressed and became more dramatic, still others must have arrived. The Boise Western Union office announced that it was prepared to handle 200,000 words a day through its telegraph keys if necessary. In an interesting commentary on the journalistic competition of the day, the Pinkerton Agency reported that the Portland *Evening Telegram's* representative at the trial, F. L. Perkins, could read telegraphy and hung around the Western Union office intercepting the private messages to and from the defense attorneys.[13]

It is difficult to establish exactly what kind of feeling prevailed in Boise at the time. Most accounts admit that the town was full of strangers, including gunmen and detectives, and that certain rumors relative to violence circulated freely. But it is hard to know which of these rumors had substantial facts behind them. Kendrick Johnson, who was only eleven years old at the time of the trial, recalls:

[13] Pinkerton report, May 13, 1907.

> All of Boise was seething with excitement, and hundreds of miners from northern Idaho poured into Boise. Those unable to obtain accommodations camped on the outskirts of town and even on the courthouse lawn. Rough, crude, and even brutal, these men brought with them an atmosphere of tension and strain for the people of Boise. Threats of violence was [*sic*] rampant, for these men were indignant at the arrest of three of the top officials of the WFM—champion of the miners. Boise citizens went carefully about their affairs, fearful for their safety and even for their lives. The impending trial was discussed only in the privacy of their homes or offices because any unfavorable remarks about Moyer, Haywood and Pettibone sparked more trouble in an already agitated town. I remember that through the eyes of a small boy, the excitement was intense. The constant talk of danger fired my imagination and I saw dynamiters under every hedge and behind every tree. While I was mortally afraid, I was more afraid that something would happen and I would not be near enough to see it. My father, uncle and grandfather were lawyers in Boise and because of my father's friendship with Steunenberg, I felt a personal interest in the excitement.
>
> Boise had smouldered to an explosive atmosphere by the time the trial opened in June. Miners crowded and shoved to gain entrance to the courtroom and wild rumors were rampant. Each evening at the dinner table father and mother discussed the latest developments. I can still feel the delicious thrill of fear and excitement as they commented on the rumor that families of the jurors were being called upon by men affecting to be peddlers or book salesmen and being subjected to only thinly veiled threats in the form of reminders that in similar trials in Colorado, jurors whose vote was adverse to the miners unaccountably did not long survive.[14]

Contemporary newspaper accounts tried to describe the feeling in Boise at the time. The *New York Times* observed before the trial that Boise was quiet, "But under the surface there is a strong undercurrent of apprehension and nervousness. Violence is the ever present fear."[15] A week later, however, the same newspaper displayed a calmer attitude when it spoke of Boise as "interested and concerned" with the proceedings, and anxious to see a "square deal" come out of the trial.[16]

The *Oregonian* had similar observations on Boise. It reported

---

[14] Kendrick Johnson, "Trial of 'Big Bill' Haywood," *The Nevada State Bar Journal,* July, 1959, pp. 123-24.

[15] *New York Times,* May 3, 1907, p. 2.

[16] *New York Times,* May 9, 1907, p. 1.

that perfectly reasonable men were worried that Harry Orchard would be murdered in the high and prominent witness chair.[17] Charles Koelsch, the Ada County prosecuting attorney, heard this fear expressed by James McParland who pointed out the large number of WFM men in the courtroom.[18] The *Oregonian* also reported that an "expert jury fixer from Chicago" was in Boise under an assumed name.[19] To give credence to both of these rumors simultaneously is to give the WFM credit for a remarkable degree of thoroughness!

One of the most colorful accounts of Boise at that time was written by John F. MacLane who was the law partner of W. A. Stone of the prosecution staff. MacLane described Boise generally:

> It boasted a number of modern homes, a good hotel, comfortable office buildings, and other modern conveniences. There was also an open-air summer theatre reproducing, during my first year, Gilbert & Sullivan operas, with Fatty Arbuckle in the title roles,—a baseball league which produced Walter Johnson, and one of the best polo teams in the west.
>
> But it still had a typically western pioneer town atmosphere. The bars never closed, or at least I never found them so, open gambling was conducted in the lobbies of the hotels, and recognized, if not licensed, prostitution was a conspicuous feature of the local scene. One block of Main Street was lined with honky-tonks,—a miniature of the Barbary Coast.[20]

Boise was growing rapidly at the time. In 1900 its population was 5,957; by 1910 it was 17,358. At the time of the trial Eastern newspaper reporters were surprised to find a small city,

> . . . nestled against the foothills of the adjoining mountains, with clean streets, good hotels, commodious office buildings, substantial residences, attractive gardens, and sidewalks lined with parking and shade trees . . .
>
> Their anticipation of an atmosphere of excitement and hostility to the defense was also disappointed. True, as I myself can testify, there was in the air a feeling of tension and suspense, but it was suppressed, and not apparent to anyone not enjoying the intimacy of the town residents. This tension had existed for some time and was heightened by the presence in the town of a vast guard of news

---

[17] *Portland Oregonian,* May 3, 1907, p. 1.

[18] Conversation with Charles Koelsch, Boise, Idaho, August 1, 1960.

[19] *Portland Oregonian,* May 10, 1907, p. 1.

[20] John F. MacLane, *A Sagebrush Lawyer* (New York: Pandick Press, 1953), p. 3.

> men, foreign lawyers for the defense, detectives and their armed guards for both prosecution and defense, and the coming and going of numbers of persons of more or less celebrity expected to be connected with the case as witnesses or in some other capacity. Lawyers and detectives for both prosecution and defense had armed guards, some of them widely known for their past records. There were two such guards stationed for several months at the entrance to Hawley's offices and no person was permitted to pass without identifying himself and justifying his entrance. I assume the same was true at defense headquarters. Among the guards for the State was Ralph Bledso, famed throughout the west as a former leader of miners and subsequently as a law abiding and enforcement official. Another was Bob Meldrum, deputy sheriff of Cripple Creek, Colorado, who was principally famous as a gun man. . . . The State's chief detective McParland was constantly accompanied by a famous western character named Siringo, known as the "cowboy detective." . . .
>
> These were but a few of the accomplished personal guards who lent an interest to the scene. Their presence was explained, if not justified, by the rumors which filled the air. Orchard was to be kidnapped from the penitentiary or seized when he left it and shot; Hawley was number two man on the list of the condemned; Governor Gooding was another; Darrow and others connected with the defense were marked by the prosecution for slaughter. But nothing came of any of these rumors and in fact there was at no time on the part of the prosecution or defense the slightest evidence of any attempt to interfere with an orderly trial.[21]

The one writer who has pursued the subject matter, but not the validity, of these rumors the furthest is Irving Stone. He says flatly that "Hysteria gripped Boise."[22] He describes detectives lurking everywhere, sharpshooters on Table Rock behind the penitentiary, and gives substance to all the rumors mentioned by MacLane. He goes so far that Koelsch was once prompted to observe, ". . . the stories contained in the biography of Darrow, to which I referred earlier in my talk, [Stone's *Clarence Darrow for the Defense*] are a libel upon this community."[23] Koelsch reports that when Stone interviewed him to get material for this book that

---

[21] MacLane, *ibid.*, pp. 153-154.

[22] Irving Stone, *Clarence Darrow for the Defense* (Garden City, N. Y.: Doubleday & Company, 1949), p. 230.

[23] Koelsch, *op. cit.*, pp. 34-35. The "talk" referred to by Koelsch is his speech before the Idaho Mining Association in Boise, April 5, 1946, which is printed in pamphlet form.

he, Stone, already had his mind made up about what Koelsch should say. Stone was argumentative, and Koelsch finally had to ask him to leave.[24]

Another blow to Stone's theory of hysteria in Boise is struck by the very subject of Stone's book. Clarence Darrow in a signed dispatch to the *New York Times* said in May of 1907:

> The little city of Boise seems to be entirely unaware of its prominence in the world. The outsider who dropped into this city after crossing the prairies and the plains might imagine that he was in a New England Congregational town on a Sunday morning. No one seems excited. The people go about their business as if there was nothing new or nothing old that could possibly affect their lives. The stories of excitement and danger and assassination that have been put out through the country seem to be entirely born of the imagination of the newspaper men.[25]

And this from the man who had a few weeks earlier complained of the inflamed passions of Idaho!

Apparently people around the United States did get the impression through newspaper stories that Boise was a dangerous city at the moment. William E. Borah found it necessary to write to his father assuring him that he was perfectly safe in remaining as a prosecutor, and pointing out that Boise was quiet.[26] Bulkeley Wells wrote to a friend in Denver that "It is absolutely quiet here in Boise, suprisingly little interest except of a sober nature is taken in the trials . . ."[27] Confirmation for this view of Boise comes from Mrs. J. C. Mills who remembers the town as quiet but tense during the trials.[28]

The *New York Times* sensed, however, that violence was still possible. It noted that if any show of force was made, "There will be 300 armed men ready in ten minutes—men who will stand no nonsense whatever."[29] Harry Shellworth of Boise attests to this arrangement. He recalls that Boise was quiet but explosive;

---

24 Conversation with Charles Koelsch, Boise, Idaho, August 1, 1960.
25 *New York Times,* May 7, 1907, p. 2.
26 Letter, William E. Borah to William N. Borah, May 28, 1907.
27 Letter, Bulkeley Wells to Maurice Corbett, May 23, 1907.
28 Conversation with Mrs. J. C. Mills, Boise, Idaho, August 10, 1960.
29 *New York Times,* May 9, 1907, p. 1.

the town was a community of friends who had a silent mutual understanding that they would support any collective act of physical force needed to insure law and order; a hardware store had guns and ammunition ready for the townspeople if needed. Shellworth, incidentally, can also speak for the presence of detectives in the community. At the time he was in the unique position of courting the daughter of the prison warden, and as a regular visitor at the penitentiary he found himself being shadowed on several occasions.[30]

It is difficult to understand how the town could have been so explosive without something touching off violence. Fortunately, there were some prudent steps taken to minimize friction such as the mayor's banning of street speaking, and the trial itself was remarkably free of incidents or rulings which might have touched off a reaction. But still, to have had that many people in town expecting trouble was almost an assurance that it would come. Perhaps the explanation of this paradox lies in an observation made by James Hawley, the son of the prosecuting attorney, and an observer of the events of 1907. Hawley remembers his brother Edgar Hawley, along with John Nugent of the defense, each day checking off the names of the opposing side's gunmen who were present in court, in order to see how many were there and where they were located. According to James Hawley, a standoff developed on the armed power of the two sides, comparable to the U. S.—Russian standoff after World War II.[31] This mutual fear and respect may well have kept the peace during the long trial.

Once the trial was underway there were no significant demonstrations in Boise or elsewhere. It was generally believed that Haywood and Moyer ordered the Western Federation of Miners to avoid any activity that would create unfavorable public opinion. Even the outspoken Goldfield, Nevada, miners complied, perhaps out of deference to the two top officials of the union, or perhaps because the local labor troubles there had resulted in long prison sentences for two miners and another murder indictment for Vincent St. John.

---

[30] Conversation with Harry Shellworth, Boise, Idaho, August 10, 1960.
[31] Conversation with James Hawley, Boise, Idaho, July 27, 1960.

The defense found it necessary to keep certain people out of Boise during the trial to avoid prejudicing its position. Eugene Debs wanted to come, and on several occasions was reported en route. But apparently Darrow was able to keep him away. Bill Haywood speculated afterward that Darrow did not want to share the Socialist laurels with anyone else,[32] but in fact all of the other defense personnel, including Moyer and Pettibone, were just as anxious as Darrow to keep Debs out of Boise. Attorney Fred Miller was quoted as hoping Debs would stay away so that the extraneous issue of Socialism would not be raised during the trial.[33]

Another radical did arrive, however, to be greeted with mixed feelings by the defense staff. Peter Breen of Butte, the old 1892 Coeur d'Alene dynamiter, came to Boise about the time that the jury selection was finished. Darrow wanted to add him to the staff, but Richardson felt that he was too radical (Breen had been making some "good riddance" speeches about Steunenberg in Montana). Breen eventually joined the defense forces, but he seems to have done no more in the trial than Miller, Nugent, Wilson, and Whitsell—the other less important attorneys for the defense.

Like any significant rhetorical event, the Haywood trial reached a large audience in history as well as a large contemporary audience. The trial was unusually well reported. Not only did the newspaper writers turn out thousands of words each day, but an enterprising pioneer motion picture producer filmed parts of the trial for showing in "Hale's Touring Car . . . Admission 10 cents." The official version of the trial, the transcript, was taken down by several stenographers.

There was an interesting sidelight in connection with the work of recording the official transcript. One of the stenographers, a man named Libby who had been brought to Boise by E. F. Richardson, was accused of being "crooked" by the Denver office of the Pinkerton Agency. Acting on information from A. E. Carl-

---

[32] William D. Haywood, *Bill Haywood's Book* (New York: International Publishers, 1929), p. 207.

[33] *Portland Oregonian,* May 23, 1907, p. 2.

ton of the Cripple Creek Mine Owners' Association to the effect that Libby had altered testimony in the past and had been thrown out of the court of Judge Ben Lindsey, a Pinkerton official advised that steps be taken to prevent the use of this man as a stenographer in the Haywood trial.[34] But apparently nothing came of this warning, inasmuch as Libby went on to serve as a stenographer. No writer has suggested that Libby—or anyone else—perverted the accuracy of testimony in the trial transcript, but for the sake of historical objectivity the facts of the pre-trial warning from the Pinkertons concerning Libby should be noted.

With the jury chosen, the larger audience watching with interest, and Boise literally ready for anything, the stage was set for the great trial to begin. On June 4, 1907, the state of Idaho began its case against William D. Haywood as James H. Hawley presented the opening statement for the prosecution.

[34] Pinkerton report, May 12, 1907.

9

THE CASE for the STATE

In American courtrooms the doctrine of *presumption of innocence* normally puts the prosecution at a disadvantage in cases depending upon circumstantial proof. This disadvantage, however, can be partially offset by a compensating advantage peculiar to the prosecution—the element of surprise. The prosecution, at least early in the trial, can keep the defense guessing. This state of affairs developed in the Haywood trial, where the state of Idaho successfully prevented the defense forces from knowing what kind of evidence they would need to defend against.

Hawley and McParland had released only fragmentary portions of the Orchard and Adams confessions during the pre-trial period. Consequently, the defense attorneys knew very little about the state's strategy. Immediately prior to the trial Darrow and Richardson found it necessary to move for a bill of particulars in which the nature of Haywood's alleged involvement in the Steunenberg assassination would be defined. But Judge Wood denied the motion, pointing out that Idaho law made no provision for such action and ruling that the indictment was specific enough. Thus, when James Hawley opened the state's case on June 4, 1907, the defense attorneys got their first real opportunity to discover what the prosecution intended to prove. But even this opportunity was not a satisfying experience to Darrow and Richardson, inasmuch as Hawley's statement was deliberately brief and vague.

Hawley had told newsmen previously that he had prepared no set speech for stating the case to the jury, but would simply ". . . think the matter over and jot down some headings and from these headings I will talk. I may write one portion of the opening statement, and if I do, I shall read it when I come to it."[1] Judging from the transcript of the opening statement made by Hawley, none of the speech was written out, for all of it appears to be in the same homely style characteristic of Hawley's extemporizing: the long, rambling sentence construction, the parenthetical expressions and digressions, and the plainness of language.

Hawley spoke for about an hour and a half. The *New York Times* was not impressed:

> As an oratorical effort the speech of Jim Hawley, in opening the prosecution of William D. Haywood for the murder of ex-Gov. Steunenberg, this morning was far from justifying the reputation of the chief prosecutor as a jury pleader. But as a time consumer it was a distinguished success. It was a fine exhibition of ability to skirt around the edges of the state's case without getting sufficiently near to details to permit the defense to derive any benefit from what was disclosed.[2]

Hawley began by reviewing the facts of the indictment against Haywood, pointing out that it was returned by a Canyon County grand jury. He was careful to point out that Harry Orchard, whom everyone regarded as the state's star witness, was also indicted at the same time for the same crime. This statement would tend to counter any potential defense assertion that Harry Orchard had been promised immunity at the time of his confession.

Hawley then identified briefly some of the principals of the case, particularly Frank Steunenberg and the three defendants. He reviewed the change of venue proceedings, and the selection of Haywood as the first to be tried. He discussed the Idaho law regarding accessories to a crime, and made it clear that the state would not attempt to show that Haywood was actually present at

---

1 *Portland Oregonian,* June 4, 1907, p. 1.
2 *New York Times,* June 5, 1907, p. 1.

the scene of the crime. He announced that the state would show instead the existence of collusion, of a conspiracy to murder Frank Steunenberg.

At this point, without mentioning his own role in the formation of the union, James Hawley explained the organizational structure of the Western Federation of Miners. He particularly stressed the power of the Executive Committee in the day-to-day affairs of the union, and went on to show the even greater power of the two officers, the president (Moyer) and the secretary-treasurer (Haywood). Hawley then asserted that the policies pursued by these leaders had led to the death of Steunenberg and other men.

At this point, Darrow objected that this kind of assertion was out of place in an opening statement, but the objection was overruled. When Hawley went on to assert that the "Inner Circle" of the union existed to perpetuate the power of the leaders through terror, Darrow interrupted again with the comment that no reference to evidence supporting these allegations had been made by Hawley. "It is a pure piece of rhetoric," said Darrow, "if it is rhetoric."

A long wrangle developed between Darrow and Hawley at this point over what was permissible in an opening statement to a jury. Judge Wood indicated that generally he would have to hear all of the contentions of the opening statement before he could rule whether any given assertion was *argument*—which was not permissible—or a *statement of proposed proof* which was permissible. When Darrow announced his intention of objecting whenever necessary, Hawley in exasperation told Darrow that he was free to object to or take exception to the entire opening statement if he so desired.

This clash between Darrow and Hawley was the first of a number to occur between these two attorneys. Apparently it was a part of Darrow's strategy. Bill Haywood explained:

> Darrow, in this case as in others he had defended, picked out a 'goat' among the prosecution lawyers. In this instance it was Jim Hawley upon whom he concentrated his sarcasm. He was at times

> so venomous that Hawley's son threatened him with personal violence. Darrow was not always the smiling, suave, persuasive individual that he is sometimes described. His grandest moments were when he was in the attitude of attack.[3]

This view of Darrow's hostility toward Hawley is also expressed by Charles Harrison[4] and by Martin Maloney.[5]

Hawley resumed his opening statement with another reference to the issue that had triggered the long interruption, the "Inner Circle" of the Western Federation. He spoke of the hiring of assassins by this group, and he developed in some detail the circumstances of Steunenberg's death at the hands of these assassins. He alluded to the facts to which Orchard would testify, relative to the reason for Steunenberg's death. He referred to an established scale of wages for crimes committed by direction of the "Inner Circle." He mentioned several crimes in Colorado that the state would connect with Haywood and the "Inner Circle" as a part of the broad conspiracy of retaliation against the enemies of the Western Federation. He traced the travels of Harry Orchard as an agent of assassination for the union, and finally he indicated that the state would show the financial support of Orchard and Steve Adams by the union during their careers as paid assassins.

It was not much for the defense to go on. Darrow announced to the court that the defense would not make its opening statement until the state's case was concluded. This maneuver permitted the defense to use all of the time taken by the state's presentation to prepare for its own opening statement, which could then be adapted to meet any evidence introduced in the meantime. But there was no way of knowing from Hawley's statement how the state planned to prove its contentions, other than through the testimony of Harry Orchard.

The state's first job was to prove the facts of the crime as

---

[3] William D. Haywood, *Bill Haywood's Book* (New York: International Publishers, 1929), p. 212.

[4] Charles Y. Harrison, *Clarence Darrow* (New York: Jonathon Cape & Harrison Smith, 1931), p. 131.

[5] Martin Maloney, "Clarence Darrow," in Marie Hochmuth, editor, *A History and Criticism of American Public Address*, Vol. III (New York: Longmans, Green and Co., 1955) p. 306.

stated in the indictment. Idaho law required that four basic facts of the death be established: 1. That Frank Steunenberg was dead. 2. That he met death in Canyon County, Idaho. 3. That William D. Haywood unlawfully, wilfully, feloniously, and with malice aforethought killed him. 4. That Steunenberg died within a year and a day.

Obviously, the first, second, and fourth facts could be established through routine examination of Caldwell citizens who were eye witnesses to Steunenberg's death. Several neighbors and a doctor testified to the facts of the ex-governor's death, and the defense made no attempt to weaken their testimony. When other Caldwell residents testified to having seen Harry Orchard "casing" the Steunenberg residence during the fall of 1905, defense cross-examination did manage to draw out the admission that Orchard did not seem to be trying to conceal his actions. Such an admission could be valuable to the defense later when it attempted to show Harry Orchard as a Pinkerton agent trying to get caught.

Further testimony of Caldwell residents and hotel keepers established that Orchard and Jack Simpkins had roomed together on several occasions that fall in various local hostelries under the names of Hogan and Simmons. Pictures of both men were identified by the witnesses, and the hotel registers bearing their signatures were placed in evidence. Again, cross-examination testimony revealed no particular secrecy in their actions.

The state's case was quite thorough at this point. Anticipating difficulty in establishing that the signature of "Simmons" on the hotel registers was really that of Jack Simpkins, the state called C. H. Wentz of Wardner, Idaho. Wentz testified that he had taught Jack Simpkins to write, and he then positively identified the signatures on the hotel registers as those of Simpkins. Thus, the state established rather early in the trial the fact that Jack Simpkins, member of the Executive Committee of the Western Federation of Miners, was in Caldwell under an assumed name and in company of Harry Orchard as the murder was being planned.

After the testimony of these first prosecution witnesses had established that the crime had been committed and that Orchard and Simpkins had been together in Caldwell, the drama of the trial intensified when Orchard was called as the next witness. This was the moment the newsmen had been waiting for, inasmuch as only one brief interview with Orchard a few weeks earlier had been granted since his imprisonment. Now for the first time could the world hear and see Harry Orchard whose gross criminality had been widely alluded to by Governor Gooding during the pre-trial period. Even the more conservative newsmen were compelled to describe the moment in purple prose. C. P. Connolly of *Collier's* wrote:

> At 10:39 by the court-room clock, the last of the witnesses who testified to the scenes surrounding Caldwell's widely heralded tragedy left the stand. Senator Borah had announced *sotto voce* to the court: "The next witness will be here in a few moments." Hawley had gone into a side room, from which he now emerged and took his seat. "Call Harry Orchard," he said—and the name seemed to catch slightly in his throat. The door behind the labor leader and the little girl, which Hawley had closed a moment before, opened, and the towering form of a guard entered at the head of a procession of six. Behind him walked a very much shorter figure, whose chunky shoulders swayed with a suggestion of physical strength. . . .[6]

The infamous Harry Orchard had made an impressive arrival in the courtroom. But before the day was over the reporters would be describing Orchard not as a demon, but as a personable, sincere, well-dressed chap who seemed incapable of committing the fantastic list of crimes he was reciting.

James Hawley started immediately into the examination of Orchard, asking him whenever practicable to answer in narrative form as completely as possible. It was obvious that the examination was well rehearsed; the state had been planning this moment ever since the day that McParland obtained Orchard's confession. And Orchard himself had recently engaged in writing his autobiography for *McClure's Magazine,* and had refreshed his memory on many events of the previous five years. Under examination by Hawley, Orchard told his story. The salient facts of this examination follow, particularly those allegations that are either confirmed or refuted by other witnesses later in the trial.

[6] C. P. Connolly, "The Moyer-Haywood Case," *Collier's,* July 27, 1907, p. 14.

Orchard first admitted that he was really Albert E. Horsley, originally from the province of Ontario in Canada. He was 41 years old. He gave a rather sketchy early history of himself up until the time of his coming to the Coeur d'Alene country. He described in greater detail the events of April 29, 1899, including the fact that Paul Corcoran had told his Burke miners that day that the central union had ordered the trip to Wardner. After leaving the Coeur d'Alenes, Orchard wandered about the West from job to job, finally arriving in Cripple Creek in the summer of 1902. He described the Cripple Creek strike and the beginning of his own career of violence with the Vindicator mine explosion.

He related how he had gone to Denver after the explosion and how he had met Haywood and Moyer for the first time. According to Orchard, the union leaders already knew of him by reputation through another miner, Bill Easterly. At this first meeting the two men told him to go ahead with further acts of violence which "couldn't go any too fierce to suit them." After collecting $300 Orchard then went back to Cripple Creek where his next significant act was the construction of a bomb that was later placed in the coal bunker of the Vindicator mine. When he was ignored for the train-wrecking job, Orchard was miffed and went to detective Scott of the railroad with the warning that an attempt would be made.

Shortly thereafter, Orchard went with Moyer to Ouray as a bodyguard. When Moyer was imprisoned at Telluride, Orchard came back to Denver. Haywood and Pettibone next wanted Governor Peabody killed because of his interference with the courts in the Moyer case. Haywood recommended Steve Adams as the man to help Orchard assassinate the governor. Orchard and Adams followed Peabody about, but were unable to get any closer to him than an encounter with Peabody's wife and daughters as they left their carriage one evening at home.

Next came the assassination of Lyte Gregory, a detective working for the mineowners, in Denver in the spring of 1904. At the suggestion of Pettibone, and with the advance approval of the Executive Committee of the union, Orchard and Adams shot the detective late one night. Each man collected $100 for the assassination.

Then the two men committed their greatest crime, the Independence depot explosion. After collecting several hundred dollars from Haywood in Denver, Orchard headed for Wyoming to hide out. At Pat Moran's saloon in Cheyenne he sent Moran back to collect more money from Haywood. After hiding out in Wyoming and spending his bank roll, Orchard eventually returned to Denver. In the fall of 1904 he was sent to California to kill Fred Bradley. In San Francisco, Orchard drew money from Pettibone by telegram and registered mail. Orchard put strychnine in the Bradley family's milk, but Bradley refused to drink the milk because of its bitter taste. Then Orchard bought powder, constructed a bomb, and finally dealt with Bradley that way. Late in 1904 after wounding Bradley, he returned to Denver disguised as a soldier.

Adams and Orchard then plotted to kill Judge Gabbert of the Colorado Supreme Court. Another attempt was made on Peabody in the meantime, but this attempt was foiled by the appearance of a coal wagon as the would-be assassins stood ready to pull the wire which would trigger the bomb. The two men also scouted Frank Hearne of the Colorado Fuel and Iron Company, David Moffat of the First National Bank, and Judge Goddard of the Colorado Supreme Court as potential victims. Orchard, in the guise of an insurance salesman, then went to Canon City to try again to kill Peabody, carrying an enormous dynamite bomb in his valise. Another insurance man, Vaughn, got curious about the ticking noise in Orchard's bag, and Orchard told him that it contained a bomb.

Returning to Denver, Orchard made another attempt to kill Judge Gabbert. The bomb worked, but it killed an innocent passer-by, a man named Wally, instead of Gabbert. Orchard also planted a bomb at Judge Goddard's gate, but this bomb failed to explode. He then prepared to assassinate Sherman Bell, the ex-adjutant-general of Colorado. For better transportation on this job (Orchard had been shuttling bombs about on Pettibone's bicycle) Haywood and Orchard bought a horse and buggy. Moyer stepped in at this point and stopped further violence in Denver. However, he wanted Johnny Neville killed at Goldfield, Nevada, because he was blackmailing the union over the Independence depot affair.

HARRY ORCHARD, the mild-mannered professional dynamiter who confessed to killing for a fee 18 men in two years time. His victims included Frank Steunenberg, onetime governor of Idaho. Cheat, steal, burn, lie, kill—this had been Orchard's code of conduct. Could the world now believe him when he implicated Bill Haywood as the paymaster behind the murders?

FRANK STEUNENBERG, the murder victim, had been fourth governor of the state of Idaho. At his funeral, Borah described him as "Rugged in body, resolute in mind, almost massive in the strength of his convictions—he was of the granite hewn." Had Steunenberg's resoluteness in the labor troubles in 1899 marked him for death in 1905? Had Haywood and the Western Federation of Miners hired Orchard to assassinate him? These were the issues of the trial.

FREMONT WOOD, the Ada County district judge who refused to disqualify himself from the Haywood trial even though his law partner was a defense lawyer. His own determination to preside over an impartial and fair trial and his inability to judge the intentions of the jury ultimately cost Wood the respect and reputation he had built through a long career in Idaho.

WILLIAM D. HAYWOOD, defendant, the tough one-eyed miner who managed the day-to-day affairs of the most militant union in America, the Western Federation of Miners. Before the trial his name became a watchword of the radical movement throughout the world. From the trial emerged an accurate and startling picture of the union, but the full, accurate, and even more startling picture of Bill Haywood would not emerge until long after the trial was history.

JAMES H. HAWLEY, the "plain, blunt" man of the prosecution. An Idaho legend as a miner, lawyer, and politician, Hawley found himself prosecuting the very organization he had helped to establish—the Western Federation of Miners. As dean of the "sagebrush lawyers" Hawley used his enormous personal popularity to prop up the state's circumstantial case against Haywood.

EDMUND F. RICHARDSON, the forgotten man of the Haywood defense. A veteran of the legal battles of the Western Federation of Miners, Richardson tried to keep the Haywood trial a case in law, but he was forced to watch it turn into far more than that. He was forced, too, to share the leadership of the defense with a man as strong-willed as himself, but possessed of completely different ideas.

WILLIAM E. BORAH, the brilliant young Senator-elect from Idaho who served as associate prosecution counsel in the Haywood trial. Borah postponed taking his seat in the Senate until his prosecution of the Haywood case was finished, but before he would ever reach the Senate floor he had to go through the ordeal of being the accused as well as the accuser.

CLARENCE DARROW: "My mind is not unbiased in this great struggle. . . . For thirty years I have given the best ability that God has given me. I have given my time, my reputation, my chances — all this to the cause which is the cause of the poor. I may have been unwise, I may have been extravagant in my statements, but this cause has been the strongest devotion of my life. . . . Never in my life did I wish anything as I wish the verdict of this jury."

But Haywood wanted Steunenberg killed, and this assassination took priority. Haywood told Orchard that he had sent three men previously to kill Steunenberg but each had failed.

Orchard then detailed to the jury the events of his trip to Caldwell. After stopping at Caldwell briefly, he went on to Portland, Seattle, and North Idaho. He met Jack Simpkins in Wardner, and mentioned to him a plan suggested by a mutual friend Dave Coates, to kidnap the children of a mineowner named Paulson and hold them for ransom. Orchard gave the Peabody bomb to a man named Cunningham whom Vincent St. John had vouched for. Orchard and Simpkins then went to Caldwell together. They set one bomb for Steunenberg on the street, but it was tripped by a passer-by and did not go off. Simpkins then left town, and Orchard finally managed to kill Steunenberg with the gatepost bomb. Shortly after being arrested and jailed, he had received a telegram from Spokane and a letter from Denver, but he was not permitted to explain the contents of these messages to the jury until the original documents had been introduced as evidence.

In the only part of the direct examination which was out of order chronologically, Orchard recalled a conversation with Haywood in which Haywood had said that Adams and another man had been sent to California at one time to get Bradley. On the way back to Denver, Adams was arrested in Ogden, and Haywood sent him $75 to get out of jail. Also, Adams had been sent to Pocatello with "Pettibone Dope" to be thrown into a trainload of scabs who were on their way to Cripple Creek. At this rather odd stopping place, Hawley abruptly turned the witness over to the defense for cross-examination.

Richardson's cross-examination of Orchard lasted 26 hours spread over a week's time. The attorney took him over all of the events of the confession, drawing out much more detail than Hawley's direct examination had produced. But Richardson was unable to make much of a dent in Orchard's story. In fact, the net effect of the cross-examination seemed to be further strengthening of Orchard's story. Clarence Darrow later commented:

> He [Richardson] was a man of much force of character and full confidence in his own ability to accomplish whatever he set out to do.

> So, in a loud voice and antagonistic manner he re-examined Orchard for several days on every detail of his direct examination. Orchard remained perfectly cool and, like most witnesses, repeated on cross-examination the story already told. However, Mr. Richardson succeeded in laying the foundation for the impeachment of Orchard, by unbiased witnesses, regarding many statements made in direct examination. As a rule, it is futile to go over in cross-examination the testimony already given. But although Mr. Richardson was an able man, he was somewhat lacking in subtlety.[7]

Although there were trial observers who disagreed with Darrow's view of the futility of cross-examination in general, most of them did agree that Richardson's examination of Orchard was futile. Oscar King Davis of the *New York Times* even suggested that Richardson would have done better by waiving cross-examination completely.[8]

Richardson opened his cross-examination by exploring Orchard's background more fully. Orchard readily admitted that he was a bigamist, with a wife in Canada and another one in Cripple Creek. He explained his early life in great detail in answer to Richardson's barrage of questions. But from the beginning the defense attorney uncovered information that did not particularly aid the defense cause. For example, Orchard admitted that he once owned a 1/16th interest in the Hercules mine in the Coeur d'Alene country, but that he had sold the interest in 1897. And yet on numerous occasions later in the trial the defense attempted to show that Governor Steunenberg's actions in 1899 caused Orchard to lose his interest in this mine that later made its owners rich, and that avenging this loss was Orchard's motive in killing Steunenberg.

Similarly, during the early part of the cross-examination Richardson pursued the point that Orchard had once told Pettibone about his exploits in Canada, particularly about running off with another man's wife. Orchard admitted that he might have said some things to Pettibone that were not exactly true, and Richardson then developed the idea that this was the kind of

---

[7] Clarence Darrow, *The Story of My Life* (New York: Charles Scribner's Sons, 1934), p. 151.

[8] *New York Times,* June 9, 1907, p. 2.

bragging that men do in moments of camaraderie. Borah, at this moment and in seeming innocence, asked, "What year was this?" When Orchard answered "1904," Richardson recognized what had happened. In pursuing this line of questioning, in which he was trying to show Orchard as a braggart, he had succeeded instead in showing an intimacy between Orchard and Pettibone during 1904 at which time Orchard had said he was busily pursuing victims for the "Inner Circle."

In answer to Richardson's questions, Orchard had no qualms about admitting other crimes or questionable behavior. He readily admitted "highgrading" ore in the Vindicator mine—secreting high quality ore in his clothing for sale to assayers. He was equally candid about his role as a double agent during the train wrecking episode in Cripple Creek. He had been involved in arson, burglary, several varieties of larceny, and swindling. He had frequently lied when it suited his purposes. Orchard showed very little emotion when Richardson hammered away at the baseness of some of his crimes. With reference to the Independence depot explosion this exchange took place:

Q. You expected to kill fifty or sixty men that night?
A. I did not know how many we would kill.

Q. The more the merrier?
A. I did not think about that.

Q. And you did not care?
A. I don't know as I did.

Q. Just as soon kill a hundred men as one?
A. I was not thinking about that.

Similar exchanges took place with reference to the poisoning of the Bradley family's milk, and concerning a bomb Orchard had once set in the Idanha Hotel for Steunenberg.

The quiet unspectacular manner in which Orchard admitted his criminality impressed the newspaper writers covering the trial. Some of them who had expressed doubts concerning Orchard's truthfulness during the direct examination now became convinced that the man was sincere and telling the truth. Orchard had a remarkable memory for the events to which he had testified; on several occasions he corrected Richardson and even the court reporter when previous testimony was read back incorrectly. The newspaper men checked their own notes when this happened, and agreed that Orchard's version was correct and the official transcript wrong.

Davis of the *Times* analyzed Richardson's difficulty in questioning Orchard:

> It is an extraordinary cross-examination, based and continued upon an extraordinary error. The trouble with Richardson now is that he is proceeding upon the theory that he is cross-questioning the same Harry Orchard who was associated with his clients in their alleged crimes of a few years ago. . . .[9]

Davis went on to say that Orchard was not now a criminal and was perhaps a stronger moral force than Richardson. While this was an extreme point of view, many of the newsmen agreed that the "modern miracle," Davis' description of Orchard's conversion, had indeed taken place and that Orchard was a man of truth for the first time in his life.

Apparently Richardson had misjudged his witness. As a result, the defense attorney frequently changed his approach, trying to discover some weakness in Orchard's story. The *Oregonian* was prompted to observe:

> Again today the aimlessness of the defense in the Haywood case was illustrated on several occasions. It has been apparent all through the cross-examination of Orchard and has been commented upon by all observers that Mr. Richardson flounders around sadly and leads into contradictions.[10]

The *Oregonian* cited several of these contradictions. For one, Richardson's questioning had frequently sought to show Harry Orchard as a successful card player always having money, and thus not needing any from the Western Federation of Miners, his alleged employer. From time to time Richardson also tried to show that Orchard was living in poverty, thus proving that he could not have been receiving money from the union officials.

[9] *Ibid.*, p. 1.

[10] *Portland Oregonian*, June 13, 1907, p. 1.

Then, too, there was a persistent attempt made by Richardson to imply that Harry Orchard was an agent of the Cripple Creek mineowners, a man who seemingly would not be well accepted by his fellow miners. And yet Richardson drew out the admission that Pettibone had invited Orchard to spend a month with him as a houseguest, and that Orchard accepted the invitation and lived with Pettibone in the summer of 1905 until it was time to leave for Caldwell and the murder of Steunenberg.

The climax of the cross-examination was reached when Richardson covered the events following Orchard's arrest in Caldwell. As the *Times* described it:

> It was when Orchard began to tell of the events that followed his arrest in Caldwell that Richardson commenced to bore in hard in the apparent effort to show that Orchard had been induced to make his confession by the promises of Detective McPartland [*sic*] and others, and in the hope of securing immunity from punishment for himself. Every resource at the lawyer's command was used in that effort.
>
> His voice boomed out its loudest, and he employed with utmost vigor the tactics of blustering, bullyragging and browbeating which had not succeeded at any point before. Then he lowered his tones and tried the other sort of attack with wheedling insinuation. He sneered and scoffed.
>
> He distorted answers and tried the old method of testifying to his own deductions, putting them into the form of statement-questions, acting as if he expected Orchard to agree to them at once. But Orchard resisted every attack.[11]

At the moment when Richardson pressed for details of his decision to confess, Orchard came close to losing the remarkable composure he had displayed throughout the trial. His eyes were moist and his voice choked, but he managed to describe his meeting with McParland in the penitentiary. He denied again that he had been promised immunity in return for the confession; instead, he explained, his confession was an attempt to square himself with society. Shortly thereafter, realizing that Orchard was gaining sympathy in the courtroom, Richardson abandoned his questioning.

MacLane summed up the cross-examination this way:

> I think it was one of the most dramatic episodes that ever occurred in a criminal trial. The man pictured as a human monster, a veri-

[11] *New York Times,* June 14, 1907, p. 2.

> table hound of hell, a self-confessed murderer of over 20 men, a thief, a betrayer of women and a deserter of his children without a single redeeming quality, convinced the world generally by his quiet and dignified demeanor and courteous treatment of his adversaries that he had experienced a complete change of heart, a spiritual conversion, and a desire to atone for the crimes that he had done.[12]

With the cross-examination of Orchard completed and the state's case reasonably intact, it was time to call the witnesses who could supply the needed corroboration to Orchard's testimony. The first witnesses called were those people who could confirm details of the Bradley incident in San Francisco. The Bradleys' ex-maid testified to meeting Orchard at Guibbinni's grocery-saloon across the street from the Bradley house, and also to the milk incident. The milkman testified that the Bradley milk was the only milk for which a complaint was registered that day, and the city chemist testified to the extremely lethal amounts of strychnine he found in the milk when he analyzed it upon request of the dairy.

Three postal employees testified to the registered letter which was mailed by Pettibone's clerk in Denver to Orchard in San Francisco. Guibbinni identified Orchard as the man who hung around his establishment in 1904, but he swore that he had seen Orchard in front of the Bradley house minutes after the explosion whereas Orchard had said he made his getaway prior to the explosion.

Clarence Harrah, who had been the cager in the Vindicator mine during the Cripple Creek strike, testified to seeing men who took a shot at him when he followed them back into a level of the mine. This confirmed Orchard's testimony concerning his first attempt to ignite the carload of powder in the Vindicator mine. An Ogden city detective then told of arresting Steve Adams in 1903 and taking him to the telegraph office where Adams wired Bill Haywood for help. This testimony confirmed the details of a conversation between Orchard and Haywood to which Orchard had earlier testified. A Denver banker identified a series of bank drafts written by Haywood and payable to Jack Simpkins, one of which was for $100 and was written on December 21, 1905.

---

[12] John F. MacLane, *A Sagebrush Lawyer* (New York: Pandick Press, 1953), p. 160.

Miss Cora Peabody testified to seeing two men who approached her carriage and peered inside. But Richardson succeeded in rattling the governor's daughter to the point where she could not fix the date of this occurrence within a six-month period of time, and her testimony added no real confirmation to Orchard's testimony regarding the attempt on Governor Peabody. The governor then testified, but, oddly enough, he was asked very little by the prosecution and nothing by the defense. He did report, however, once seeing Harry Orchard in Canon City.

Major Naylor of the Colorado militia then produced part of a broken revolver found at the scene of the Vindicator explosion, and a piece of wire from the same spot. Orchard had testified to rigging the bomb in such a way that the lifting of the shaft guard rail would pull on a wire tied to the trigger of a revolver aimed at a quantity of dynamite. In questioning Major Naylor, Richardson tried to establish the harsh conditions of the military occupation of Cripple Creek including the reprisals and deportations. But Naylor professed no knowledge of many of the incidents mentioned by Richardson.

A fireman from Wallace testified to finding the "Peabody bomb" in the river where Cunningham, the man to whom Orchard had given the bomb, reportedly had thrown it. The bomb case was then identified in court by the Denver plumber who made it for Harry Orchard. Vaughn, the man with whom Orchard had written insurance, confirmed the story of the heavy suitcase in Canon City with the ticking noise inside. Orchard had shown him the clock mechanism and told him it could cause mine explosions. For this and other reasons Vaughn thought Orchard was "bughouse." But the hail insurance, he maintained indignantly, was good insurance rather than "fake" insurance as Orchard had testified.

Several damaging communications were introduced at this point by the state. First was a letter to Orchard's wife in Cripple Creek written by Bill Haywood on November 18, 1905, saying that Orchard was last heard from in Alaska. Orchard had testified to getting Haywood to write this letter to deceive his second wife who was making inquiries about him. At the same time that Haywood wrote the letter, Orchard was really in Caldwell and Haywood knew this—at least according to Orchard's testimony.

Then Sheriff Nichols of Canyon County produced a copy of the letter which Orchard had received in the Canyon County jail. Orchard had testified that this letter was from Pettibone, although it was unsigned. The significant portion of this letter read: "That was sent to Jack Dec. 21 for you. He should send it to you so that you ought to have it by this time." Nichols also testified to the receipt of the telegram announcing the arrival of attorney Fred Miller in Caldwell. Orchard later explained on redirect examination that he had been told in Denver never to write or telegraph Western Federation headquarters for help if he found himself in a jam, but to wait for the legal help which would soon arrive.

At this point the defense was permitted to put Harry Orchard on the stand for the purpose of asking impeaching questions. Richardson asked five such questions, or rather one question with five variations. It was: Had Orchard ever threatened Frank Steunenberg in the presence of Max Malich, Eugene Engley, Lottie Day, Dr. I. L. McGee, or Dave Coates? To each question Orchard replied negatively. Richardson also asked if Orchard had ever visited "Kid" Waters, an MOA detective in Cripple Creek. Again, Orchard said "No."

While Orchard was still on the stand the state completed its redirect examination. Hawley drew out the information that Orchard had once written a series of three letters to his Cripple Creek wife to be mailed by various WFM officials at various times and places to further mislead the woman. Two of the letters were taken to San Francisco for mailing by Paddy Maloney, and Marion Moore took one to Alaska. The arrangements for the letter sent by Haywood were also made about this same time.

More documentary evidence was then introduced in the form of a series of articles from the *Miner's Magazine* showing the animosity of the union leaders toward Frank Steunenberg. A heated debate developed over the admissibility of these articles as evidence. Richardson read from a number of anarchist publications at the time of the Haymarket incident to show what truly threatening writing was like, and pointed out that the *Miner's Magazine* articles were much milder in tone. Borah replied that Richardson was arguing the effect rather than the admissibility of the literature.

The jury, said Borah, should determine the effect but the judge should rule on the admissibility. After due deliberation, Judge Wood ruled that most of the articles were admissible as tending to show motive, excluding only those pieces written after Steunenberg's death. The articles were then introduced as evidence. They contained such references to Steunenberg as

> . . . we have never known him to articulate the truth.
> . . . such Christless whelps as Steunenberg, Merriam and Sinclair . . .
> . . . Hessian descendant that would disgrace Ananias . . .
> monstrosity
> filthy reptile
> perjurer
> hireling and a traitor.

In another example of prosecution thoroughness, the letters of recommendation that had been written for Orchard at the time of his insurance career were introduced. One letter had been written by Horace N. Hawkins, law partner of Richardson, who had met Orchard only once. As Hawkins' wholehearted endorsement of Orchard was read in court, Richardson grinned sheepishly. The recommendations, incidentally, were written for Thomas Hogan rather than Harry Orchard, indicating that the WFM attorneys as well as the "Inner Circle" knew of this alias.

Harry Orchard's landlady during his San Francisco adventures testified to finding lead and wood shavings in his room, a screw-eye in his door, and a very heavy suitcase. She thought he was an inventor. Judge Goddard then took the stand to describe how he had found the bomb by his gatepost after he had learned of the bomb through Orchard's confession. Bulkeley Wells had opened the bomb, and after test-exploding some of the dynamite the Pinkerton Agency in Denver sealed the bomb in a container which was opened prior to the trial.

W. T. Stuart, who had been chief engineer of a mine in Silver City in 1899, testified to hearing Haywood threaten Frank Steunenberg at that time. This testimony seemed to disturb the defense considerably; they did manage to establish by cross-examination, however, that Stuart remembered this occurrence because he had always thought of Bill Haywood as a model citizen prior to this time.

A representative of the telegraph company then testified to the telegraphic money order transactions between Orchard in San Francisco and Pettibone in Denver. Inasmuch as Pettibone had allegedly signed an alias to the application form, it was necessary to identify Pettibone's handwriting. Charles Kingsley, a Boise attorney who had qualified himself as a handwriting expert, then identified Pettibone's signatures on the Postal Telegraph applications by comparing them to his signature on the letter of recommendation that he, too, had written for Orchard-Hogan.

The final prosecution witness was a Negro liveryman from Denver who told of selling a rig to Orchard and Haywood. Orchard had testified that this rig was purchased for transportation in the attempt to be made on Sherman Bell. On June 21, with this witness' testimony, the state then rested the case that it had been building since June 4.

During this time the state had successfully confirmed many of Orchard's movements, but Borah and Hawley must have realized that their case had serious shortcomings, too. They had shown that Orchard planned the Steunenberg killing in company with a member of the Executive Committee of the Western Federation of Miners. The letter of December 30 to Hogan and the bank draft of December 21—the date referred to in the letter—seemed to indicate that high union officials knew of the activity of the two men in Caldwell, but the absence of the original letter as evidence weakened the inference.

Apparently, several members of the Western Federation had cooperated to help Orchard deceive his wife through the four letters. But this fact would hardly be regarded as highly material in establishing a conspiracy to commit murder. Orchard's intimacy with the "Inner Circle" of the union was established largely through defense cross-examination, and only two witnesses provided any link between Haywood and Orchard, and that hardly enough to imply conspiracy. The state's case required a cumulative proof of the relationship between Orchard and the "Inner Circle." Additional links might easily have been established by more of the detective work for which the Pinkerton Agency was famous. For example, newspapers reported during the time the state was making its case that the revolvers found on Harry Orchard at the time of his arrest had been traced to a Denver hardware store where they had been purchased by George Pettibone.[13] But this fact was not brought out in evidence during the trial. Perhaps the prosecution attorneys recognized that, while it could implicate Pettibone, such evidence would do nothing toward showing Haywood's connection with the murder.

Some motive for the killing of Steunenberg had been shown by the articles in the *Miner's Magazine,* and from Stuart's account of Haywood's 1899 remark in Silver City. But whether these reactions were strong enough to suggest the malice needed for murder was another question. Richardson had fought bitterly against the admission of the magazine articles and the Stuart testimony. Perhaps additional evidence on the question of a specific motive for Haywood to kill Steunenberg might have been very damaging to the defense. Borah had received a letter from a Pueblo, Colorado, attorney, James F. Drake, naming two men who had heard Haywood threaten Steunenberg in a speech in Pueblo in 1900, and who would be willing to so testify. There is no evidence that the Pinkertons ever checked on this lead, although they did trace a similar lead on a Coeur d'Alene miner named Sinclair (not Bartlett Sinclair) who had written Hawley saying that he had heard Haywood threaten Steunenberg.[14]

Although subsequent events of the trial strengthened their case, at this point Borah and Hawley had not made a particularly good case for the existence of a conspiracy to kill Steunenberg. Proof of conspiracy is always difficult to obtain, for several reasons: direct evidence such as a contract rarely exists, the testimony of a member of the conspiracy requires corroboration, and circumstantial evidence is often compatible with a reasonable theory of innocence. But in the Haywood case the state passed up some readymade proof of conspiracy which might have helped its case. This proof was in the form of official statements growing out of

---

[13] *Portland Oregonian,* June 12, 1907, p. 1.

[14] Letter, James F. Drake to William E. Borah, undated, in 1907 letter file of Borah Collection, Idaho Historical Society; Sinclair mentioned in letter, James McParland to G. J. Hasson, Pinkerton Supt. at Spokane, May 21, 1907.

the Paul Corcoran case which Borah and Hawley had successfully prosecuted a few years earlier. In reviewing this case the Idaho Supreme Court had said:

> For a period of some eight years the organization known as the "Miners' Union" had had almost complete control of the affairs of Shoshone County; the election of all officers of the county had been controlled by that organization; all business was subject to their domination and dictation; crimes of the most heinous character had been committed with impunity; and so intimidated had been the law-abiding portion of the county, who were vastly in the minority, that any investigation of such crimes was practically impossible. That this condition of things had existed from 1892 is a matter of history.[15]

It would have been relatively easy to establish for the Haywood jury that the "Miners' Union" mentioned in this unusually opinionated court decision was the Western Federation of Miners and its Coeur d'Alene locals. At least two of the jurors, Sebern, who was new to Idaho, and Gilman, who had been in the Philippines in 1899, might not have had any idea that such judgments had ever been pronounced on the union. The committee of the U. S. House of Representatives which investigated the Coeur d'Alene troubles expressed a similar judgment, and actually used the words "damnable conspiracy" in describing the situation.[16] Not only did the state fail to quote this report, but it failed to react when Haywood, replying to a Darrow question, said the committee made no report.

While it would have been impossible to argue that Haywood was a part of this "damnable conspiracy" inasmuch as he was not in North Idaho at the time, the state still might have introduced this evidence to show that at the time Steunenberg incurred the wrath of the Western Federation of Miners the union had officially been branded a criminal conspiracy in Idaho, and that Haywood had actively supported the union's Coeur d'Alene policies. In the absence of such evidence the state could only infer that a conspiracy had been demonstrated by the acts and words of the defendant. But virtually all the incriminating acts and words of Bill Haywood were testified to only by Harry Orchard.

---

[15] *In re Corcoran,* 59 Pacific 19.

[16] House Report 1999, *op. cit.,* pp. 24-25.

This dilemma faced the state's attorneys as they rested their case. Although their friends were worried, Borah and Hawley seemed quite confident.[17] Could they have possibly known that the defense would soon supply much of the corroboration the state had been unable to supply? Or were they sure that their own witnesses, held in reserve for rebuttal purposes, could materially strengthen the state's case? Regardless of what they had in mind, Borah and Hawley must not have had any inkling of the danger the state's case could have been in at that moment, had the defense played its hand with more finesse.

---

[17] *Portland Oregonian*, June 16, 1907, p. 1.

10

THE CASE *for the* DEFENSE

AT THE END OF THE STATE'S CASE against Bill Haywood the defense attorneys presented a motion for a directed verdict of acquittal. This is a routine procedure common to defense strategy in this type of trial and marks in reality the beginning of the defense's case. Richardson and Darrow spoke in favor of the motion, but they apparently had no great expectations of having it granted in their favor. It was not until many years later that it became known how remarkably close they came to ending the Haywood trial at this point.

Contrary to a fiction widely reported by popular writers on the trial,[1] it was Richardson and not Edgar Wilson who made the actual motion for acquittal. Richardson cited seven reasons for the motion, all of which boiled down to the argument that there was no testimony, other than that of Harry Orchard, to connect Haywood with the death of Frank Steunenberg. In the absence of the jurors, Richardson then launched into a two-and-a-half hour argument in support of the motion.

---

[1] e.g., Walter Lord, *The Good Years* (New York: Harper and Brothers, 1960), p. 170; Irving Stone, *Clarence Darrow for the Defense* (Garden City, N. Y.: Doubleday & Company, 1949), p. 231.

This speech was perhaps Richardson's best effort of the entire trial. The newspaper writers were duly impressed. The *Statesman* reported that "Mr. Richardson yesterday made a fine effort. He talked as if he had his heart set upon accomplishing his purpose." The Boise paper observed that Richardson talked directly to the judge, not gazing to either side, and ". . . while his logic did not meet the approval of the court, while, in the end, his motion was denied, Mr. Richardson yesterday made a decidedly good impression upon those who heard him."[2]

The *Oregonian* called Richardson's speech "a very able argument" and "a long, carefully prepared and eloquent speech." Toward the end of the speech Richardson indeed became quite eloquent and "reached the point of declamation."[3] The *Times* was impressed, also, but it thought that Richardson was not dealing with the issues. Said Oscar King Davis, "Mr. Richardson spoke with emphasis and vigor, and made a forceful argument. But it was also applied to a theory of the case different from that on which the prosecution has proceeded, and on which the great bulk of the testimony has been introduced."[4]

It is true that Richardson interpreted the case in a somewhat different light. He based his whole argument on the fact that Orchard was an accomplice and that the testimony of accomplices must always be viewed with suspicion. He cited section 7871 of the Revised Statutes of the State of Idaho:

> A conviction cannot be had on the testimony of an accomplice unless he is corroborated by other evidence, which, in itself, and without the aid of the testimony of the accomplice, tends to connect the defendant with the commission of the offense; and the corroboration is not sufficient if it merely shows the commission of the offense or the circumstances thereof.

Richardson then went on to read from various court decisions in states having almost identical statutes, as well as from highly regarded law books which consistently endorsed this principle. He also cited cases in which the decision included the fact that one

[2] *Idaho Statesman,* June 22, 1907, p. 1.

[3] *Portland Oregonian,* June 22, 1907, p. 4.

[4] *New York Times,* June 22, 1907, p. 3.

THE STEUNENBERG BOMB (above) as reconstructed by Orchard. Once a time bomb, it was finally exploded as the string from the gate pulled the stopper from the vial of acid.

FRANK STEUNENBERG'S HOUSE in Caldwell shortly after the bombing, showing the effects of the bomb on the gate.

HARRY ORCHARD being transferred from the prison to the courthouse. (above) Next to Orchard is James McParland; man with the cane is Charles A. Siringo.

THE JURY: (front, l-r below) Gilman, Robertson, Powell, Gess, Clark; (back) Smith, Sebern, Burns, Russell, Messecar, McBean, Schrivener.

THE PROSECUTION STAFF: Borah, Stone, and Hawley. (above) A fourth man was once in this picture—the official prosecutor, district attorney Van Dyne of Canyon County—but an enterprising retoucher dubbed him out, adding ammunition to the defense's charge that the official channels of prosecution had been bypassed in the state's determination to hang Bill Haywood.

THE DEFENSE STAFF (l-r below): Edgar Wilson of Boise, Leon Whitsell of Wallace, John Nugent of Silver City, Fred Miller of Spokane, Clarence Darrow of Chicago, and Edmund F. Richardson of Denver. Another attorney, Peter Breen of Butte, was absent from this picture.

THE HAYWOOD TRIAL opened in Boise, Idaho, on May 9, 1907. As it moved along to its dramatic climax through June and July, the small, hot, crowded court room became a focal point of national interest. Above photo, which appeared in Collier's magazine, shows William D. Haywood on the witness stand on July 11. It provides a rare view of his right, and blind, side. In the photo below, Harry Orchard, the man who rigged the bomb which killed ex-Governor Steunenberg, gives testimony under cross-examination. Attorneys for the defense sit around the table beyond court reporters, Clarence Darrow chin in hand.

accomplice cannot corroborate another accomplice, a suggestion to the prosecution that Steve Adams' testimony would not confirm that of Harry Orchard.

In support of his argument on the testimony of accomplices, Richardson cited dozens of court decisions relative to the inconclusiveness of such testimony without the independent corroboration of other witnesses or evidence. Then he began to review the witnesses called by the prosecution, pointing out for each one that without the testimony of Harry Orchard the facts established were innocent enough and did not connect Haywood with the death of Steunenberg in any way.

A particularly moving version of this statement was that which Richardson used after discussing the testimony of the San Francisco chemist who reported analyzing the Bradley milk. With reference to this testimony Richardson concluded:

> Eliminate Orchard from it, as you are compelled to do under these authorities, and there is nothing in that testimony which is corroborative of Harry Orchard—corroboration, as we have seen, upon an independent fact or independent circumstances, or any number of such facts and circumstances, is not the kind of corroboration which is contemplated by the very just and the very salutary statute of the state of Idaho.

In a remarkable variety of ways Richardson said essentially the same thing at the end of his discussion of each of thirty-five state witnesses. Significantly, he said nothing about the documentary evidence which the state had introduced in the form of letters, telegrams, bank drafts, magazine articles, and court decisions. Richardson's entire argument was predicated on the idea that no witness' testimony, taken by itself, could connect Haywood without using the testimony of Orchard. He concluded by saying in essence: The law is clear; do not leave the decision to the passions and prejudices of the jurors; let us dispose of the case here and now.

Senator Borah replied briefly to Richardson for the state. He commended the defense attorney for his "moving and eloquent" speech and agreed that the cases cited by Richardson were pertinent. But Borah stressed other portions of the same court decisions that held that the whole case need not be corroborated independently, but merely corroborated in some material way. Then he singled out the question of proving conspiracy as the real issue of the Haywood case. He began a discussion of the two ways that a conspiracy could be shown in this case, but he interrupted his explanation to remind the jury that in a conspiracy the act of one becomes the act of all. With this important concept introduced—but hardly established—Borah then resumed the point he had been making relative to proof of conspiracy. This proof, he said, could come from the testimony of a member of the conspiracy or from the cumulative effect of a combination of circumstances. He argued that outside of Orchard's testimony the state had made such a circumstantial case for conspiracy from its evidence on the movements of Jack Simpkins, the letter transactions, Orchard's consistent return to Denver, and other well-established facts.

Borah spoke confidently and briefly—only about twenty minutes. The *Statesman* found the Senator somewhat "disappointing" on this occasion.[5] James Hawley did not speak to the motion for acquittal, so Borah was followed immediately by Clarence Darrow. This was Darrow's first real speech of the trial, and the newsmen and spectators were curious to hear what this man from Chicago had to say.

Darrow was also brief, but he hit back hard and effectively against some of Borah's allegations. "After the fiery, fierce eloquence of Richardson," reported the *Statesman,* "Darrow's plain, old fashioned, easy, quiet manner on the start was resting, refreshing. But after awhile, the Chicago attorney also became heated. He began climbing the hillside of oratory and, in his closing sentences, he was at the top and was shouting down to those below his sentiments in a megaphone voice."[6] On the way up this "hillside of oratory" Darrow made some very effective points; he challenged the state's conspiracy case. "If there is a conspiracy in this case," he asked, "what is it? When was it born and who were the parties to it?" A few moments later he asserted,

---

[5] *Idaho Statesman,* June 22, 1907, p. 1.
[6] *Ibid.*

"It takes something besides intemperate language, something besides feeling, something besides a cause for prejudice to make out a conspiracy to kill, and there has been nothing else in this case." Darrow thus complemented Richardson's predominantly legal case with a simple but effective argument that struck hard at Borah's reorientation of the issues. The *Oregonian,* however, found Darrow "sneering and sarcastic" in this speech, and gave much more space to Richardson's argument than to that of either Borah or Darrow, whom it called "the picturesque figure of the afternoon's arguments."[7]

When Darrow finished, Judge Wood spoke up immediately. "Gentlemen, the court is clearly satisfied that this case should be submitted to the jury." The judge went on to explain that normally he would give his reasons for so ruling, but since three other trials under the same indictment were still pending he would not do so in this situation.

Nearly twenty-five years later Judge Wood reported the reasons for his action:

> At the close of the argument on the motion for advisory verdict the Court immediately denied the motion without further consideration. The evidence or lack of corroboration, I found, was given little thought, but two facts loomed prominent in the mind of the Court which could not be escaped. One was the appearance of Edgar Wilson in the cases as attorney for the defendants; the other was the fact that at the instance of and on application of the attorneys for the defendants, the State had already been put to a great expense in bringing the witnesses from outside states to testify on behalf of the defendants.
>
> In considering this case from a retrospect of more than twenty years, I admit I feel that had Edgar Wilson been absent from the case as attorney for the defendants the decision of the Court on the motion for advisory verdict might have been different and the trials there terminated. In reaching this conclusion I desire to say that there would be no inconsistency between this position and the subsequent rulings of the Court in the Haywood case and in the Pettibone case holding that there was sufficient corroborating evidence to warrant the submission of the cases to the consideration of the jury. The principal portion of the corroboration in the Haywood case was developed through the witnesses of the defendants

[7] *Portland Oregonian,* June 22, 1907, p. 4.

> when making their defense and while there was little or no corroboration against Haywood in the original presentation by the State, it was my opinion that the corroboration was ample when the case against Haywood was submitted as well as upon the conclusion upon the trial of the defendant, Pettibone.[8]

In other words, Judge Wood admitted that the presence of his law partner, Edgar Wilson, on the defense staff might well have been the consideration which kept him from granting the defense motion for acquittal. Not only that, but the subsequent defense witnesses made a real case against Haywood where one had not existed when the state finished. Thus, one can only disagree with Clarence Darrow who observed after the trial that ". . . the money paid to Wilson was the best investment that we made."[9] Had Darrow not engaged Edgar Wilson the trial might have been halted after a rather overconfident state's case built largely on Harry Orchard's testimony, and the Western Federation of Miners and its methods might never have been exposed to a critical public.

After the motion for acquittal had been denied, Darrow opened the case for the defense with a three-and-a-half hour statement on June 24, 1907. This speech received a mixed reception. The *Oregonian* called it

> . . . a disappointment. Like the cross-examination of Orchard by E. F. Richardson, it seemed to lack purpose, and those who expected a strong and plausible line of defense failed to find their expectations realized.
>
> Mr. Darrow . . . beyond entering some denials and making some charges . . . accomplished very little, while his effort made a bad impression everywhere. . . . Throughout Mr. Darrow's arguments were the contradictions that were so prominent in the work of Mr. Richardson in conducting the cross-examination of the chief witnesses of the state.
>
> The effect on the jury was noticeable. The jurors lost all interest after Mr. Darrow had talked an hour. One seemed to be trying to follow him through, but the others were plainly "tired."[10]

---

[8] Fremont Wood, *The Introductory Chapter to the History of the Trials of Moyer, Haywood, and Pettibone* (Caldwell, Idaho: The Caxton Printers, 1931), p. 24.

[9] Conversation, Clarence Darrow and J. H. McLennon of the *Denver Republican,* reported in letter, James McParland to William E. Borah, August 14, 1907.

[10] *Portland Oregonian,* June 25, 1907, p. 1.

But the *New York Times* found it a "clever, striking performance, interesting from first to last, and a shrewd, forceful presentation of his case." Said the *Times:*

> The speech was a combination of argument, based on a series of counter-charges meant to disprove or destroy the force of the allegations of Orchard, of explanation of parts of Orchard's story, of flat denial of other parts, and of admission of still other parts.

The *Times* reported that Darrow received close attention from the jurors, particularly because of his use of humor.

> Darrow in action is an engaging personality. He strives to present the appearance of complete fairness, and succeeds in it extremely well. He stands immediately in front of the jury, often with one foot on the iron rail that serves for a footrest for the front row of jurors. He speaks most of the time in an ordinary conversational tone, stepping back a little when he soars to brief flights of oratory or wants to lend vigor to his words by using more voice. His manner of address is exceptionally pleasant. He does not confine himself strictly to the tedious business of hard, cold legal argument. There is variety and wit both in what he says and in his way of saying it. . . .
>
> All told, Darrow made a good speech. He had a hard row to hoe. There were a lot of awkward explanations to make and of awkward admissions as well, but he made them all, giving them as little prominence as could be, and steering away again quickly as successfully, and hammering in his denials and his promises of "respectable" evidence.[11]

The *Times* seemed to have recognized the difficulty of Darrow's position, and to have credited him with doing a good job under the circumstances. But the *Idaho Statesman,* like the *Oregonian,* was disappointed. "It was neither a feast of reason nor an oratorical treat," said the Boise paper. It also observed that the jurors were interested only part of the time.[12] The Associated Press accounts of Darrow's speech, it is interesting to note, reported only what was said, and made no evaluation or criticism of content or delivery.[13]

Darrow opened the speech by reviewing Hawley's sweeping indictment of the Western Federation of Miners and its "Inner

---

[11] *New York Times,* June 25, 1907, p. 3.
[12] *Idaho Statesman,* June 25, 1907, p. 1.
[13] *Portland Oregonian,* June 25, 1907, p. 3.

Circle" in the state's opening statement. Darrow admitted the union had done some of the things mentioned by Hawley, particularly that it had ventured into politics and that it had hired lawyers on numerous occasions to defend members accused of crimes. Speaking of the formative days of the union he said, "And of course they hired a lawyer and paid large fees, and they hired the best they could—they hired Mr. Hawley; and he laid it out for them and advised them and was the godfather of them . . ." Apparently Darrow had declared a truce at this point and was speaking sincerely rather than sarcastically of the prosecution attorney. A few minutes later, in speaking of the efforts of the union to elect sympathetic men to public office, he said in a similar vein that "They endeavored . . . to elect a United States senator—among the rest, they tried to elect Mr. Hawley and unfortunately failed on that . . ."

Darrow then reviewed the union's role in the fight for the eight-hour law in Colorado and other western states. He traced the progress of mine labor with respect to working conditions, safety, medical care, and welfare benefits which had been won through the union's efforts. He pointed out the organized opposition which had existed to many of these measures, and described the process of blacklisting which had been practiced against union men who were too outspoken in their demands. The mineowners, said Darrow, had attempted to destroy the Western Federation by blaming the union for every crime, act of violence, or mine disaster which had occurred in the West; ". . . since they were organized every illegitimate child that was born west of the Mississippi has been bundled up in its swaddling clothes and hurried up to Denver and laid on the front door step of the Western Federation of Miners—for a purpose."

Darrow then began a discussion of Harry Orchard's story, using a narrative form rather than the traditional "we shall show" technique. Reviewing the Coeur d'Alene troubles, he observed that it was Jack Simpkins who really had the motive to kill Steunenberg because of the harsh treatment he had received in the bull pen. It must have been this kind of argument that prompted the *Oregonian* to comment on the "contradictions" in the speech, since the defense had already indicated that Orchard had a personal motive to kill Steunenberg. Furthermore, announced Darrow, Orchard did not go to Wardner for the blowing up of the Bunker Hill and Sullivan concentrator. A few moments later Darrow asserted that Orchard tried to sell his interest in the Hercules mine while fleeing from the troops, an act which seemed inconsistent with Orchard's nonparticipation in the riot—at least to some of the critical newsmen at the trial.

Darrow denied that Paul Corcoran gave a speech to his Burke miners in their hall on the morning that the dynamite train was hijacked. He concluded this portion of his historical review by pointing out that at the time of the second Coeur d'Alene troubles Haywood and Moyer were still mining, neither of them in the Coeur d'Alenes, and Pettibone had long since left the mines for the safer life of a Denver storekeeper.

Next Darrow turned to Cripple Creek and what he called the "waterloo [*sic*] of the Western Federation of Miners in the state of Colorado." He traced Harry Orchard's Cripple Creek adventures and the situation in general during the long strike. He announced that the defense would show Orchard's relationships with the detectives, Scott and Sterling, and would offer another theory of the Vindicator mine explosion. He implied that the Independence depot explosion was planned by the mineowners with the knowledge of the militia and the civil authorities.

He spent considerable time reviewing the events of June 6, 1904, in the Cripple Creek district and the deportations that followed. Next came the "awkward explanations" that the *Times* thought Darrow handled so well. He explained Orchard's financial transactions with Pettibone as innocent enough, growing out of the fact that Orchard left a lot of money with Pettibone while fleeing from Cripple Creek, money that was later sent to Orchard on several occasions. The Lyte Gregory killing could not have been the work of the Western Federation, said Darrow, since the union had no grievance against the man. The Bradley explosion was a gas explosion, not a bomb set by Harry Orchard or anyone else. The Western Federation of Miners was no more hostile to Judges Gabbert and Goddard in Denver than were thousands of Coloradoans who had abused the two men orally and in print as loudly as had the union. It was Orchard, not Dave Coates, who proposed the kidnapping of the Paulson child. The $100 sent to Simpkins was part of some money that Simpkins had left with Haywood some time earlier.

Still using a conversational style, Darrow concluded his opening statement by announcing that it was the Western Federation of Miners, rather than Bill Haywood, that the state seemed to be prosecuting. If this was intended to be a startling conclusion, it must have fallen a bit flat, for Darrow's statement itself had been almost completely a defense of the Western Federation of Miners and a counterattack on the mineowners rather than a defense of Haywood.

Following Darrow's opening statement, Harry Orchard was recalled by the defense for further impeaching questions. The questions were similar to the previous set. Did he ever have a conversation with an old man named Elliott on the train near Caldwell in which he told the man that he was an agent of the mineowners' association? Had he ever told Dr. McGee in Wallace in 1904 that he was "spotting" in the Coeur d'Alene mines? Had he ever threatened Steunenberg in San Francisco in the presence of D. C. Copley? Had he ever threatened Steunenberg in the presence of a Cripple Creek miner named Sullivan or to a Coeur d'Alene miner named Haugh? Had he tried to sell his interest in the Hercules mine to a stage driver in the Coeur d'Alenes in 1899 immediately following the Bunker Hill explosion? Had he threatened Steunenberg in the presence of a Cripple Creek miner named Redd? To each of these questions Orchard again replied negatively.

The defense then introduced a picture of Harry Orchard and two other men, taken in a photography gallery in Salt Lake City about 1899 or 1900. In the picture Orchard stood with a smoking revolver over the bodies of the two other men, whom he identified as miner friends. He explained the picture as the sort of comic pose frequently struck by people who visit such establishments, and denied that it represented any latent desire to be a desperado.

The first defense witness, Mrs. Mary J. King, then took the stand. She had run the Star, a roominghouse in Cripple Creek. She testified that Sterling, the MOA detective, stayed at her place and was visited frequently by Harry Orchard who always used the back stairs. Another roomer was Mrs. McKinney, wife of the man being tried on the train-wrecking charge. Mrs. King on cross-examination admitted that her sons were Western Federation men. Mrs. King's daughter confirmed the visits by Orchard to Sterling. The next witness was the woman who took over the Star when the Kings left, a Mrs. Fechyew. She reported that McKinney visited Sterling in the roominghouse for several days after he got out of jail.

C. W. Aller, the railroad station agent of the Florence & Cripple Creek Railroad, testified to seeing Sterling visiting Scott, the railroad detective, at Scott's office in the depot. Orchard came to the depot to see Scott on several occasions. The three men met, according to Aller, at the office a few weeks before the Independence depot explosion.

Dr. I. L. McGee of Wallace, who appeared as an impeaching witness, offered testimony that might have been more effective if it had not been so completely contrary to the general facts of the Orchard confession, much of which had already been confirmed by defense witnesses. McGee testified that he had seen Orchard in Mullan playing cards on the day of the Bunker Hill and Sullivan explosion, which supported Darrow's allegation that Orchard had not made the trip to Wardner. Then Dr. McGee began the testimony aimed at impeaching Orchard. He related the conversation in Wallace in which Orchard told him he was "spotting." Dr. McGee said initially that this talk was in 1905, but then he fixed the date definitely as July of 1904. It was this insistence on the year 1904 that weakened McGee's testimony. The doctor said he saw Orchard with Cunningham, whereas Orchard had testified that he did not know Cunningham prior to giving him the "Peabody bomb" in Wallace in 1905. Furthermore, the movements of Harry Orchard in 1904 were well confirmed by other testimony, and there was no indication that he had been in the state of Idaho that year.

Other impeaching testimony came from two Western Federation miners from Cripple Creek, Redd, and Sullivan, who testified that they had heard Orchard use threatening language against Steunenberg. The defense also used Mrs. Lottie Day to confirm a similar threat made in her presence. Mrs. Day had originally been brought to Boise by the prosecution attorneys, but they had decided not to use her because she was not considered reliable. When Darrow and Richardson learned that she had heard Orchard make such a threat, they called her as an impeaching witness. But on cross-examination she revealed that Haywood had come to the Belmont roominghouse in Denver looking for Orchard who was living there under the name of Dempsey. Haywood introduced Orchard to Mrs. Day as Dempsey, and then the two men spent a long time together in Orchard's room. This meeting was a few days before the Independence depot explosion.

Still another impeaching witness was John Elliott, a resident of the Idaho Old Soldiers Home. He testified to meeting Orchard on a train and discussing the Colorado labor situation with him. Orchard told him that he was an agent of the mine owners and that something startling, relative to labor troubles, was going to happen soon in that part of Idaho. On cross-examination Borah drew from Elliott the statement that Orchard had a mustache at the time, whereas prosecution witnesses and defense photographs had established earlier that Orchard was smooth shaven. Elliott also admitted that he had twice been committed to a mental institution.

Although no specific impeaching question had been put to Orchard about anti-Steunenberg language in the presence of John O'Neill, O'Neill was called to testify to a conversation with Orchard in which such language was used. O'Neill was the editor of the *Miner's Magazine,* and obviously very proud of the fact. Borah got him to admit that the magazine reflected official policy and feeling of the Western Federation of Miners. Borah asked O'Neill if he had written certain editorials which he then proceeded to read. O'Neill readily admitted authorship, apparently unaware that Borah had succeeded at last in getting into the record those bitter "Farewell, Steunenberg" editorials which Judge Wood had ruled inadmissible.

The next witness was considered remarkably reticent and unobservant by the newspaper correspondents. He was W. F. Davis, the man Orchard had named as being in charge of the dynamiting of the Bunker Hill and Sullivan concentrator. Davis denied any knowledge of the explosion, insisting that he did not make the trip to Wardner. He remained in Gem, saw the train from a distance of about twenty feet, but noticed nothing unusual about it. Davis also described a conversation with Orchard during which Orchard used abusive language in talking about Steunenberg, but he could remember relatively few of the circumstances of the conversation. Some of the newspaper writers made the interesting observation that Davis and several other WFM witnesses were believable when they described the treatment they had received at the hands of the mineowners in Colorado, but considerably less believable when they denied the allegations of Orchard's testimony.

Perhaps the most inconclusive episode of the entire Colorado labor troubles had been the attempted train wreck. The locomotive engineer of that train, W. W. Rush, was the next defense witness, but he was unable to throw much light on this question. The defense apparently called him to testify to the fact that the detectives, Scott and Sterling, had asked him before the attempt to indicate a suitable spot where a train might easily be wrecked, suggesting that the two men planned it themselves. But Orchard had admitted telling them that an attempt was forthcoming, so Rush's testimony did not implicate the MOA in the incident any more than it did the WFM.

Ed Boyce, onetime president of the Western Federation of Miners, was then utilized by the defense to describe the tough, uphill fight of the union to win its demands. He described how he and other WFM men had been blacklisted and deported by mineowners' associations in various western mining camps. However, on cross-examination by Hawley, Boyce admitted that he did not know of any MOA in Idaho since 1899, nor in several other western states. When Boyce described the gains won by the miners through the union, particularly on the eight-hour day issue, Hawley got him to admit that part of the credit for these advances must go to other unions and to reform legislation in a number of states. Hawley also obtained from Boyce the admission that the Western Federation of Miners in Idaho had been unable to improve wages over the scale that prevailed 25 years earlier.

Another of Orchard's alleged accomplices, W. B. Easterly, then took the stand. He admitted that Orchard had contacted him in Silver City from Caldwell, but insisted it was relative to selling insurance around Caldwell and not in connection with killing Steunenberg. He said that he had heard Orchard threaten Steunenberg once in the Cripple Creek district. On cross-examination by Borah, Easterly admitted that he knew of this threat, but did not tell the Idaho authorities either before or after the crime that the man who had made this threat was then in Caldwell. Asked why, Easterly said he was not an "informer." However, Borah got him to admit as soon as Orchard turned against the WFM, Easterly "informed" Nugent. As Borah kept hammering away at this point, Easterly then changed his story and said that he told Nugent immediately after the crime.

A Cripple Creek miner named Schultz was then called. He denied going into the Vindicator mine with Orchard, but Orchard had already said that the Schultz present at the trial was not the man he knew in Cripple Creek. On cross-examination Schultz admitted that once in Cripple Creek he had met another Joe Schultz who looked like a miner.

Several witnesses then testified to seeing the bloodhounds from the Colorado penitentiary being brought to Independence to track the dynamiters of the depot. Two of these witnesses reported seeing the dogs on two occasions follow the scent from the depot to the nearby cabin of Al Bemore, who was known to have engaged in detective work for the mineowners. One witness reported seeing Bemore among many people at the depot the morning after the explosion, before the dogs were brought into the area. The dog handler had earlier testified to the trails the dogs had followed; he reported that the dogs had finally picked up a good scent and were going down the road to Colorado Springs when Sterling called off the dogs with the statement that Steve Adams was known to be the dynamiter.

A keystone of the defense's case was a new theory of the Vindicator mine explosion, built on circumstances suggesting an accident rather than a bomb. Thomas Wood, a miner in the Vindicator, testified to putting half a box of powder on top of a water barrel at the shaft on the 8th level on the day before the explosion. He saw the powder the next morning at about eight o'clock as he went to work. At about ten o'clock he saw Beck and McCormick on the 8th level. The explosion occurred about twenty or thirty minutes later. As Wood made his escape he noticed that the powder was gone. He testified that he had seen a revolver dangling loosely from Beck's pocket when he saw him just before the explosion, suggesting that he might have dropped the revolver while moving the powder off the cage at the 6th level. Wood said he found part of a revolver during his escape, but that he saw no wire on the safety bar. On cross-examination he admitted that he had not been called as a witness at the coroner's inquest, and that he had worked only a day and a half in the mine and had never been on the 6th level. After getting these admissions from Wood, Borah passed up several good chances to weaken this testimony. Wood had described his escape by climbing in near panic up a long series of rickety ladders from level to level; and yet the man knew exactly how many men were with him and how much time it took. He saw no powder where he had left it, and he managed to find a shattered revolver on a level he had never visited. He was, perhaps, too observant; he reported seeing no wire on the guard rail, but why should he be looking for it? He even said that he looked for parts of "the infernal machine" before help came, but found none. Again, why should he be looking for a bomb, as a man fleeing for his life out of a mine in which he was virtually a stranger, from what he had testified was an accidental explosion? Perhaps Borah was counting on rebuttal testimony to weaken Wood's story, but he did let some seemingly incredible statements go unchallenged at this point.

The next witness was D. C. Copley, onetime member of the Executive Committee of the Western Federation of Miners. Copley had met Orchard in San Francisco when he was showing moving pictures of the Cripple Creek situation in behalf of the union. At that time Orchard had used harsh language in discussing Steunenberg. On cross-examination Copley revealed that

Lyte Gregory had been an enemy of the Western Federation in the Idaho Springs trouble where Copley had been one of the defendants.

A WFM miner, Haugh, then swore that he met Orchard in Wallace in 1904 or 1905 and that Orchard used threatening language against Steunenberg at that time. Haugh also testified to conditions in the "bull pen" at the time of the 1899 troubles. Another Coeur d'Alene resident, a stage driver named Ramey, then testified that Orchard had tried to sell him his interest in the Hercules mine following the Bunker Hill explosion in 1899.

After several witnesses described the deportations in the Cripple Creek district, another of the defense's star witnesses was called. This man was Morris Friedmann, who had once been a stenographer in the Pinkerton offices in Denver and who had recently written a book entitled, *The Pinkerton Labor Spy*. Friedmann described how he had made copies of many of the reports sent in by Pinkerton operatives to the Denver office for editing; he also named eight or ten of the Pinkerton operatives who were working on mine and smelter assignments, including several who were officials of WFM locals. What promised to be a damaging blow to the prosecution fizzled, however, when Friedmann admitted that the Mine Owners' Association was not a Pinkerton client. The reports which were introduced in evidence contained no suggestion of any Pinkerton plotting against the Western Federation of Miners, but they did contain numerous references to violence that the Pinkerton operatives had heard union men discussing.

Other important witnesses confirmed one of the allegations of Darrow's opening statement. Darrow had announced that Harry Orchard did not go to Wardner on the dynamiting expedition. The defense now produced two witnesses, Flynn and McHale, who testified to playing poker with Orchard in Mullan on that day, confirming Dr. McGee's earlier testimony to that effect.

Several United Mine Workers organizers then testified to the role that Lyte Gregory had played in the coal mine strike in southern Colorado, suggesting that the coal miners rather than the metalliferous miners had reason to retaliate against the detective. The deportations in Telluride were then described by Judge Stevens, the district judge who had originated the habeas corpus writ for Moyer. According to Stevens, the district had been quiet until martial law was imposed, at which time the military showed a complete disregard for civil law. Stevens seemed to be a reasonably objective witness until he professed no knowledge of several widely known murders which had been committed in connection with the labor troubles of the area.

Two more impeaching witnesses testified to Orchard's threats against Steunenberg. One was Eugene Engley, onetime attorney general of Colorado in the "Bloody Bridles" Waite administration and later an attorney for the WFM in Cripple Creek. With every answer Engley managed to make a speech about Socialism or Populism, and both sides seemed relieved when he was through. Max Malich then explained the circumstances of Orchard's denunciation of Steunenberg in his presence. He admitted that he and Orchard discussed blowing up Malich's boardinghouse, as Orchard had testified, but insisted that it was Orchard who brought it up. He also admitted that the building burned shortly after he had insured it, but he made it quite clear that he was at his ranch on the western slope when the fire occurred.

In one of the trial's more ironic moments, Edward McParland, brother of the Pinkerton detective, testified how he, a shoemaker in the town of Victor, had been deported from the Cripple Creek district with the trainload of men taken to the Kansas border. While this testimony added nothing to the evidence, it did help the defense build a negative image of the prosecution as heartless, inhuman, almost fratricidal.

Pat Moran, the Cheyenne saloonkeeper, denied going to Denver for Orchard or being in Denver at that time of the year. Dave Coates, onetime lieutenant governor of Colorado, testified to another denunciation of Steunenberg by Orchard. He also admitted that Orchard had talked to him about kidnapping the Paulson child, but swore that it was Orchard's idea and that he had threatened to denounce Orchard if he did not abandon the scheme immediately.

In other testimony, another Cripple Creek boardinghouse keeper reported seeing Orchard, Scott, and Sterling together on the night of the second train-wrecking attempt. Marion Moore then took the stand and admitted that he took Harry Orchard's letter to Alaska; what the defense had in mind in calling Moore is not clear. Another questionable strategy was the calling of Mrs. "Kid" Waters, wife of a MOA gunman who had been prominently mentioned in testimony on several occasions. Mrs. Waters as an impeaching witness testified that Harry Orchard had visited her husband in Cripple Creek. On cross-examination, however, she said that they also had frequent visits from Lyte Gregory who was an MOA detective. Darrow, of course, had insisted in his opening statement that Gregory had no connection with any Western Federation labor troubles.

The man who had sent the registered letter to Orchard in San Francisco, Pettibone's clerk, then testified that what he sent on that occasion was Orchard's Masonic charm and his union card. Still another Coeur d'Alene resident reported that Orchard had tried to sell his interest in the mine to him in 1899, just before the Bunker Hill trouble.

At this point the defense introduced a long series of depositions relative to the Bradley explosion, taken in San Francisco during the early days of the trial by Owen Van Duyn for the prosecution and Fred Miller for the defense. The reading of these depositions slowed down the proceedings of the trial considerably as lawyers and jurors tried to make sense out of complicated explanations and pictures of the building and the damage to it. Because of the conflicting testimony and because of the inherent limitations of deposition testimony—the inability of either side to recall witnesses to clear up doubtful testimony—this portion of the Orchard story has always remained somewhat enigmatic.

The owner of the building, Walter Linforth, first described the explosion damage. He said that the tenants had complained of gas fumes prior to the explosion and that a defective gas meter had been discovered after the explosion. Linforth, incidentally, had won a law suit against the gas company for damages from the explosion, but the gas company had since appealed the case after learning of the Orchard confession. Apparently the testimony relative to this pending court decision in California was kept from the Haywood jury so as not to influence their determination of facts. Linforth and several other witnesses weakened Orchard's testimony considerably on one point: Orchard had said he climbed to a flat roof on the rear of the Bradley flat to await the delivery of the milk he wanted to poison. The San Francisco testimony made it clear that this roof could be reached only through the attic of the building; an adjacent building which provided access to the roof was built after the date on which Orchard made the alleged attempt at poisoning the milk.

Fred Bradley, the victim of the explosion, admitted that his frequent trips to lonely mining camps in the West provided many opportunities for anyone who wanted to kill him. He described how on the morning of the explosion he had come down the stairs with a lighted cigar in his mouth, opened the door, and was momentarily blown down by an explosion which seemed to be a flash at the end of his cigar. He had time to think that it must have been a trick cigar, and to feel his ear to see if it were severed. Then he was lifted by an explosive force and hurled into the street. He maintained, however, that he heard but one explosion. Coming down the stairs he had smelled no gas, but while lying briefly on the floor he felt overcome by gas. He smelled no powder, an odor he was familiar with through his mining experiences.

Tracy Cummings, an occupant of another flat, said he left the building about a minute and a quarter before the explosion and saw no bomb and no one around the building. J. B. Reilly, a neighbor, reported walking by the building ten or fifteen minutes before the explosion and seeing a Japanese servant cleaning the steps. Reilly visited Guibbinni's corner saloon where Guibbinni served him his regular morning drink. On his return trip Reilly saw the servant finishing his cleaning and gathering up his equipment. The explosion occurred when Reilly reached his own house at the end of the block. The witness reported seeing no one else on the street, and no street cars.

Through these two witnesses the defense was trying to establish the impossibility of Orchard's going to the Bradley door after Cummings and Reilly had passed, planting the bomb, catching a passing street car, and being out of earshot of the explosion —as Orchard had described the bombing in his confession and testimony. On cross-examination Reilly admitted that he knew Orchard as Barry from seeing him around Guibbinni's saloon for several weeks previous to the explosion. He also admitted that the cable car which started down a steep hill a block away could be very noisy, particularly to a person riding the car.

The Bradleys' former cook then testified that she had not gone to the theatre with Orchard as he had asserted, but that he had offered her tickets. Orchard had gone up the Bradley back steps to deliver groceries on two occasions, but had not been in the house. The explosion, she reported, did not seem very loud or sharp where she stood in the back of the house.

Mrs. Cummings, mother of Tracy Cummings, testified to the impact of the explosion. She also reported that her son left the house ten or fifteen minutes before the explosion, but Van Duyn for the prosecution apparently overlooked this significant contradiction of the son's testimony.

A group of San Francisco firemen testified to hearing the blast at their stations, six and three blocks from the house respectively. The blast was quite loud, they said, but they admitted they had never heard a gas explosion to which they could compare the intensity of this explosion. One fireman called it the loudest explosion he had ever heard, including some heavy dynamite blasts during the great San Francisco fire and earthquake which had occurred since the Bradley explosion. Thus, by a strange quirk of fate these San Francisco firemen were quite familiar with dynamite at the time of the trial in 1907 whereas they had not been at the time of the explosion in 1904. As men now familiar with dynamite fumes they testified that there was no odor but gas after the Bradley explosion. This was indeed valuable evidence for the defense.

Several men who had had a part in building or rebuilding the structure then testified that the explosive force seemed to be concentrated between the studding of one wall, and that they found no lead fragments at the scene of the explosion. This fact would also tend to confirm the gas theory.

The defense had located another Coeur d'Alene miner in San Francisco who testified in the deposition that he had known Orchard in San Francisco in 1904. Orchard, in trying to interest this man in a "mining proposition" in the Coeur d'Alenes, had used threatening language in explaining how Steunenberg's actions were responsible for the loss of his property in Idaho.

With the completion of the reading of the depositions the case for the defense was almost complete. Only two more witnesses were called, but they were important ones in that they were the defendants, Moyer and Haywood. The defense attorneys must have felt that there were so few direct links between Orchard and the two union officials that it would be safe to allow them to testify. Moyer denied ever having a conversation with Orchard relative to any act of violence. He admitted that Neville had come to the Western Federation office seeking money, but he explained that the saloon keeper wanted to be reimbursed for the losses that he suffered by having to leave the Cripple Creek district.

Moyer created a good impression as a witness. He was courteous and articulate, offering reasonable explanations for several embarrassing points in the prosecution case. When he produced the telegram from Jack Simpkins to the union headquarters, reading "Cannot get a lawyer to defend Hogan. Ans.", it was the state's first knowledge that such a telegram existed. Moyer explained that the union officials in Denver had read newspaper accounts of the killing of Steunenberg by a man named Hogan, but were not sure it was the Hogan they knew until Simpkins' cipher telegram arrived. Moyer also explained the correspondence between Haywood and the Silver City local, and copies of the telegrams and letters were introduced. He readily admitted that Fred Miller came to Denver to collect a $1,500 retainer to defend Orchard and that Simpkins had sent Miller.

On cross-examination by Borah, Moyer admitted that the union had made no inquiry to determine whether Orchard was guilty or not. He also professed no knowledge of the draft of

December 21, 1905, to Jack Simpkins even though he, as president of the union, would have had to sign the check by which it was purchased.

Hawley and Borah treated Moyer with considerable respect during his cross-examination. They must have realized that they could have impeached him as a witness, as they later did with John O'Neill of the *Miner's Magazine,* because of his previous felony conviction, but they permitted him to make a complete explanation of his version of Orchard's tale.

Haywood, too, was accorded a full opportunity to testify, and there was no attempt made by the state to show the embarrassing details of his arrest even though the defense had brought out the details of Moyer's arrest to show the Pinkerton machination behind it.

Darrow asked about Stuart's testimony that Haywood had said Steunenberg should be "exterminated;" Haywood on the witness stand explained that he believed he had said "relegated," a word connoting retirement from political activity. The question of the draft to Simpkins came up again. This money, said Haywood, was money that Simpkins had left with him for safekeeping and was not Federation money. He denied ever talking violence with Orchard, and denied meeting Orchard with Lottie Day at the Belmont. He explained the Steve Adams transaction as money of his own which he had sent Adams to help him get started again after an unsuccessful prospecting trip, and that Adams had eventually paid back about $30 of this money after locating in Oregon.

Haywood admitted that he had written to Mrs. Orchard because she had been seeking information about her husband. The last time he had seen Orchard, Haywood had chided him about not taking better care of his wife. On this occasion, Orchard had talked about going to Alaska. It was on this information that Haywood wrote the letter to Mrs. Orchard.

Haywood testified to the conditions imposed upon the union in Cripple Creek, particularly the permit system. On cross-examination Borah read from a WFM poster which threatened miners who did not stand by the union during the strike. When Borah asked if the WFM didn't have a "permit system of its own," Haywood replied that it did not, since the WFM used a union shop approach rather than a closed shop. Haywood's cross-examination ended with his statement that he knew nothing about Miller's trip to Caldwell. He did admit, however, that three attorneys came to Caldwell unsolicited by Harry Orchard—Sullivan, a labor attorney from Denver, Miller, a WFM attorney from Spokane, and Nugent, a WFM attorney from Silver City.

This testimony concluded the defense case. Although Moyer and Haywood had been effective witnesses, the performance of many of the defense witnesses tended to justify Judge Wood's conclusion regarding the damaging effect of the defense presentation. This effect was apparent to other contemporary observers, too. C. P. Connolly, himself a former prosecuting attorney in Butte, wrote during the trial:

> There is no escape from the conclusion that at the close of the case for the defense, a much stronger chain of evidence had been forged against Haywood than the prosecution had succeeded in welding. And the credit for laying the State's well-concealed traps for the defense to stumble into must be given to the detective McParland, an old-fashioned man in appearance and habit, who works silently and seriously, and with a passion for winning.[14]

At the end of the defense evidence Harry Orchard had been corroborated on as many counts as he had been refuted. The poisoning of the Bradley milk as Orchard had told the story seemed impossible in view of the evidence regarding the flat roof, but Orchard's stalking of Bradley was more clearly established. Generally the evidence supported the gas theory of the Bradley explosion, but there were some confusing aspects of Bradley's testimony that could best be explained by the dynamite theory.

Orchard's close relationship with detectives had been shown by several witnesses, but his relationship to Haywood had also been made more intimate by the testimony of at least one witness. Orchard's feeling toward Steunenberg had been described by no

---

[14] C. P. Connolly, "The Moyer-Haywood Case," *Collier's*, July 27, 1907, p. 14.

less than a dozen witnesses, but the official hostility of the Western Federation of Miners toward Steunenberg had also gone into the record on several occasions.

Lyte Gregory had been clearly identified as an enemy of the Western Federation which would confirm Orchard's testimony, but the Vindicator mine explosion had been explained as an accident, which tended to contradict Orchard. The explanation of the Independence depot explosion promised by Darrow in his opening statement had not materialized, but the evidence with which he had promised to place Orchard in Mullan on Bunker Hill day had been presented.

Perhaps, most significantly, the basic contradiction in the defense case had not been resolved by the testimony of the witnesses selected by the defense. If anything, it had been widened. Defense testimony had asserted that the mineowners and their detectives were out to destroy the Western Federation, and that Harry Orchard was in league with them. But other defense testimony revealed Harry Orchard as the vindictive hate-filled victim of Steunenberg's policies in the Coeur d'Alenes. And still other testimony—supporting neither theory—held Orchard blameless in the bombing of the Bunker Hill and Sullivan concentrator. The personal revenge theory and the counter-conspiracy theory were both plausible defenses, but when some of the witnesses supported one theory and some of them supported the other, the total defense argument must have been somewhat implausible to the jurors.

Regardless of which theory their testimony supported, many of the defense witnesses had too much reason to want the testimony to go against Harry Orchard and for Bill Haywood. Darrow had promised in his opening statement to call "respectable" witnesses, meaning people who were not affiliated or in sympathy with the Western Federation of Miners. But, with the exception of those who testified through the San Francisco depositions, most of the witnesses had strong ties with the union. They perhaps wanted to support the labor movement more than they wanted to see the truth emerge. When subsequent rebuttal testimony discredited some of these defense witnesses, the state looked upon their original testimony as perjury rather than as bad memory.

11

LAST EVIDENCE and LOST EVIDENCE

CLARENCE DARROW and E. F. Richardson must have recognized that many of their witnesses made admissions more damaging to Bill Haywood and the Western Federation of Miners than they were to Harry Orchard and the state's case. Perhaps more important, this defense testimony enabled the state, through its rebuttal witnesses, to open the lid on a veritable Pandora's box of WFM activities which otherwise would never have been revealed.

The first rebuttal witness for the state was William Dewey, whose testimony was in direct conflict with that of W. F. Davis for the defense. Dewey was a unique witness in that he was the first man, other than Harry Orchard, to admit participation in the Bunker Hill and Sullivan dynamiting in 1899. Dewey swore that Davis accompanied the mob to Wardner after serving out guns and ammunition to the miners at the union hall at Gem on that day. On cross-examination Richardson tried to discover how Dewey came to appear as a volunteer prosecution witness in view of the fact that no other man had ever risked admitting participation in the explosion. What Richardson was after was an admission that immunity had been promised, but when he got from the witness was a statement that he had gotten tired of hearing defense witnesses, particularly Davis, pervert the truth. Dewey related how he had gone to his mine foreman in the Cripple Creek district to ask how he might set the record straight. The foreman sent him to the Pinkerton office in Denver where he was given transportation and expenses to Boise.

Another rather ironic moment occurred when a miner named Gainey appeared as a state rebuttal witness. Specifically he contradicted Flynn who had claimed to be playing cards with Orchard in Mullan on April 29, 1899. Gainey testified that he saw Flynn in May of that year, and that Flynn told him then that he had not seen Orchard since February. Gainey was an old friend of Orchard's. By a strange twist of fate he had been one of the miners injured in the Independence depot explosion. In an emotional exchange of correspondence as well as in a personal reunion, the badly crippled Gainey had since forgiven Harry Orchard for his role in the tragedy.

The testimony of John O'Neill was formally impeached by the introduction of his prison record at the "Dakota penitentiary" on a manslaughter conviction. The testimony of John Elliott was thoroughly discredited on several counts. Railroad officials testified to the nonexistence of the train described by Elliott; a Caldwell resident swore that Orchard was smooth shaven at the time; a Salt Lake hotel keeper said that Orchard was staying at his establishment at the time of the alleged conversation with Elliott; and several witnesses testified to Elliott's unbalanced mental condition.

August Paulson, one of the owners of the Hercules mine, testified to the fact that Orchard had actually transferred his interest in the mine to Dan Cardoner on March 7, 1898, and the deed proving this transaction was introduced in evidence. Two other witnesses then confirmed previous rebuttal witnesses, although by itself this new evidence would not have been strong enough to impeach the defense witnesses whom it contradicted. A Denver roominghouse keeper reported that Orchard had been staying with him during the time in 1904 when Dr. McGee said he saw Orchard in Wallace, but this man kept no records. And a Coeur d'Alene mine employee testified to paying a brief visit to Gem during Bunker Hill day and seeing only two men in town, neither of whom was W. F. Davis.

On the basis of accumulated evidence the state of Idaho arrested Dr. McGee for perjury on July 13, 1907. Shortly thereafter, W. F. Davis and C. W. Aller were arrested on the same charge, and the state announced its intention of also prosecuting McHale, Flynn, Moran, Mrs. King, Reilly, and several other defense witnesses. Aller was arrested because he had testified that Orchard, Sterling, and Scott met at Scott's office just before the Independence depot explosion which occurred in June of 1904. On rebuttal Scott testified that he left the employ of the railroad in March of 1904 and did not work for it or use the office again until August of that year. A Denver hotelkeeper testified that Scott was staying there the latter part of April and for some time thereafter. Upon cross-examination this woman said that she had a "particular reason" for remembering Scott, but the defense did not press this point further. On redirect examination Borah asked what the reason was. She replied that she remembered Scott because threatening notes were frequently left on his door. A Denver railroad official then testified to seeing Scott in Denver regularly during April, May, and June of 1904, and a Cripple Creek railroad official testified to not seeing Scott during this time in the Cripple Creek district.

Rebuttal witnesses also aided the state's version of the San Francisco events. An official of the Boise Gas Company testified that a glowing cigar would not ignite gas. After a rather technical explanation of the combustion of manufactured gas, this witness then made his point effectively by noting that the Boise gas works did not have a "no smoking" rule. Further support for the state came when Mr. and Mrs. Guibbinni both testified that they did not serve a drink to Reilly on the morning of the Bradley explosion as Reilly had testified.

Harry Orchard took the stand again to deny that he had ever been called "Shorty," the name by which Pat Moran had said he knew the man who visited his saloon with Neville in June of 1904. Moran had denied making a trip to Denver for Orchard at this time, but a rebuttal witness, a Denver plumber named

Bynum, said he saw Moran on a streetcar in Denver in June of 1904. While Orchard was still on the stand the defense made its only rebuttal effort by inquiring about the mental condition of several of Orchard's relatives. Orchard admitted that he had a mentally unbalanced uncle, but denied knowing anything about his grandfather having an abnormal sense of criminal guilt.

The question of Lyte Gregory's enmity toward the Western Federation of Miners was clearly settled by the rebuttal testimony of E. M. Sabin, an attorney of Idaho Springs, Colorado. Sabin said he knew Lyte Gregory well and that Gregory had been engaged by the prosecution to secure evidence in the case in which 14 WFM members including D. C. Copley were tried for the blowing up of the Sun & Moon mine transformer house. Richardson drew out the fact that at the time of this explosion Sabin and 80 other members of the Citizens' Alliance in Idaho Springs were placed under an injunction to keep the peace, but Sabin denied that this was the reason the Federation had been prosecuted. A series of interesting exchanges then took place between Richardson and Sabin who had been the two opposing attorneys three years earlier in Idaho Springs. For example:

Q. But those cases were all tried by special prosecutors and the District Attorney had nothing to do with them?

A. Yes; but it was because the District Attorney was what you called him at the trial—a nonentity.

Richardson succeeded in getting Sabin to admit that the Western Federation men were acquitted, but Sabin managed to convey the impression that the men were nevertheless guilty.

On the final day of rebuttal testimony the state again damaged the defense case considerably. A Burke pharmacist testified to seeing Harry Orchard in Wardner on Bunker Hill day. The state attempted to introduce the *Idaho State Tribune* account of that day to show the organized nature of the mob, contrary to Darrow's description of it as a disorganized crowd, but Judge Wood unexpectedly ruled it inadmissible.

The ex-powderman of the Vindicator mine, Ramsey, then testified to several facts which contradicted Thomas Wood's explanation of the mine explosion as an accident. Ramsey said he had never seen Beck or McCormick carry a pistol in the mine. As the powderman he inspected the mine morning and night to see that there was no powder left out, and he had seen none prior to the explosion. Furthermore, there was no water barrel on the 8th level. Wood had said that Beck and McCormick went up to the 6th level from the 8th, but Ramsey testified that he saw the two men descend the shaft and heard them tell the cager to stop at the 6th level. Ramsey also reported that he subsequently found traces of some 40% powder where Beck and McCormick were killed, and that the mine regularly used only 35% powder. This would tend to confirm Orchard who had described bringing powder into the mine for this bomb.

On cross-examination Ramsey confirmed two other details of the Orchard confession which had puzzled the Pinkertons and the prosecution for some time. He reported finding the bomb disguised as a lump of coal in the coal bunkers of the mine. Orchard had said he manufactured this bomb and gave it to an old man named Dempsey who reported back to him that it had been thrown into the bunkers. Until Ramsey's testimony there was no corroboration of this part of Orchard's story. Similarly, Ramsey testified that several tons of powder had been stored deep in the mine for safe keeping in the early days of the strike. This powder must have been the cache that Orchard and Schultz had found on their first excursion into the mine. Richardson tried to develop the fact that Ramsey's testimony at the time of the coroner's inquest into the explosion was somewhat confusing, but Ramsey explained that he was quite upset at the time inasmuch as one of the victims, McCormick, was his stepfather.

Although Borah and Hawley agreed with Judge Wood that much of the state's evidence was immaterial at this point, the state's attorneys then called several witnesses to testify to conditions in Telluride during the strike there. This was done presumably to get something into the record in opposition to what defense witnesses had said. The most valuable testimony came from the onetime tramway boss of the Smuggler-Union mine, a man named Sackett. He described the union troubles of 1901, and introduced a remarkable document in evidence, the Agreement of July 3, 1901:

> It is hereby agreed between the Miners' Union, by V. St. John, president, and the Smuggler-Union Mining Company, by Edgar A. Collins, assistant manager, that all work on said mine shall cease for a period of three days, ending Friday, and that said Miners' Union will refrain from violence as to person and property for the same period. The said Smuggler-Union mine may employ four guards during the period.

If the character of the Western Federation of Miners had not been clearly established by the evidence up to this point, this agreement must have settled any doubts. Here was a 20th-century American labor contract in which the union promised to refrain from violence for three days! The American public, regardless of individual differences of opinion on the labor question, could agree that the Western Federation of Miners was indeed an amazing organization.

Sackett went on to tell of the killing of Arthur Collins, the disappearance of several men, and the intimidation of nonunion miners. On cross-examination he admitted that he had been a "whitecapper" and helped escort men out of town. He justified the Citizens' Alliance in Telluride as necessary in returning the town to the rule of law and order.

The final witness for the state was the old carpenter, Stewart, whose beating had been the event that initially brought the troops to Cripple Creek. He testified that he was threatened, then beaten, by Ed Minster, Charley Campbell, Steve Adams, Sherman Parker, and others, resulting in his hospitalization for several months. Psychologically, Stewart was a good prosecution witness with whom to end the parade of nearly 200 people to the witness chair. He was elderly, likable, hard-working, and courageous, the sort of person with whom the jurors could readily identify themselves. With Stewart the evidence was all in; it remained to be seen how much of it the jury would be told to ignore.

On July 18, with the jurors not present, Darrow, Borah, and Richardson argued the admissibility of certain evidence before the judge, particularly the defense evidence which tended to show the existence of a counter-conspiracy. The debate was quite informal, characterized by good feeling between the opposing attorneys. Darrow opened the argument by citing court decisions and legal authorities on the right of the defense to show that other persons might have greater motive for the crime than the defendant. Thus, argued Darrow, if *A* is charged with killing *B* and implicates *C* in the crime, *C* can not only deny the charge but can show that *D* had more reason to kill *B* than did *C*. Substitute Harry Orchard for *A*, Frank Steunenberg for *B*, Bill Haywood for *C*, and the combined forces of the Pinkertons, the Mine Owners' Associations, the Citizens' Alliances, and the Colorado militia for *D*, said Darrow, and this legal interpretation accurately applies to the Haywood case. After an effective legal argument up to this point, Darrow became somewhat careless with his assertions. For example, when he flatly stated that the defense had shown a member of the counter-conspiracy to be responsible for the Independence depot explosion, Judge Wood asked what evidence to that effect had been introduced. Darrow replied that the evidence showed that Sterling, the MOA detective, had been in close touch with Orchard just prior to the explosion and later had called off the hounds when they finally found Orchard's trail. Judge Wood allowed Darrow to proceed, but it was apparent that he felt that Darrow was drawing conclusions not justified by the evidence.

Borah agreed with Darrow's legal citations that generally the defense had a definite right to look for other persons or conspiracies with more reason to murder the deceased than the defendant had. But he said that the Haywood defense had not demonstrated the existence of such a conspiracy. He pointed out that the counter-conspiracy argument could not apply to the defense's theories of the Vindicator mine explosion, the death of Lyte Gregory, the attempts on Goddard, Bradley, and Peabody, or the death of Frank Steunenberg. It could apply only to the bombing of the Independence depot, where the defense had inferred that Sterling and the bloodhounds connected Harry Orchard to the Mine Owners' Association. Borah explained that the link between Sterling and Orchard was not clearly established, nor had the evidence properly qualified the bloodhounds. Citing court decisions, Borah argued that bloodhounds were no longer competent witnesses in this country.

Richardson replied for the defense. He admitted that the Independence depot was the only real incident of the counter-conspiracy germane to this trial. He also admitted that Harry Orchard must have blown up the depot, but the question was—for whom? Richardson then discussed the qualifications of the bloodhounds. Having a little fun with Borah, he recalled how witnesses had testified that these hounds had been trained at the penitentiary which was a unique place to qualify expert witnesses. Without citing legal precedents, he also went over the *A, B, C, D* argument relative to the counter-conspiracy.

Judge Wood then ruled on the admissibility of the disputed evidence. He first ruled out Orchard's testimony relative to a conversation with Pettibone regarding Steve Adams' trip to North Idaho and the claim jumper affair. Neither side suffered from the loss of this testimony. But when Judge Wood then ruled out testimony relative to any acts of a counter-conspiracy in Colorado, the defense was dealt a hard blow. Judge Wood was unequivocal in his ruling; he said, "In the opinion of the court, however, no evidence was introduced by the defense even pointing to or indicating that the acts of violence testified to by Orchard, if actually committed by anyone, were committed by any other person or persons than as testified to by the last named witness." He made it equally clear that no evidence had indicated that a counter-conspiracy was responsible for these acts of violence. The state, said Wood, would be permitted to argue that the acts of violence were a part of a general "Inner Circle" conspiracy, of which the death of Steunenberg was a part, in order to permit the prosecution the latitude envisioned by the law in such cases.

This excluded evidence, announced Judge Wood, would be singled out in an appropriate instruction to the jury. But the instructions would not be given to the jurors until the arguments were completed by the four lawyers. This meant that, for all practical purposes, there were few limitations on what could be said in summation. So, when James Hawley opened the argument for the state on July 19, 1907, it was still a wide-open battle of theory against theory, witness against witness, and lawyer against lawyer, rather than a narrowly restricted process of legal decision-making.

PART THREE

*In spite of the oft-repeated statement that the era of forensic oratory has passed, there is a perennial interest in speeches of lawyers summarizing and interpreting evidence for the benefit of juries, judges, investigating committees, and courts of impeachment. Both laymen and lawyers, familiar through the press with the facts in notable cases, exhibit curiosity as to the handling of those facts by the respective counsel in their opening and closing addresses. This is because the dramas of the courts are inherently interesting, continually exemplifying the adage that truth is stranger than fiction. And while the inflated, flamboyant, grandiloquent style of forensic oratory has indeed gone, the very purpose of opening and closing addresses causes them to retain the essence of true oratory, which is to make the auditor think and feel as the speaker thinks and feels. To the lawyer, skill in summing up cases is as necessary today as it ever was. It may even be contended that the complexity of modern cases calls for a higher order of skill than was formerly necessary. Whatever the case may be, it must always be analyzed and simplified, so that it may be clearly understood by the average man. Eloquence, moreover, if genuine and natural, is still useful.**

---

* Preface to Frederick C. Hicks, editor, *Famous American Jury Speeches* (St. Paul: West Publishing Co., 1925).

12

JAMES H. HAWLEY for the PROSECUTION

ALTHOUGH THE HAYWOOD trial marked the first time that James Hawley had spoken to a national audience, Idaho courtroom audiences had known and respected his speaking for more than thirty-five years. Hawley had a wide acquaintance throughout Idaho, extending from preterritorial days down through the twenty-seven-year history of the territory and the seventeen-year history of the state. Not only was he dean of the sagebrush lawyers, but he was also one of the most colorful characters of the West.

To understand James Henry Hawley one must know something of his adventurous youth. He was born in Dubuque, Iowa, January 17, 1847, to Thomas and Annie Carr Hawley. His mother died when he was quite young. His father, who was somewhat of a rolling stone, went off to California as a '49er and later spent some time in Texas. When the Civil War began in 1861 James Hawley was restless to leave home but he was only fourteen, too young for soldiering. The call of adventure was irresistible, however; he left Dubuque at this age with relatives who were going to California via the Isthmus of Panama. For a brief time he stopped in California, but in 1862 he worked his way north with a hostler bound for what was soon to be Idaho territory. As a lad of fifteen he arrived in Placerville in the Boise Basin, six weeks after the town's founding on the heels of a great placer gold strike. He immediately became a prospector and miner. By 1865 he was successful enough to sell his holdings for a good profit and go to San Francisco, determined to get a college education.[1]

After two years at San Francisco City College pursuing an applied science course, James Hawley graduated in 1867. As his part of the graduation exercises he demonstrated his individualism by giving an original oration while most of the other graduates declaimed various literary selections.[2] His wanderlust still unsatiated, Hawley then went to sea for 18 months, visiting the Orient, where he got into some difficulty in the Taiping Revolutionary Army in China. After an English consul had rescued him from being beheaded, Hawley sailed for home, working his way back to San Francisco as second mate of a clipper ship. By 1869 he was back in Idaho once again and thinking seriously of his future in the mining camps.

In 1870 James Hawley was elected to the lower house of the sixth territorial legislature. After two terms in the House of Representatives he was elected in 1874 to the Council, the upper house, in the eighth legislature. Service in these pioneer legislatures must have been frustrating, however, since the lawmakers had the thankless job of raising money and writing laws for the territory, the administration of which was in the hands of "carpetbagger" governors appointed in Washington. But, as Hawley himself observed later, "Thank God, this condition was happily ended when Idaho took her place in the galaxy of states."[3]

In 1871 while living in Quartzburg, Hawley had acquired his first lawbook, a work entitled, *Every Man His Own Lawyer* by Wells. He began reading law and shortly thereafter, early in 1871, was admitted to the territorial bar. Hawley practiced law

---

[1] Conversation with Hawley's son James, Boise, Idaho, July 26, 1960.

[2] Graduation program in Hawley papers, Idaho Historical Society.

[3] James H. Hawley, "Idaho's Territorial Governors—A Reminiscence," in Hiram T. French, *History of Idaho* (Chicago: Lewis Publishing Co., 1914), p. 88 of Vol. I.

from 1871 until 1878 when he became district attorney for the second judicial district, including most of the territory between the Salmon and Snake rivers and most of Idaho's population. In 1884 he was named by President Cleveland to be U. S. Attorney for the territory, a position he held until 1887. During these years he built a reputation as a fearless prosecutor, noted for his fairness and courtesy to all, including those whom he prosecuted. While serving as U. S. Attorney he was called upon to prosecute the Mormons for polygamy, but he remained personally liberal towards the Mormons as contrasted with the intolerance of the DuBois wing of the Democratic party in Idaho. During this same time Hawley used his influence to settle amicably a labor disturbance at Broadford on the Wood River, the only labor-management friction in Idaho prior to the Coeur d'Alene troubles.

James Hawley was a conservative in the sense that he believed in a minimum of restriction on individual freedom of choice. For several years prior to the trial he had actively opposed the Sunday closing laws in Boise. Even though he had had his 10,000 gallons—the mythical quota of alcohol the sagebrush lawyers consumed before giving it up—Hawley believed in the right of others to consume it unhindered by restrictive legislation. He was a man of free-thinking tolerance. His attitude toward the Mormons has already been cited; his personal life contains other examples. Although he married a Catholic, Mary Bullock, and his children were raised in the Catholic faith, Hawley chose to remain outside the church. He was intolerant only of wrongdoing, and in this regard he did not object to the worldly pleasures prudishly condemned by many religions, but rather those breaches of morality which were inimical to society and to the law.

As a criminal lawyer James Hawley was an Idaho legend. It has been said that during his career he was involved in more murder cases as prosecutor or defense attorney than any other American lawyer in history. MacLane puts the number at something over 300.[4] James Hawley, Jr., son of the great sagebrush lawyer, once pressed his father for confirmation of this story.

[4] John F. MacLane, *A Sagebrush Lawyer* (New York: Pandick Press, 1953), p. 87.

"Son," said the elder Hawley, petulantly, "I once dismissed 113 murder indictments at one time."[5]

Koelsch calls Hawley "perhaps the most experienced criminal lawyer west of the Mississippi."[6] His work in the defense of the 1892 dynamiters and of Diamondfield Jack has already been cited in this study. But, lest one get the impression that Hawley was primarily a criminal lawyer, it should be noted that some of his most important cases were civil actions involving as Darrow once said ". . . most of the important litigation of Idaho."[7] Hawley and other sagebrush lawyers were particularly involved in numerous civil cases in which the doctrines of riparian rights were established, aspects of law which had been neglected in the old California code that had been the basis of territorial jurisprudence.

Hawley's breed of men were civilizing influences on the frontier; they brought about change and they generally accepted change. Jim Hawley had carried a revolver during his early career and a Bowie knife later in life. But as the lawless frontier became organized and law abiding, Hawley gave up his miner's garb for the same conservative business clothing that an eastern attorney might wear, save for the broad-brimmed hat he continued to wear. Physically, Hawley was a striking man—six feet, four inches tall, weighing well over two hundred pounds. He wore what was variously described as a walrus, handlebar, or cavalryman's mustache. He cut a handsome figure at the Haywood trial, even though he was then in his sixty-first year.

His age, the heat, and the strain of the trial had combined to make Hawley ill for several days prior to his summation speech. As he confided to a friend:

> The Haywood case has been a very wearing one, and I have been doing three men's work constantly, and as old age is beginning to tell somewhat on me and as my stomach will not permit stimulents [*sic*] in the same old way I feel a little ragged.[8]

---

[5] Conversation with James Hawley, Jr., Boise, Idaho, July 26, 1960.

[6] Charles F. Koelsch, *The Haywood Case* (Boise: Idaho Mining Association, 1946), p. 24.

[7] Clarence Darrow, *The Story of My Life* (New York: Charles Scribner's Sons, 1934), p. 144.

[8] Letter, James H. Hawley to Frank H. Parker, July 22, 1907.

In spite of his condition Hawley began the opening argument for the prosecution on Friday, July 19, 1907, at about 2:30 in the afternoon. He talked for about two hours during this session of court, plus three hours on Saturday morning, and another three hours on Saturday afternoon. It was warm in Boise during this time, the temperature reaching 85° on Saturday. Hawley's reaction to the two-day speech was revealed in a letter to a friend:

> The strain of the trial, especially the rebutting evidence and its preparation made me quite unwell, and did not feel in good shape when called Friday to commence the argument; I stood [up] under it alright however, and finished on Saturday, after occupying only eight hours, and I think I made a good impression upon the jury.[9]

If a speech of "only eight hours" was the product of a sick James Hawley, it is interesting to speculate what a well one might have done!

Contemporary press comments spoke favorably of Hawley's argument. After the Friday afternoon portion of the speech the *Statesman* observed:

> Mr. Hawley, who has been ill for several days as a result of the strain of the long trial, commenced his address in a voice almost inaudible to anyone except the jury. . . .
> But it was not long before all traces of weakness in Mr. Hawley's voice had disappeared. Never before a jury did Mr. Hawley's presence appear more impressive than yesterday afternoon after he had fairly started. Never was his voice more aggressive, his manner and argument more convincing. His sentences were powerful and well delivered, sent to the jurors with a ring that was convincing.[10]

Hawley's argument was for the most part a point-by-point review of the violence of Harry Orchard for the Western Federation of Miners as established by the evidence of the trial. It was prefaced with a discussion of the truthfulness of Orchard and the characteristics of a criminal conspiracy. It concluded with an attack upon the leaders of the Western Federation of Miners as the perpetrators and conspirators behind the criminal acts of Harry Orchard.

---

[9] Letter, James H. Hawley to Jacob Fillius, July 22, 1907.
[10] *Idaho Statesman,* July 20, 1907, p. 1 .

At least three prominent writers, in remarkably similar language, have accused Hawley of using gross invective in this speech. Irving Stone said it first in these words: "Hawley's summation was nearly solid invective against the federation . . ."[11] Then Vernon Jensen spoke of "almost solid invective against the W. F. M." which would "tend to bear out the assertion that the W. F. M., not Haywood, was on trial."[12] Finally, Stewart Holbrook described it as "a speech filled with invective against the Western Federation which some present thought did little more than bear out Darrow's assertion that it was the federation and nothing else that was on trial."[13] These criticisms must have been made from a superficial examination of the speech or from opinions expressed in the labor press of the day (or perhaps from each writer's over-dependence on the others' books). For, in reality, Hawley was not "grossly intemperate" but remarkably moderate under the circumstances.

In the long address there are only a few points at which Hawley used language which could possibly be construed as "invective." Early in the speech, in discussing the credibility of Orchard, he pointed out that the contradictions of Orchard were either by interested parties or by perjurers. Perhaps this statement was unjustified, but it was true that most of the defense witnesses were interested parties and that the state of Idaho was then engaged in trying several of these people for perjury. Toward the end of the speech Hawley referred to the Western Federation as a "stench in the nostrils of the decent people of the West" and to the criminal element in the union as "scum" that floats to the surface. These isolated examples represent the extent of the harsh language used by Hawley.

With respect to the charge that the Western Federation of Miners was on trial rather than Bill Haywood, Hawley's position was somewhat ambiguous. In his peroration he said:

---

[11] Irving Stone, *Clarence Darrow for the Defense* (Garden City, N. Y.: Doubleday & Company, 1941), p. 235.

[12] Vernon H. Jensen, *Heritage of Conflict* (Ithaca, New York: Cornell University Press, 1950), p. 215.

[13] Stewart Holbrook, *The Rocky Mountain Revolution* (New York: Henry Holt & Co., 1956), p. 254.

> It will be charged that we are making war upon the Western Federation of Miners, that we are making war upon unions and upon union organizations, but it is not true. No man has a greater respect than I for organizations and those engaged in the different branches of labor to assist themselves both so far as wages and hours of work are concerned.

He went on to point out that the Western Federation of Miners, as then constituted, could not be classed with conventional labor unions, because such unions were not criminal organizations.

> I don't mean to say, gentlemen, that the majority of the members of the Western Federation of Miners are criminal, but I do mean and say that this organization has fallen into the hands of men who are criminals . . . and that an organization such as this should be warred upon by every good citizen until it is absolutely and positively obliterated as a factor either in economic or political matters . . .

Thus, Hawley issued a call to arms against the kind of unionism that the Western Federation of Miners represented. Thus, Stone, Jensen, and Holbrook are correct in concluding that Hawley's summation was an attack upon the WFM, but their descriptions of the argument as "solid invective" and as "grossly intemperate" are not accurate.

It is not difficult to understand why Hawley felt as he did on this matter. His explanation of the prosecution strategy in the Paul Corcoran case (see p. 39) made it clear that the state in 1899 was trying to reach the union, which was not a legal entity, through the union official, who was. The Haywood case was a similar attempt. Only the most naive observer could view the Haywood trial as purely a murder case. But Hawley was careful to bring the union leader to the fore at regular intervals throughout the summation speech in order that the state's legal case against Haywood not be overlooked by the jury in their condemnation of the Western Federation.

Hawley opened his argument with the traditional compliment to the jury for their long and valuable service to the state during the trial, and the customary reminder of the importance of the trial: "We have been engaged here in making history, I might say; this case will be looked upon as one of the most important in the criminal annals of the country." In indicating what he planned to cover in his argument, Hawley said:

> . . . I will simply attempt to call your attention to the various points that strike me as being worthy of your consideration as shown by the evidence of the different witnesses. I have none of those elements or qualifications that constitute the orator, and therefore I will be compelled in a plain, blunt way to give you my ideas in regard to these matters, and let you form your own conclusion in regard to the matter after listening not only to what I have to say in regard to them but the remarks of counsel upon the other side as well.

"A plain, blunt way" describes accurately the style of James Hawley's forensic speaking. There is very little figurative language, imagery, or polished utterance; the ideas are expressed in simple, sometimes even ungrammatical, word combinations. For example, in taking up the history of the Cripple Creek labor strife, Hawley began:

> They were paying the highest wages, but some trouble arose in regard to a smelter away down below there, and they called what they call a sympathetic strike. They throwed thousands of men out of employment; they impeded the business relations of a vast section of the country simply to show their power, simply to force people in another section of the country engaged in another branch of business to do their bidding.

Perhaps the most characteristic feature of Hawley's style was the long rambling sentence which frequently contained parenthetical expressions or digressions. There were sentences in Hawley's summation of 133, 148, 191, and even one of 224 words. An objective word-count of comparable portions of each of the four summation speeches indicates that Hawley's sentences averaged 41 words, considerably more than those of Borah and Darrow but about on a par with those of Richardson. This passage from Hawley's review of the Vindicator mine incident is fairly typical of the length and construction of his sentences:

> And his truthfulness in this respect is shown by the cager—you remember the young man who was brought here and stated that after a shift was going up on the cage he was walking through the mine in that level and saw two men and followed them back a ways and got close to one of them and two shots were fired at him and he retreated and saw them no more. That corroborates Orchard to the fullest extent. Now, Orchard knew this mine for he had been highgrading there. That seems to be a small matter perhaps—it seems to be countenanced, though, by the men who have control of this association—but on account of his highgrading there he had a knowledge of this mine and was therefore called in to assist in this enter-

> prise because he had been through it and knew where the rich streaks were and he was acquainted with the mine.

Other stylistic and rhetorical features of Hawley's speaking are readily seen through an examination of the various major points developed in the speech. In the introduction Hawley affirmed the fact that he represented only the state of Idaho in this prosecution and no one else, denying the implication of the defense that there were other forces responsible for the prosecution of Haywood. He indicated that his presentation would necessarily be lengthy because of the amount of evidence to be revealed.

The truthfulness of Harry Orchard was Hawley's next theme. He did not dwell at great length on the Orchard conversion, but he did say that it was the "saving power of Divine Grace" that prompted Orchard to confess. In order to avoid an overemphasis on this feature of the Orchard story, Hawley pointed out that the state had not introduced any testimony relative to Orchard's conversion, but that the defense cross-examination had been responsible for all references to it in the record.

Moving into a discussion of conspiracy and the Idaho law on accomplices, Hawley then identified all of the violence from and including the Bunker Hill explosion to the death of Governor Steunenberg as incidents of the general conspiracy which the state was attempting to prove. Discussing the Bunker Hill explosion, Hawley noted that no word of criticism had ever appeared in the *Miner's Magazine* relative to the acts of the union men on that occasion. This remark precipitated the first of two objections by Clarence Darrow during the speech, but no name-calling developed at this point.

Next came a review of the long chain of events in Cripple Creek, beginning with the Vindicator mine explosion. The testimony of Ramsey was reviewed favorably, and that of Wood was generally belittled. In a series of short, parallel sentences—unusual for Hawley—he said:

> Mind you, gentlemen, what Tom Wood says in regard to the effect of that explosion upon that cage. Mind you, he intends to impress upon you that the bottom of the cage was blowed in. Mind you, that he intends to impress upon you the damage was done to the guys

> and all that, trying to deceive you upon those matters because it was necessary to make it appear that a very considerable damage had been done on that occasion, and all these matters.

Hawley argued that the explosion could not have been an accident, as the defense had inferred, because the body of Beck, the man allegedly carrying the pistol that might have accidentally set off the dynamite, was intact, whereas McCormick's legs had been blown off. Using a rather unusual expression Hawley concluded:

> Now what follows from all that? That this finely constructed theory in regard to the pistol being the pistol that was on Beck's body is the veriest humbug. It could not have been Beck's.

The Vindicator mine was the last topic of the Friday portion of the speech. On Saturday the first topic concerned the train-wrecking incident. Inconclusive as it might have been, Hawley had to offer a reasonable explanation of it. He admitted Orchard's double role at this stage of his career but denied the frequent Orchard-Sterling meetings testified to by the roominghouse keepers. Pointing out that these women did not know Orchard at the time, Hawley talked in a down-to-earth way about the fallibility of human memory:

> Why, gentlemen, just think of some person that you saw that was a stranger to you three or four months ago that you was casually brought into contact with, that you had no reason to recollect, and see if you could swear positively with any degree of certainty as to the identity of that person unless there was some controlling cause, some incident that would fasten the recollection absolutely in your mind. You cannot do it, and when a person comes upon the stand and swears that four years afterward in regard to a matter which would not imprint itself upon the memory they were positive as to the identity of an individual with whom they were not acquainted, I say, gentlemen, the very narration of the testimony itself shows an absolute falsehood or an attempt to deceive the jury upon the part of the person who related it.

Next he discussed the attempted assassination of Governor Peabody of Colorado. All of Hawley's rhetorical elements were blended carefully at this point. His ideas were striking, yet reasonable: the Western Federation of Miners wanted Peabody removed "to learn a lesson to their enemies . . ." Orchard and Adams were selected to accomplish the governor's death because they were the kind of men who could handle such a mission. Hawley's style became more pungent; in arguing that the Western Federation was behind the attempt, he again utilized effectively the series of shorter sentences building to a climax, in this case, rhetorical questions. Even his delivery became more intense. This must have been one of the moments to which the *Statesman* referred when it said, "Throughout the day Mr. Hawley used an almost conversational tone, only at intervals becoming enthused and warmed by the topic under consideration and then letting his voice soar until it could be heard in other parts of the building."[14] Said Hawley:

> I ask in all seriousness, gentlemen of the jury, what there is in this evidence and the facts and circumstances developed in that line, I ask you whether there is anything to warrant an idea upon your part or any person's part that Steve Adams or that Harry Orchard had any ill will of any kind whatsoever towards Governor Peabody? I ask you, gentlemen, where in this record there is anything to indicate to you that Harry Orchard would have any motive in murdering the governor or that Steve Adams would have any desire to take the chances of being punished for a great crime simply for the satisfaction of sending Peabody into the next world? I ask you, gentlemen, as reasoning men, as men that know that no crime is committed without a motive or an object on the part of the perpetrator, what earthly object would either Orchard or Adams have had in this attempt upon Peabody's life. Who did have a motive? Who had an object? To whom was this man an object of enmity? Who was it that would profit by Peabody's death? Who were the enemies of the governor of the state of Colorado? Who was it, I ask, that would be benefitted by his removal, and the substitution of another in the high office that he held? The Western Federation of Miners.

If Orchard and Adams did not make this attempt on Peabody, continued Hawley, it would be easy for the defense to so prove, merely by calling Steve Adams as a witness. At this point Darrow objected, and the two men had a long and heated verbal exchange with the word "falsehood" flying about freely. Both sides were touchy on the question of Steve Adams, who reposed at the moment in the Ada County jail in the basement beneath the courtroom. The state wanted to be able to question him so that his confession would get into the record, at least in the form of a series of questions, even though the answers might all be denials. The defense, on the other hand, was not anxious to use Adams, even though seemingly he could flatly deny some of the most important

---

[14] *Idaho Statesman,* July 21, 1907, p. 1.

parts of the Orchard confession, because they were not sure they could trust him to stick by the Federation. Oddly enough, during this exchange between Darrow and Hawley the court did not intervene, apparently letting the two men get it out of their systems so that the speech could resume.

Hawley then moved into a discussion of the Independence depot explosion. Taking note of the fact that Aller's testimony concerning the Orchard-Scott-Sterling meeting had been discredited, Hawley talked about the matter that must have bothered the defense attorneys considerably—the refutation of many of the defense witnesses by the state's rebuttal witnesses. Speaking of these defense witnesses, Hawley used a bit of sarcasm when he said, "One by one, gentlemen, the roses fall." Also, at this point, he utilized the one source of humor from which each of the lawyers were to draw, the hound dogs, for a brief moment of levity.

Following the Independence depot in the chronology of events and thus in Hawley's organizational pattern as well, the next incident on which conflicting testimony had gone into the record was the Cheyenne-to-Denver trip of Pat Moran for Harry Orchard. In discussing the refutation testimony that strengthened the state's case on this point, Hawley manifested the hesitancy over names which would be natural in a case where scores of persons had testified.

> But we have another witness brought upon the scene. Moser,—or Bynum,—Bynum, gentlemen, who has known Pat Moran for a number of years.

He went on to discuss how Bynum's testimony clearly established that Pat Moran was in Denver on or about the day on which Orchard had said the trip was made. But the names continued to bother Hawley as he concluded this discussion:

> I believe, gentlemen of the jury, that all these circumstances show conclusively, or the testimony of Moser—I called him Bynum a moment ago—

At this point W. A. Stone of the prosecution staff came to his rescue and called out, "It was Bynum."

> Yes, that is right—that the testimony of Bynum shows conclusively that he falsified when he made those statements . . .

The pronoun "he" in this sentence was supposed to represent Moran, but it must have sounded to the audience as though it were Bynum who lied. On several other occasions, because of Hawley's rambling sentence structure, there were ambiguous antecedents in the speech, but perhaps none as awkward as this one.

As the concluding topic of the Saturday morning portion of the speech, Hawley turned to the Bradley affair in San Francisco. He noted with some satisfaction that the defense had no explanation of the poisoning attempt, which indicated that Darrow and Richardson did not know about it prior to the trial. But Hawley had no satisfactory explanation to offer for the discrepancy in Orchard's story with respect to the flat roof, so he glossed over it with a reference to part of Guibbinni's testimony that suggested that the roof was accessible at one time or another. Hawley reviewed the gas vs. bomb controversy, and argued fairly effectively as an ex-miner that the physical effects of the explosion as described by the witnesses suggested a dynamite explosion. This argument concluded the Saturday morning session of court.

Starting the afternoon session, Hawley apologized for the amount of time he was taking. He pointed out that it was more of a hardship for him to talk, since he did not feel well, than it was for the jury to sit and listen. He explained that it was his responsibility to cover *everything* in the case from the prosecution's point of view, so that the defense would have an adequate opportunity to deny and refute whatever they chose to cover in their summations.

Hawley then considered the testimony of Dr. McGee who was then being tried for perjury—a fact the jury was not permitted to know. Hawley pointed out that McGee could easily have been mistaken in his dates when he claimed to have seen Orchard in Wallace in 1904, but that the doctor insisted on fixing the date as July 1904, by referring to a local convention of the Republican party which took place at the same time. Rebuttal witnesses for the state had fixed the date of that convention as September, rather than July, and San Francisco witnesses had testified that Orchard was in that city in September. Thus, concluded Hawley, McGee was not mistaken in his recollection, but was deliberately lying.

Still covering the events in chronological sequence, Hawley turned to the killing of Lyte Gregory. When he made the statement that Haywood and Pettibone had put Orchard on the trail of Gregory, Richardson interrupted to point out that Haywood had not been implicated by the testimony. Hawley was willing to agree:

> It cuts no figure, because the acts of one of these are the acts of all, as the court will inform you. But I may be mistaken as to his having advised with Haywood in regard to this matter although my recollection is the other way. But counsel for the other side thinks it is the way he states and very likely he is correct, but we will have that investigated in so far as that matter is concerned. It will be brought to your attention by associate counsel in summing up the case. But we will take it for granted that I am in error in that, and if I misquote anything it is not intentional and I will thank counsel upon the other side to call my attention to it in the courteous and gentlemanly manner that I was interrupted at this time, to call my attention to any oversight or any mistake.

Hawley then dealt briefly with the other incidents of Orchard's stay in Denver in the first part of 1905 including his relationship with Max Malich, his attempts on Gabbert and Goddard, his further attempts on Peabody in the guise of an insurance salesman, and the purchase of the team for the attempt on Sherman Bell. Hawley then began to consider Orchard's trip to Caldwell; he was particularly interested in the "Peabody bomb" that Orchard had carried to Caldwell in the hope of using it on Governor Steunenberg. With one of his longer sentences he described what happened to the bomb:

> He gives it to this man Cunningham who has figured somewhat in the evidence, gives it to him and he has no personal knowledge of what become of it. But we find, gentlemen, digressing from this for a while and following up the evidence of this bomb, we find that a few days after it was noised throughout the state that Orchard had made a confession that the man who had the custody of this bomb in that section up there at Wallace became fearful that investigations would be made in reference to its whereabouts, and that bomb was in a day or two afterwards found in the ice in the Coeur d'Alene River, undoubtedly thrown in there upon the ice and been covered by a fresh influx of water that caused it to be frozen in, and it was found there and was taken to the sheriff's office and was brought here and has been placed in evidence, and Roach the plumber, you recollect, swears it is the identical bomb he made and it is identified throughout and it is a strong corroborating

proof so far as the testimony of Orchard is concerned, in regard to his movements and in regard to the objects that he was seeking to accomplish with the assistance of that formidable implement.

One observer noted that during Hawley's description of the final and successful attempt on Steunenberg's life, "Lips in other parts of the room trembled. Many eye lashes were wet with tears."[15] This reaction must have taken place during the most emotion-laden part of Hawley's narration of the events in Caldwell:

> But that does not work, and it goes on until the 30th day of December, until the holiday season has arrived, until that era of peace and good will which prompts even the most savage man to respect the peace and quiet of his neighbor and feel at peace with them and with all the world, and there, gentlemen, at that time, right before the new year commenced he sees the opportunity to plant the bomb in front of the gate and blows the governor into eternity. There, gentlemen, was an act that probably shocked the people of this state, probably shocked the people of the United States, all the people of the civilized world in a greater degree than anything that had ever happened. Here was a man, the foremost citizen of the state of Idaho, thought well of by every right minded citizen not only of this state but in the entire West, a man who had retired practically from active political life and was attending to his own business in the interest of his family there brutally murdered on account of some matters that had happened seven years before, killed at his own gateway, murdered in the presence of his own family.

The circumstances surrounding Orchard's arrest and confinement in Caldwell were then reviewed briefly, particularly the letter from Pettibone, the attorneys converging on Caldwell (on this point Richardson found it necessary to correct Hawley again to the effect that the Denver attorney, Sullivan, was not a Western Federation attorney), and the $1,500 retainer paid to Fred Miller by the union. If Orchard had killed an ordinary citizen, said Hawley, and not an enemy of the Federation, the union would not have spent fifteen cents in his defense. Jack Simpkins' absence from the trial was in itself an incriminating circumstance, continued the prosecutor, and the union membership by re-electing him to his position on the Executive Committee while a fugitive from justice was acting in a manner which seemed to support the state's contention that a criminal conspiracy existed.

---

[15] *Ibid.*

Orchard had no personal motive to kill Steunenberg, reiterated Hawley. The sale of the 1/16th interest in the Hercules mine to Cardoner was final and absolute. Those people who testified to having heard Orchard threaten Steunenberg could not be accepted at full value. Three of them, Redd, Sullivan, and Mrs. Day, were complete strangers to Orchard when they heard the alleged threats. Why, asked Hawley, would Orchard make threats to these people and never express the same feelings to his friends, Haywood and Pettibone? Hawley ignored the fact that he had just discounted Mrs. Day as a witness when he went on to point out how valuable her testimony was in establishing that Haywood visited Orchard at his room. Next he noted that Elliott had been thoroughly discredited, and Davis, Easterly, and Copley were too deeply implicated themselves in the violence of the Western Federation to be trusted as witnesses. Coates was not honorable enough to tell Paulson that Harry Orchard planned to kidnap his children, said Hawley, and thus could not be relied on. For Eugene Engley, Hawley reserved special comment, one of the rare examples of sarcasm in the speech:

> And the next man is General Eugene Engley, and you notice the unction with which the title came from the lips of my friends upon the other side. General Engley is an ex-Attorney General of Colorado. He was one of that misfit outfit that floated in to power at the time that "Blood to the Bridle" Waite was governor of that state. He wanted to go in to the difference between philosophic anarchy and scientific socialism and would have been talking now if he had not been shut off by counsel.

The review of the evidence completed, Hawley began to talk very directly with the jurors about the responsibility they faced in making their decision. With respect to the doctrine of reasonable doubt he told them ". . . you are not privileged . . . to hunt up a doubt . . ." He asked on several occasions simply for the "honest judgment" of the jury on the question of guilt, and he assured them that he would be satisfied with that judgment.

It was, at last, the psychological moment for injecting the personal element into the speech. With obvious sincerity and restraint, Hawley talked about his own role in the formation of the union.

> I have had, gentlemen, some experience with unions. I have been

> brought necessarily into contact with them on many occasions, and while it is not a matter of argument, or of reference that should be made, I would be pardoned I think for saying that at all times I have been a friend of these people and these organizations when they have been carried on in a manner such as the law permits, and I hope to be to the end of my days. True it is that at the inception of this organization, and before it was as important as it is at present, I was consulted by members of the different unions, including Mr. Boyce, when I appeared for them in certain matters affecting the interests of some of those members, before the federal courts. But for that, gentlemen, I have no explanations to offer nor apologies to make, because I acted right, and if my advice had been followed by those organizations at that time, or the organization which was formed shortly afterwards had been carried on in the way it was intended by the men that formed them they would have been a factor for good in the development of the west, instead of being an engine of oppression.

After a final review of the evidence, characterized by effective use once again of the short series of sentences, Hawley concluded his argument with an ethical appeal taking advantage of his stature at the Idaho bar.

> Gentlemen, I wish that I could look over this evidence and find some way of satisfying myself that this man here upon trial was innocent and that these other men associated with him in this indictment were also innocent of this offense. I have no desire, gentlemen, to have the scalp of any innocent man hanging at my girdle. I don't, gentlemen of the jury, desire that any man shall be convicted through my efforts, or through any effort of mine in whole or in part, that is innocent of any offense. But I have arrived at a time of life, gentlemen, that I believe would, I think, preclude one from desiring through overenthusiasm in a case that he is advocating to have a man punished for a serious offense who is guiltless of it. A young man may become inspired by his case, may reason that the only evidence worthy of belief is that which goes in upon his side, and may be so actuated by a desire to win that he may overlook those matters which should have been considered by him and which would show the innocence of the party accused. But I think after we have been in this business for nearly two score of years as I have been, we get beyond that stage and I hope that I have got beyond that stage, because I tell you frankly, gentlemen of the jury, if I did not believe in my heart that this man was guilty I would so state. I wish I could find some way by which I could conclude from this evidence that I was satisfied of his innocence, because I would a thousand times rather have a man vindicated than to have him dragged through the mire and dirt of a conviction. But we can come to but one conclusion, and that is that he is not only respon-

> sible for this atrocious murder but that for more than a score of other murders that have been proven here he is equally responsible. . . .
>
> I ask you to take this evidence and carefully consider it. I ask you to give it that weight and consideration that under the instructions of the court it will be entitled to. I ask you that you honestly, in your own good judgment, apply the law to the evidence and thus find your verdict. And I for one, gentlemen, will say in advance that with the utmost confidence in this jury and every member of it, I will be satisfied whatever that verdict may be. Gentlemen, I thank you for your attention, and so far as I am concerned as an active participant in this case, it is with you.

If the ultimate measure of a man's rhetoric is its effect upon the audience, the critic—contemporary or latter day—must try to determine what that effect was. In terms of contemporary evaluation, perhaps the most interesting appraisal of Hawley's effect on the jurors was written by John Carberry of the *Boston Globe:*

> Hawley obviously exerted an influence over the 12 men by his homely style, his grievous faults of grammatical expression and the absence of all pretense at polished utterances. They liked to see him sitting on the table only a few feet from the front row of jurors; they smiled at his mining camp humor; they drank in his common place analysis of the evidence and they acknowledged by those subtle indications their belief in his honesty and sincerity when he fervently declared his only motive to be a firm conviction that Haywood was responsible for the death of the ex-governor of the state.[16]

A similar observation was made by the *Evening Capital News* of Boise which said, "His argument was clear, logical and doubtless will have a great weight with the jury. At only a few points did he attempt any degree of oratory . . ."[17] The *Statesman* agreed that it was effective because it was simple, earnest, and sincere. This was particularly true of the conclusion of the speech where,

> The jurors, it was particularly noticeable, seemed to hang upon every word he said. They leaned forward in their seats, oblivious to the fact that beads of perspiration were rolling down their faces. They forgot to use their fans. And so with the entire audience. Save but for the voice of the speaker and the gentle whir of the electric fan complete silence reigned. And Mr. Hawley's close was one that will long be remembered. He seemed suddenly to have

[16] *Boston Globe,* July 24, 1907, quoted in MacLane, *op. cit.,* p. 165.
[17] *Capital News,* July 20, 1907, p. 1.

> thrown off some weight. He cut loose. He was not trying to orate, he seemed to have thoughts surging to his lips which he could not talk fast enough to give utterance to.[18]

Oscar King Davis of the *New York Times* confirmed the close attention given by the jurors to Hawley in spite of the stifling heat and the swarms of flies in the courtroom. In evaluating the speech he used such terms as "clear statement . . . clever presentation . . . strong, able speech . . . forcible. . . skillful plea."[19] An *Idaho Statesman* news story called the speech ". . . one of the most masterful and forceful opening addresses that has perhaps ever been made to a jury in a murder case in the history of this country. It was an address that will go down in the history of court proceedings as one of the greatest efforts of its kind."[20] It is interesting to note, however, that the personal scrapbook of Calvin Cobb, the staunch Republican publisher of the *Statesman,* contains clippings on the three other summation speeches but none on Hawley's.[21] Neither was there any *Statesman* editorial comment on Hawley's speech as there was on the three other summations. This might suggest that Calvin Cobb could not get as enthusiastic about the Democratic lawyer-politician as could H. L. Crane, the reporter who wrote the news story.

In any event, the forensic battle was now underway as a result of James H. Hawley's thorough, eight-hour argument. The gauntlet of accusation had been thrown down, and it was now time for E. F. Richardson to accept the challenge by picking it up and hurling it back at the prosecution.

---

[18] *Idaho Statesman,* July 21, 1907, p. 9 .
[19] *New York Times,* July 20, 1907, p. 3, and July 21, 1907, p. 12.
[20] *Idaho Statesman,* July 21, 1907, p. 1.
[21] Calvin Cobb papers in Idaho Historical Society.

13

EDMUND F. RICHARDSON for the DEFENSE

OF THE FOUR PRINCIPAL ATTORNEYS of the Haywood trial Edmund F. Richardson was in 1907 the least known. Today his name evokes little response from the historian, a result of the fact that death ended his promising career only four years after the trial whereas the three other attorneys lived on to enjoy greater fame for a number of years. But as a participant in this great trial Richardson was every bit the equal of Hawley, Darrow, and Borah. As such, he deserves better treatment than he has had at the hands of most historians of the trial, including even eyewitnesses such as Bill Haywood and Kendrick Johnson, who have ignored him in describing the trial.

Edmund F. Richardson was born on a farm near Sandisfield in the Berkshire hills of Massachusetts on July 29, 1862. His parents moved to Springfield, Massachusetts, where he spent his boyhood and attended school. At the age of sixteen he taught the Lenox grammar school. The following year he was employed by a store in Springfield where he remained until he was twenty-one. During this time he read law in the evenings.

In 1884 he went to San Francisco to become a law clerk for a firm of attorneys. He continued his reading of the law, and in

1885 he was admitted to the California bar. The next year he moved to Colorado, locating first at Del Norte in the San Luis Valley. He remained there for nine years, during which time he had a successful and highly profitable practice and served as county attorney. During this time he carried out what was later described as "his most telling achievement" in long and complex litigation involving the repudiation of bonded indebtedness by a number of Colorado counties, a case which was eventually decided in the United States Supreme Court.[1]

In 1895 Richardson moved to Pueblo for a brief time, and later that same year went to Denver upon the invitation of Thomas M. Patterson, who shortly thereafter was elected to the U. S. Senate. The firm of Patterson, Richardson, & Hawkins was formed on September 1, 1895, later to become Richardson & Hawkins when the senator retired in 1906. It was one of the most prominent Denver law firms in the early years of the 20th century, particularly active in what has been euphemistically described as "anti-corporation" litigation. Richardson's most notable cases of this type were the previously noted Moyer habeas corpus appeal and the Sun and Moon dynamiting in Idaho Springs. The volume of his work is attested to by the statement in an early biographical sketch that, "For many years probably no lawyer in the state of Colorado has actively participated in the trial of as many and as important cases as has the subject of this sketch [Richardson]."[2]

Unquestionably, Richardson would have gone on to greater fame as a lawyer following the Haywood trial, had not his life been cut short in an automobile accident in Colorado in 1911. His obituary contains the best available clue to the man's personality, describing him as a "likable, genial 'man's man,' bluff and hearty in personal dealings, alert, keen, aggressive, and a tireless fighter in court," a man who "scorned oratorical and sensational methods, and sought to win on merit entirely."[3] Another early biographical sketch speaks of Richardson as a "close student and a keen ob-

---

[1] *Denver News,* May 8, 1911, p. 5.

[2] *Press Biographies, Representative Men of America,* March-July, 1906, p. 166.

[3] *Denver News,* May 8, 1911, p. 5.

server of men and methods" and as "a man who would scorn to adopt any of the unscrupulous methods of obtaining money so common with some attorneys."[4]

At the time of the Haywood trial Richardson was 44, a tall and robust man of striking appearance. He was partially bald, with ample dark hair at the temples but none on top. Like Hawley, he wore a mustache, but his was of more modest dimensions than that of the prosecutor. His manner of dress was somewhat conspicuous in the sweltering Boise courtroom in that he always affected the old-fashioned wing collar whereas most westerners preferred turned-down collars by this time.

Richardson had the misfortune of drawing two of the hottest days of the ten-week trial for his summation speech. On Monday, July 22, 1907, the temperature was near 90° in Boise. It was so hot in the courtroom that Judge Wood ordered two split sessions, one of three hours in the morning and another of three hours beginning at six in the evening. Richardson's ten-hour argument occupied both of these Monday sessions, plus two similar sessions on Tuesday when the temperature hit 90°. Without doubt, this was a hostile climate for the vigorous and long-winded kind of oratory that Richardson practiced.

Richardson's argument was, for the most part, a moderately worded attack on the evidence supporting the state's case. Early in the speech Richardson was conciliatory and complimentary toward the prosecution, but in the final evening session he became testy and less temperate. Nevertheless, most of the argument was couched in accurate terms, neither exaggeration nor understatement. His language was more colorful and less legalistic than Hawley's, with similes and other figures occurring from time to time as he identified Pinkertons in general as "vultures" and one specifically as a "grinning hyena." Orchard became "a cheap and tawdry and a tinsel hero." Occasionally, Richardson used terms that must have been well over the heads of the jury, such as his reference to Hawley's "animadversion" toward the witness Wood,

---

[4] A. R. Pelton, *San Luis Valley* (Denver: Carson, Hurst and Harper, 1891), p. 163.

and his use in series of the verbs, to "extirpate," to "rout," and to "branch." These unusual usages, however, occurred sparingly throughout the speech. In general, Richardson conveyed his meaning well, although he was somewhat more oratorical than Hawley. As the *Statesman* described him, ". . . Richardson talked eloquently. This attorney from Denver displayed a wonderful ability as a painter and decorator of word-picture theories."[5]

Richardson began his long address by taking up immediately the death of Governor Steunenberg. After an opening reference to the assassination, he observed:

> It had been Governor Steunenberg's fortune while governor of this state to be called upon to stand in the forefront of a labor controversy which occurred in the northern part of the state. Perhaps the situation demanded of him all that he did. I don't know about that, and I am not going to discuss it. Perhaps in handling that situation Governor Steunenberg took such an advanced ground from anything that had ever occurred before in the United States of America that he received the condemnation of large numbers of the people of the United States. One thing is certain, that it gave rise to an endless amount of discussion throughout the entire civilized world. For the first time in the history of America the military bull pen was established in the administration of what were practically civil affairs. For the first time in the history of America men were deprived of their liberty with, perhaps, just cause but without due or any process of law.

Frankly admitting that 99% of the people saw a connection between these events and the death of Steunenberg, Richardson made a simple and direct appeal for impartiality on the part of the jurors. He then indicated what he planned to do in the speech on which he was then embarking, by proposing a rather extensive eleven-point agenda.

Richardson then began his first point, the discussion of the law regarding accomplices and the law regarding conspiracy. In calling attention to the positive wording of the Idaho statute that prevents conviction on the uncorroborated testimony of an accomplice, Richardson quoted directly what Borah had once said along this line in defending a similar case in North Idaho. Rich-

[5] *Idaho Statesman,* July 24, 1907, p. 1.

ardson was able to further identify his own ideas with Idaho ideas by complimenting the state on having such a clear statute:

> And among the states which have so adopted such a statute as I have described, Idaho is found, as she is in most things, in the foremost ranks. That statute was enacted long prior to the time that this case had its rise, long prior to the time that Governor Steunenberg was governor of this state, long prior to the events which it is now claimed are responsible for the action of Harry Orchard and which resulted in this trial against this defendant.

In discussing conspiracies, Richardson again took a reasonable position in admitting that the prosecution had shown a conspiracy to exist:

> So, the Steunenberg killing under their proof, under their argument, is an incident of this general conspiracy to do what? A general conspiracy to control politics, a general conspiracy to control the labor markets, a general conspiracy to fix the price of wages without consultation, perhaps, and certainly without dictation from the owners of those mines or those who operated in labor and who do not labor themselves, a general conspiracy to elect men who are friendly to them to office . . . Every one of those objects are lawful yet in this country, every one of those objects have the sanction of the statutes of this country, every one of your farmers, every one of your craftsmen have the same right, and every one of you take advantage of it just the same as the laborer does, only the conditions for you who are farmers are not as hard as they are for those who labor.

Richardson then turned to the question of the criminal conspiracy suggested by the prosecution. With a rhetorical question he struck out at Hawley's argument that the Bunker Hill and Sullivan dynamiting and the re-election of Jack Simpkins indicated the scope of that conspiracy.

> Is there any man upon this jury so insane as to believe that 40,000 citizens of the United States of America, or 4,000, or 400 citizens, or 40 citizens can be made to combine in one criminal aggregation for the purpose of destroying life and property?

When Richardson considered the second of his major points, the history of the Western Federation of Miners, he launched into a commonplace analysis of economics that was the antithesis of Clarence Darrow's position. It was plain and blunt enough to make sense to the jurors, and yet it was a singularly penetrating analysis of the complex economic issues of the times, especially the distribution of wealth. Said Richardson:

> I have heard, gentlemen, a great deal of talk and you have heard a great deal of talk. I have read a great many things and you have read a great many things about the equal distribution of the world's goods to everybody. But so far as I am aware it has never been done. And so long as men are situated as they are, the old rule that was adopted in the Hoosier School-master has been prevalent—"Git all you can while you're gitting, says I." That is the position which the capitalist takes upon the one hand, and naturally under our conditions, "Git all you can while you're gitting, says I."—that is the position that the laborer takes upon the other, and it is perfectly natural from his standpoint. I wish, you wish, perhaps everybody else wishes that somewhere, somehow, and in some way the rule could be different, that our statesmen might be able to devise a better plan, that the goods of this world should be more equally distributed. But they are not. We have got to deal with conditions as we find them, and the condition in the Coeur d'Alenes and elsewhere was that those who owned the property were antagonistic in a certain degree to those who were operating in the property. And so this organization was formed.

Even when Richardson moved in the direction of identifying the owners of the property with the class of eastern capitalists generally distrusted by western miners or farmers, he still retained a remarkable degree of objectivity. When he referred to the Coeur d'Alenes as a "Standard Oil district," Standard Oil being a contemporary symbol of exploitation, he was careful to point out that while some mines in the district were owned by the Rockefeller interests, the Bunker Hill and Sullivan was not, contrary to a number of allegations appearing in WFM publications and prounion papers for several years.

By now Richardson had entered into his third point, the background of the Coeur d'Alene situation.

Capitalizing on the good will he had built up, and the reasonableness of his logic to this point, the attorney went on to describe, in a series of parallel clauses, how the events of 1899 would have created understandable bitterness:

> I don't know but it would have been different if Governor Steunenberg had been there. But however that may be, I want to say to you, gentlemen of the jury, that if you had been driven out of that country, if you had been incarcerated in that bull pen, if you had remained there in the summer of 1899, if you had been covered with

> the vermin which were there at that time, if you had been subjected to insult by Negro soldiers, if you had been subjected to that which was done by those who were in command over the Negro soldiers, and you, and you, there would have been created in your breast a resentment and a hatred of all who had any part or parcel in that incarceration.

It was now the evening session of court. Continuing in the same spirit of reasonableness, Richardson said that the truth of some of the events of the Orchard confession might never be known, but that either way—prosecution version or defense version—Haywood had not been implicated. Moving into point number four, a review of the Cripple Creek troubles, he denied Hawley's charge that the strike was a sympathy strike by pointing out that the mill men in Colorado City were members of the Western Federation of Miners. He pointed out how unreasonable it was to believe that union men were responsible for the violence of the Cripple Creek district when they were the very ones who would lose the most from such violence. Richardson was by now into the fourth of his major points, a step-by-step review of the incidents of the conspiracy the state was trying to prove. He discussed the Vindicator explosion, reminding the jury that the bodies were found on opposite sides of the shaft, a situation that suggested the accidental explosion on the cage rather than Orchard's bomb on one side of the shaft. Like Hawley, Richardson, very humanly, had trouble with the massive amount of evidence to be quoted:

> Mr Holman, who was there as soon as Naylor was—yes, I believe before Naylor was—yes, I am sure he was there before Naylor was —and Mr. Holman found no wire and no bar at all and he so testified with respect to it.

Needling the prosecution a bit, Richardson reminded the jury that the bulk of the testimony on the train-wrecking incident favored the defense but that the prosecution could have denied Orchard's strong ties with the MOA detectives simply by putting Sterling on the stand. "What is there about Sterling's story," asked Richardson, "that he don't dare tell to this jury if he had no connection with Mr. Orchard?" A few minutes later he flung the same challenge at the state in connection with the Neville boy who had been with Orchard and Neville on their flight from Cripple Creek. Both Sterling and young Neville were in court day after day and never called, noted Richardson; finally on the last day they were called, but they were conveniently absent.

Richardson then reviewed Orchard's trip to Ouray as Moyer's bodyguard, asserting that Orchard was not handpicked to do this work, but was already planning on making a trip to this area at about the same time. The Moyer arrest and the flag desecration charge were discussed as fully as the judge's ruling permitted, with Richardson noting that the flag itself had not been imprinted. The poster on which the flag appeared had been overprinted with what Richardson reminded the jury were true statements about the conduct of the courts and the militia in Colorado.

The unpleasant task of dealing with the testimony concerning Lyte Gregory then confronted Richardson. Explaining that Lyte Gregory had never testified in the Sun and Moon dynamiting case in Idaho Springs, Richardson argued that there could be no reason for WFM animosity toward the man. In discussing this case he said:

> The evidence shows that Mr. Sabin tried the case or assisted in the trial of it. Another great lawyer by the name of Ralph Talbot, a man whose reputation is as wide perhaps as that of any man in the state of Colorado, tried the case with all the vigor that he possessed. With all of the unlimited wealth at their command, with a detective agency behind them, they labored night and day and long and well to secure a conviction in those cases, and it is no credit to the man who was defending them and he don't claim any credit for the defense at all. The case was so weak that standing alone it fell of its own weight or lack of weight on the part of the state's evidence.

The "man who was defending them" had been, of course, Richardson.

In an effective bid for critical thinking by the jurors, Richardson then changed the mood of his presentation for a satirical analysis of the state's efforts to corroborate Orchard's story. Corroboration that something took place, reasoned Richardson, is not corroboration of a man who claims he conspired to make it take place. He then told the story, which he said was in a current popular play, about the man who was visiting the St. Louis World's Fair. The man stayed out all night, and when his wife wanted to know where he had been, he said he had been riding in the great ferris wheel at the fair when its machinery broke down. Since he was at the top of the wheel, he couldn't get home until the wheel was fixed in the morning. The wife didn't believe his cock-and-bull story, so the man took his wife to the fair and showed her the ferris wheel to prove the story. This, said Richardson, was the way the prosecution was corroborating Harry Orchard, by showing merely that there was an explosion here and a violent death there.

Meeting Hawley's challenge about the witnesses who were not called, Richardson admitted frankly that both sides had people they were not sure of. It was "six of one and a half dozen of the other," said the defense attorney. Pettibone was not put on because there had been "visible connections" with Orchard demonstrated, and no lawyer would have put him on under the circumstances.

Next it was time to take up the Independence depot explosion. Richardson touched on it lightly, probably because Judge Wood had been so startled and displeased by Darrow's treatment of it during the pleas on admissibility of evidence. But Richardson managed to bring in the often-mentioned hound dogs, describing how ". . . this ignorant, this ill bred, this uneducated, this good-for-nothing bloodhound, which had no college education according to Senator Borah, was put upon the trail . . ."

Richardson then attacked the rebuttal testimony of Bynum, relative to Moran's alleged trip to Denver for Orchard's money. Richardson questioned Bynum's reason for recalling the event: the fact that he had performed some work for a third party that day, and the fact that he always considered people dressed in the same color combination that Moran wore as rather ludicrous. In a new approach the defense attorney suggested that Orchard could easily have been in North Idaho when Dr. McGee insisted he saw him there, because the direct route from Cody, where he had been in July, to California would have gone through the Coeur d'Alenes. Then, citing another example of the ferris wheel type of corroboration, Richardson scoffed at Cora Peabody's testimony:

> And if they had a million Miss Peabodys, and if her father instead of being the governor of the state of Colorado was the king of the Sandwich Islands or some other important part of the world's surface, it would not be the corroboration which is required by the statute.

As the final topic of the first day of the speech, Richardson discussed the Bradley affair. Acknowledging that a poisoning attempt had been made, Richardson pointed out that Orchard could have learned of this poisoning at Guibbinni's where he admittedly saw the milk afterwards, and then claimed the act as his own. Orchard's story of the poisoning certainly had defects in it, particularly in regard to the flat roof. Now Richardson intimated that the Pinkertons had seen a picture of the Bradley house, noted the adjacent roof, and picked it as Orchard's hiding place while waiting for the milkman, unaware that this adjacent structure was built after the poisoning attempt. It was a strong allegation on Richardson's part, but he followed it up with another of his well-reasoned conclusions that ". . . there is at least as much evidence in favor of his not having done it as there is in favor of his having done it." Since reasonable doubt is all the defense needs to show, said Richardson, this kind of testimony should convince the jury that they cannot convict Haywood.

On Tuesday morning, July 23, 1907, Richardson took up a new line of reasoning that apparently was not well received in the courtroom. The *New York Times* reacted in amazement:

> The most extraordinary thing took place this morning, when Richardson, senior counsel for the defense, declared that the fact that Gov. Peabody, Judges Gabbert and Goddard, Gen. Sherman Bell, and other opponents of the Western Federation of Miners are still alive is conclusive proof that the federation leaders never marked them for death. . . .
>
> It was a plea of confession and avoidance again as Hawley described it the other day. The jurors watched the lawyer with curious eyes as he was making it, and over Haywood's face there came an expression of seriousness as grave as any he has worn at any time during the progress of the trial, even upon that trying occasion when the indictment was read to him. It was a plea of desperation, and everybody in the defense knew it.[6]

Actually, Richardson's argument did not sound as ill-conceived as these press criticisms would imply. What he did was to point out that Orchard's story of stalking Peabody, Gabbert, Goddard, Bell, Moffat, and Hearne, all with considerable difficulty and no success, was hard to believe when one considered

[6] *New York Times,* July 24, 1907, p. 5.

how freely these men moved about, and how easy it would be to learn the habits and routine of each of them. He also argued that the kind of "Inner Circle" suggested by the prosecution would not have tolerated the hesitancy and incompetence demonstrated by Orchard.

To show that Orchard could not have been subsidized by the union treasury, Richardson examined his career as an insurance salesman. Corroborating testimony of Vaughn, the insurance agent, had established that Orchard had visited several communities in the Arkansas Valley and the San Luis Valley in the process of writing insurance. Why, asked Richardson, would Orchard have worked so hard at selling insurance in places where the WFM had no enemies if he were really an assassin for the union?

> Do you suppose that a professional and hired assassin, a man who was employed for the specific purpose of taking away human life, a man who was using the writing of insurance as an excuse for his presence in a town, do you suppose that such a man as that after five or six days, would abandon his employers, abandon his enterprise, abandon the thought of killing and go off to another and a distant part of the state to write hail insurance?

Hawley had implied that Jack Simpkins' flight was an admission of guilt. Now Richardson took Hawley to task for the inconsistency of his position in this respect. Union men who had avoided appearing at the trial were examples of the criminal attitudes of these men, according to Hawley, and yet union men who came to the trial and testified against the prosecution were likewise criminals to Hawley because they came—and said what they did. You cannot use both theories, argued Richardson. However, the effect of this argument must have been dampened by the fact that the defense itself throughout the case had used several incompatible explanations of Orchard's behavior simultaneously or in quick succession.

At this juncture, Richardson skipped ahead to his previously announced eighth point, the impeachment of Harry Orchard. He reviewed the testimony of each witness who had reported hearing Orchard make threats against Steunenberg. He singled out the testimony of Lottie Day, pointing out that the state had brought her to Boise but did not want to use her when they discovered what she knew. With respect to Hawley's sarcastic comment on Eugene Engley, Richardson noted that Engley's views were not much different from those that Borah and Hawley held in 1896, an allusion to the fact that the two prosecutors had had Populist support in the days when the silver issue had split the major parties in Idaho.

As Richardson returned to the regular sequence of his announced agenda, time ran out for the morning session. During the long, hot afternoon he apparently made the changes in strategy that were so noticeable in the evening session that followed. It would be interesting to know what actually took place during this time. Perhaps there was a defense strategy conference at which the decision was made, or perhaps Richardson went off on his own after a disagreement with Darrow. But, whatever happened, it marked a turning point in the speech. What had been a consistently interesting and effective argument became now, too frequently, an unintelligible and ineffective harangue.

Richardson opened the final session by covering his fifth and sixth points, the death of Steunenberg, and Orchard under arrest. He admitted at this stage that he did not know if Orchard was a Pinkerton, but he reminded the jurors that Orchard had made little effort to conceal himself in Caldwell. He admitted, too, that the Orchard confession was made before any religious motives had been attributed to the prisoner; a bit later he concluded that the confession had been prearranged.

For a considerable period of time Richardson then read from Denver newspaper accounts of the arrest of Orchard-Hogan in January of 1906. His purpose in doing this was not clear, unless it was to show that the union had been cooperating with law enforcement agencies. The papers had not been introduced in evidence, and they offered nothing startling in the way of new interpretations of Orchard's arrest. If anything, they showed that the civil authorities and mine owners in Cripple Creek had been looking for Orchard since his departure in June of 1904, and that they were glad to hear at last of his arrest in Caldwell. But one gets the impression that Richardson's reading of these papers was simply some sort of a delaying action, uncalled for in the eighth hour of a lengthy speech.

When Richardson turned to his seventh point, a review of Orchard's treatment in the penitentiary, he shook off the inhibiting effect of the reading of the long newspaper stories and delivered some of the most moving and eloquent moments of the speech. Of Orchard he said:

> Petted and coddled, visited by the governor, called on familiar terms "Harry" by the counsel for the prosecution and by the governor of this state and by the warden of this penitentiary, this vile, this loathsome, this damned creature who sat upon the stand and related the most blood curdling series of events that was ever perpetrated by a single individual upon the face of the earth, associating with a United States senator and with a man who if it were not for his democracy would probably be his colleague in the same senate . . .

Taking a subtle dig at the way the trial had been conducted, Richardson continued:

> These men taking charge of this prosecution, the two greatest lawyers in the state of Idaho and I am willing to concede perhaps the two greatest lawyers in all of the West—I think perhaps that the people here very generally believe that my associates and myself are not fit to try a case on the opposite side with them on account of their ability, and I am willing to concede it—come in here and take charge of a criminal case and supplant the district attorney regularly elected by the people to fill that office.

Again alluding to some sort of unholy, behind-the-scenes alliance that was responsible for the conduct of the trial, the Denver attorney utilized an interesting hyperbole from Milton's *Paradise Lost:*

> Why is it that McParland and his cohorts, the Pinkerton detectives, thicker than the leaves of Vallambrosa here in this court room since we have been trying this case are engaged in it?[7]

For one final moment Richardson recaptured the spirit of reasonableness that had characterized most of the first day and a half of his argument. In this spirit he dealt briefly with the conversion of Harry Orchard as a factor in the trial:

[7] The reference is to Vallambrosa, a shady vale near Florence in Italy. In *Paradise Lost* Milton describes the abundance of Satan's fallen angels: "Thick as autumnal leaves that strew the brooks In Vallambrosa . . ." (Book I, lines 202-203.)

> Now, gentlemen, I don't want any of you to entertain any misconceptions with respect to what I have said about conversion. I say that the greatest institution that the world has ever known is the Christian religion. I say it is the greatest factor in the progress of humanity that has ever been created, be it God-given or otherwise. I say that it has imbued human souls to do the most remarkable things and under the most remarkable circumstances. But I say, gentlemen of the jury, that it is true that the livery of Heaven is often stolen by the devil to render service that cannot be fitly placed upon the altars of religion. I want to say to you that Orchard himself says that his confession was not the result of religion.

Contrasting Orchard and Haywood, Richardson moved into the ninth of his topics. As the *Capital News* described this portion of the speech,

> He paid an eloquent tribute to the care of Haywood for the invalid wife and his family, in opposition to the obloquy cast by Orchard upon his deserted wife and child, made by his confession of crime. Richardson spent a half hour in delivering to the jury an eloquence they perhaps never heard before in stigmatizing Orchard and in praise of Haywood.[8]

Typical of the eloquence of this portion of the trial was this sentence delivered shortly before the conclusion of the long speech:

> This tinsel hero has clothed his wife and his innocent daughter with a cloak of infamy and of obloquy which will make them the subject of contumely, the recipients of sneers from now until the time that their tired bodies and their weary minds shall have gone back to the native earth from which they came.

The tenth point in the argument, why certain witnesses did not testify, had previously been disposed of, and the summary promised as the last point had been woven into the discussion of Orchard, Haywood, and the organized efforts of the prosecution to link the two men. Richardson now announced his intention of concluding with a short poetic passage by James Russell Lowell. This passage, part of the eighth stanza of Lowell's anti-slavery poem called "The Present Crisis," had been placed in evidence as a part of a *Miner's Magazine* reprint of a speech by Congressman Knowles of South Dakota, the speech and poem as evidence purporting to show a motive for the attitude of the union toward Steunenberg. If the prosecution's reason for including this ma-

---

[8] *Capital News,* July 24, 1907, p. 2.

terial in its case was obscure, Richardson's reason for concluding his defense argument with it was twice as obscure.

In any event, after a rather confusing explanation of the poem, Richardson concluded:

> . . . and with it I want to close the argument for my side of the case, that is for the part of it I represent, leaving the case in your hands, gentlemen of the jury, for such determination as you think that it warrants.
>
> I want to say to you in closing that no lawyer has a right, and in my judgment Mr. Hawley should have been corrected for putting the personal equation into his speech, he has told you that if he did not believe the defendant ought to be prosecuted and convicted he would not be here asking for his conviction; his belief is immaterial. I want to tell you if I did not believe that the defendant was innocent and ought to be acquitted I would not be here pleading for his acquittal, and the word of one with respect to that matter ought to be as good as the other and both should be rejected and the case should be determined from the evidence adduced upon the stand. I say that this case represents a phase of an industrial warfare. It bears none of the aspects, or at least but a few of them, of the criminal case. It is not a trial for the murder of Governor Steunenberg. It is a trial of the Western Federation of Miners at the instance of those who do not represent the authority of this state and who have secured the aid of the authorities of this state as they secured the aid of those authorities in Colorado and some day or other they will find that:
>
> Right forever on the scaffold,
> Wrong forever on the throne,
> But that scaffold sways the future
> And behind the dim unknown
> Standeth God within the shadow,
> Keeping watch above his own.

Richardson's speech was generally criticized harshly by the newspaper men who were covering the trial, particularly those portions delivered on the second day. The *New York Times,* as previously noted, found it an "amazing argument." The *Idaho Statesman* spoke of Richardson's "remarkable inconsistency" in building "theory after theory concerning events connected with the case" and his nonchalance in abandoning one theory for another:

> He declared that the state was right in that Orchard killed Steunenberg and he was willing to accept the stated method by which the deed was done. But he urged that the state had shown no connection

> between Orchard in that deed and the officers of the Western Federation.
>
> And when Mr. Richardson had blown this bubble-theory of the personal grudge and had filled it and had it floating before the jurors and they were looking at its beauty and were turning over in their minds whether they should pronounce it a thing of beauty or not—then the Denver attorney petulantly thrust out his finger, poked it through his own creation and the bubble broke. He had another idea. He would blow another theory-bubble that would be more pleasing to the jury. So he dipped his pipe and this time he spread before the jury the startling theory that the Steunenberg murder was all a plot of the Pinkerton detective agency. And that is the way he left it.[9]

Actually, Richardson had not developed the personal grudge theory to any great extent in his summation argument. Most of the time he had used the theory that Orchard was somewhat demented, pursuing victims with a "desultory maniacal method" and adopting coincidental explosions as acts of his own. But, admittedly, Richardson did not offer a singular and credible explanation of those acts of Orchard that had been corroborated.

There was something about Richardson's oratorical style that brought out a colorful and imaginative style in his newspaper critics. Oscar King Davis of the *Times,* developing into the most prolific rhetorical critic of the trial, not only commented on Richardson's ideas but on his delivery as well. Davis described Richardson's appearance before the jury in vivid terms:

> Richardson steams at high speed when cruising, and his coal consumption is great, so his steaming radius is comparatively short, especially on hot days like this. He has a great, big voice which he works pretty near all the time, and he accompanies it with both feet and hands in a series of leg-and-arm movements which require a good deal of stamina to sustain.
>
> He is probably the most practiced orator among the lawyers making the closing arguments, but there is not nearly so much variation in his emphasis or tone as there is in the work of either Hawley or Darrow. He speaks rapidly, but with great distinctness and his diction and pronunciation are admirable.
>
> He had the counsel table moved back and apart, so as to give him a good space to walk about in as he talked. His favorite method of attack on the jury was to back off the limit of retreating possibility, then, crouching down, to approach stealthily, speaking softly until he

[9] *Idaho Statesman,* July 24, 1907, p. 1.

> got fairly in front of the first row of jurors, and then booming out his points at the top of his voice and with explosive emphasis. He is a tall man, who throws his shoulders far back, and his head is very suggestive of Abe Hummel.[10] In gesturing he usually spreads the fingers of his hands apart, and when not using his hands in that way he often folds them on his stomach, after the manner of the Sunday School Superintendent addressing his children.[11]

Assessing Richardson's effect on the jury is more difficult than measuring Hawley's effect. In some respects it must be done inferentially and through comparison. For example, Hawley had held the attention of the jury to the extent that they stopped fanning and the courtroom was noticeably still. But Richardson reportedly encountered vigorous fanning by jury and spectators. Other than through this sort of inference—and warmer temperatures may have been a factor here—no conclusion can be drawn relative to Richardson's immediate impact on the jury. No description of the jurors' attention is available, except for comments on specific reactions such as that of the *Times* concerning Richardson's new argument on the innocence of the union leaders:

> The whole court room listened to this amazing argument with astonishment, and there was plenty of indication that it did not sit at all well with either Haywood or Richardson's associates in the defense. The jurors looked at the lawyer with weird attention, and for once there was an expression of surprise even on some of these ordinarily inscrutable faces.[12]

An interesting contemporary evaluation of Richardson's argument was offered by James Hawley. While the speech was still in progress he observed, "Richardson is talking today, but I am inclined to think he is talking over the heads of the jury. He seems to rather have the credit of an orator than making an argument."[13] In this simple analysis lies a clue to Hawley's own rhetoric of jury pleading.

It was late Tuesday evening when Richardson finished. By

---

[10] Abe Hummel was a famous Eastern criminal lawyer; he had recently been disbarred, enjoined from practicing law, and sentenced to a year in prison for subornation of perjury.

[11] *New York Times,* July 23, 1907, p. 8.

[12] *New York Times,* July 24, 1907, p. 5.

[13] Letter, James H. Hawley to Jacob Fillius, July 22, 1907.

means of his long address the defense now had a certain amount of momentum established, albeit going in several directions simultaneously. On the following day Clarence Darrow would control the force and direction of that momentum as he presented his closing argument in behalf of Bill Haywood.

14

CLARENCE DARROW for the DEFENSE

THE SPEAKING OF CLARENCE DARROW defies analysis. This is true, generally, argues Martin Maloney, because this "nonconformist by habit, . . . devil's advocate by profession" became literally an American myth in his lifetime, the sort of person whose success as a pleader could not be explained by conventional rhetorical standards.[1] Specifically, Darrow's closing argument in the Haywood case defies analysis "For," as one critic put it, "it was not an argument, nor was it a plea that will stand analysis."[2] With the realization that the task will be difficult, we must, nevertheless, attempt to consider Clarence Darrow's summation speech in the Haywood trial in something of the same light as those of Hawley and Richardson. Inasmuch as Darrow has been the subject of numerous books and articles, it will be necessary to recall here but a few of the highlights of his life and personality.

Clarence Seward Darrow was born in Kinsman, Ohio, April 18, 1957, to Amirus and Emily Eddy Darrow. The senior Darrow was a woodworker who also served as the community undertaker.

[1] Martin Maloney, "Clarence Darrow," in Marie Hochmuth, editor, *A History and Criticism of American Public Address,* Vol. III (New York: Longmans, Green and Co., 1955), pp. 262 and 307.

[2] *New York Times,* July 25, 1907, p. 5.

Clarence attended school in Kinsman, showing an interest but no great success in debate and elocution. After graduating from the academy he attended Allegheny College in Meadville, Pennsylvania, for a year, after which he returned to Kinsman to work with his father in his shop.

During the winters young Darrow taught in the district school; it was also in this period that he began to read law. At the end of three years, with the financial help of a sister and brother, he attended the University of Michigan law school for a year. He then worked in a law office in Youngstown, Ohio, while he continued his legal study. After being admitted to the bar he began to practice in the little town of Andover, Ohio. After a brief practice here, and a somewhat longer period at Ashtabula, Ohio, Darrow at the age of 29 decided to go to Chicago to further his career.

This move marked the end of Darrow's small-town days. But nothing could erase the influence of Kinsman and its provincial citizenry upon the young lawyer. Darrow spoke at some length of these influences in his autobiography, as well as in *Farmington,* a fictionalized account of life in the community. Students of Darrow generally see in Amirus Darrow's skepticism and nonconformity the genesis of Clarence Darrow's philosophy; young Darrow's ultimate departure from Kinsman becomes the symbol of his break with conventionality and the beginning of his long journey with minority groups and social outcasts. Throughout his life, says Maloney, "A verdict of acquittal was, for Darrow, a hard stroke at Kinsman . . ."[3]

Darrow's early years in Chicago were lean years. To occupy himself and to get his name before the public he became active in politics. He spoke at various political meetings and at the Single Tax Club. The turning point in his early career came when he had an opportunity to speak at a free trade convention on the same program with the great Henry George. Darrow was well received by the audience, and by the newspaper writers who were covering the convention.

---

[3] Maloney, *op. cit.,* p. 275.

From that moment on he received numerous invitations to speak. A mayoralty campaign was in progress in Chicago, and Darrow became active in the campaign. His candidate won the election, one of the few times Darrow ever supported a popular and successful man or issue. The new mayor appointed Darrow a special attorney for the city of Chicago. A series of lucky breaks catapulted Darrow to the head of the city's law department within a year's time. After two years in this post he became general attorney for the Chicago and Northwestern Railway.

When the American Railway Union strike of 1894 took place, Darrow asked to be relieved of his responsibility of prosecuting the strike for the railroad because of his sympathy for the strikers. The railroad allowed him to remain neutral, but before long Eugene Debs and a number of Darrow's friends prevailed upon the lawyer to take up the defense of the ARU officials charged with conspiracy to obstruct the mails and with violating an injunction. Darrow reluctantly agreed, resigned his position with the railroad, and began his career as a labor lawyer.

Maloney has taken note of the techniques that Darrow used in the Debs defense that became a part of his rhetoric throughout his career:

> . . . the attempt to present the facts in a case against a broad backdrop of history, and so to alter their significance; the suggestion that the prosecution is the tool of some blackly evil force . . .; the use of invective against the prosecution and especially against agencies associated with the prosecution; the insistence upon the honesty, kindliness, and in general the ordinary qualities of the client. All of these elements . . . are essential parts of Darrow's rhetorical system. In the trial of Debs, they appear on the record for the first time.[4]

After losing the Debs case, at least that portion of it involving the violation of court injunctions, Darrow's next major case was the defense of the United Mine Workers in their struggle with the anthracite coal mineowners in 1902. Darrow appeared before the arbitration commission and argued with some success the cause of the miners. He had now represented the unions of two of the country's strongest labor leaders, Eugene Debs and John Mitchell.

[4] Maloney, *ibid.*, p. 286.

It was natural that the Haywood defense committee should turn to Darrow in 1906.

Clarence Darrow's closing argument for the defense in the Haywood trial was delivered in four sessions of the court on July 24-25, 1907. The speech lasted a total of eleven hours and fifteen minutes, an hour longer than Richardson's. The weather remained warm, with the temperature reaching 88° the first day and 89° on the second. Morning and evening sessions were held on Wednesday, and morning and afternoon sessions on Thursday.

It is difficult to categorize what Darrow did in this speech. It is even more difficult to be objective in evaluating the speech and the man. Some of Darrow's admirers have become blinded to his faults. For example, Irving Stone says, "The summation speech is astounding in its organization and its mastery of every detail that had been elicited in the seventy-six days of examination."[5] "Astounding" may be the correct word for the organization—or lack of organization—in the speech, but mastery of detail was hardly one of Darrow's strong points, as his more critical admirers will readily admit. Then, too, Charles Harrison observes, "Other lawyers know full well how to play on a jury's emotions, how to simulate indignation, pity, sorrow. Darrow, too, appeals to juries in this way, but because of his social consciousness and his vast, abiding humanity there is a dignity and sincerity about his appeals that other lawyers fail to achieve."[6] How dignity and sincerity can be reconciled with invective as a rhetorical device is not made clear. Thus, it would seem that Harrison and Stone are trying to give to Darrow qualities that the more objective students of the great lawyer have not ascribed to the man.

Most of Darrow's conservative critics and detractors have, at least, conceded his effectiveness. They would, however, take exception to his ethics, his knowledge of law, and his conduct of trials. In the Haywood case, MacLane's appraisal of Darrow is typical of this point of view:

---

[5] Irving Stone, *Clarence Darrow for the Defense* (Garden City, N. Y.: Doubleday & Company, Inc., 1941), p. 236.

[6] Charles Y. Harrison, *Clarence Darrow* (New York: Jonathon Cape & Harrison Smith, 1931), p. 138.

> Clarence Darrow is too well known to require any description. As stated before, the only times I met him I did not like him. From such observations as I have had of his subsequent career I never thought that he rated as a lawyer, and I never knew any lawyer who would give him any rating. His Boise associate, John Nugent, called him "Old necessity," and when asked why he said "because necessity knows no law." But he was certainly a man to be reckoned with in criminal prosecutions susceptible of emotional defense before a jury.[7]

Judge Koelsch confirms the "Old Necessity" label the Nugent placed on Darrow. To Koelsch, Darrow was an unethical lawyer, particularly for his role in "selling out" his clients in the *Los Angeles Times* bombing case in order to protect himself.[8] James Hawley, son of the governor, regards Darrow as "largely a fraud."[9] Contrast these opinions with the opinions regarding Richardson, and the problem of objectivity in dealing with Darrow is readily apparent. Darrow seems to have been a unique personality, the sort of person with whom most lawyers, regardless of politics, could find no common bond.

Notwithstanding the fact that Darrow's summation had no clear pattern of organization, there are a number of recurrent themes which can be recognized in the argument. Among the more prominent are these:

1. Orchard is a liar.
2. Hawley is crazy for believing Orchard, and is motivated by his own greed.
3. The religious issue in Orchard's confession is a spurious issue.
4. There is a capitalist plot to kill Bill Haywood and the labor movement.
5. Violence done in behalf of the cause of labor is justified.
6. Orchard's greatest crime is in revealing his family background and bringing shame to his relatives.
7. Defense witnesses are more honest looking than the state's witnesses.
8. Orchard had a personal motive to kill Steunenberg.

Obviously, only two of these themes are germane to the issue of Haywood's guilt or innocence.

---

[7] John F. MacLane, *A Sagebrush Lawyer* (New York: Pandick Press, 1953), p. 158.

[8] Conversation with Charles Koelsch, Boise, Idaho, August 1, 1960.

[9] Conversation with James H. Hawley Jr., Boise, Idaho, July 26, 1960.

The first of these many themes, that Orchard was a liar, recurred most frequently throughout the long speech, although Darrow did not use it in his most eloquent passages. Examples of Orchard's incredibility were frequently woven by Darrow into a review of the defense testimony. For example, in upholding the testimony of the three Cripple Creek roominghouse keepers, Darrow equated the truthfulness of their testimony to the virtue of womanhood, and the untruthfulness of Orchard's conflicting testimony to the baseness of men. Using a technique that Borah had once used in the Paul Corcoran case, he challenged the jury to decide which sex was inherently more virtuous: "If you believe Orchard you never should look your wife in the face again, or yourself either." He also used hyperbole to reinforce his assertion that Orchard was a monumental liar:

> Why, gentlemen, if Harry Orchard were George Washington who had come into a court of justice with his great name behind him, and if he was impeached and contradicted by as many as Harry Orchard has been, George Washington would go out of it disgraced and counted the Ananias of the age.

Perhaps the most eloquent passage referring to the veracity of Orchard's testimony is this one which has been quoted in several condensations of the speech:

> Gentlemen, I sometimes think I am dreaming in this case. I sometimes wonder whether this is a case, whether here in Idaho or anywhere in the country, broad and free, a man can be placed on trial and lawyers seriously asked to take away the life of a human being upon the testimony of Harry Orchard.
> We have the lawyers come here and ask you upon the word of that sort of a man to send this man to the gallows, to make his wife a widow, and his children orphans—on his word. For God's sake, what sort of an honesty exists up here in the state of Idaho that sane men should ask it? Need I come here from Chicago to defend the honor of your state? The juror who would take away the life of a human being upon testimony like that would place a stain upon the state of their birth and their nativity, a stain which all the waters of the great seas could never wash away. And yet they ask it. You had better let a thousand men go unwhipped of justice, you had better let all the criminals that come to Idaho escape scot free than to have it said that twelve men of Idaho would take away the life of a human being upon testimony like that.

The next of Darrow's themes, that Hawley was crazy for

believing Orchard, was tied in closely with the attack on Orchard's testimony. Referring to Hawley, the defense lawyer said:

> He said to you, gentlemen of the jury, that he would not prosecute this case unless he believed this defendant guilty. Now, why? Is he prosecuting it because he believes him guilty, is that it? Or is he prosecuting it because he may want to put another "ell" on his house and wants some more deficiency warrants with which to do it? Which is it? Has any man a right to make a statement like that? I hope there is not anybody here who cares a fig about what Mr. Hawley thinks about this case. He may be bughouse, and he is if all of his statements are true. Or he is worse. Let me show you what he said and then judge for yourself. We are trying Mr. Hawley. We will try him on an inquest of lunacy. He said to these twelve men, men of fair intelligence and fair learning, that you would be warranted in convicting Bill Haywood if you took Harry Orchard's evidence out of this case. And still he says he is honest. Maybe it is, but if he is honest he is bughouse, and he can have his choice.

Darrow not only accused Hawley of being "bughouse" on several occasions during the speech, but he also raised the question of whether Hawley's motives were mercenary or not. Shortly after referring to Hawley's expanding his house, Darrow went on to say:

> Yes, gentlemen, Mr. Hawley has always been a friend of labor unions, when they got their cash to his office first. But when they did not, they had better hunt some other friends. Mr. Hawley is advising the state in this case. He had better stick to the state and let the labor unions be taken care of by someone of their own choice.

Throughout the speech Darrow seized upon every opportunity to contrast Hawley's summation speech with common sense. He made unflattering comparisons frequently, for example, arguing that the old soldier, Elliott, was saner than Hawley. Even when Darrow talked critically about Borah, he managed to be more critical of Hawley. Speaking of the evidence concerning Sterling and the Independence depot, Darrow observed:

> . . . and Mr. Hawley, with one of those feeble bluffs, called his name in the courtroom on the forenoon of the last day when they were putting on what they call evidence. And then he got up and asked the court to adjourn because they had run dry of witnesses and said he would put him on in the afternoon. But in the afternoon Mr. Borah was at the helm and Mr. Borah forgot. Mr. Borah forgets lots of things; that is his strong suit, one of them, I mean. And

> Mr. K. C. Sterling came here and went away and went back home and these three women have sworn that he had this infamous thing in his room at least twenty times to their knowledge, and Mr. K. C. Sterling went home without denying it. And yet Hawley says they are perjurers, perjurers. You ought to hang these women, if you could get them, get them back into Idaho. I have no doubt Hawley would go to the legislature and try to get the law changed to hang those three women because they dared testify against Orchard. Now, let me make a suggestion. After I have got all done, Senator Borah is going to talk to you, and then you will hear something. I want Senator Borah to tell you twelve men whether he believes that Mrs. King, Miss King, and Mrs. Fechyew are perjurers, or whether he believes that precious gentleman with the wings sprouting on his shoulders, Harry Orchard, is a liar. Now I want him to say—I don't mean to insinuate for a minute that he is honester than Hawley, but I do think he is slicker. I will just lay a little wager that he won't tell you twelve men that he thinks Mrs. King, Miss King, and Mrs. Fechyew were perjurers.

This passage illustrates well how Darrow digressed at every opportunity to insert sarcastic comments. These comments interrupted his reasoning on many points (hence, many of the passages to be cited are unduly long), but they had the cumulative effect of building a negative image of Orchard, Hawley, and to a lesser degree, Borah, in the minds of the jurors.

The third of Darrow's themes was that the religious issue in Orchard's conversion was a spurious issue. Conveniently ignoring the fact that the defense cross-examination had raised the issue for the first time (as Hawley had pointed out), Darrow launched out at the religious question. ". . . of all the miserable claptraps that have been thrown into a jury to give some excuse for taking the life of a man this is the worst." He was equally blunt when he announced, "I want to say a few words for the benefit not of this jury but of those sickly, slobbering idiots who talk about Harry Orchard's religion." With this unusual preface he went on to discuss religion from the standpoint of his own unorthodox views.

> Now, gentlemen, like Brother Hawley and like Brother Richardson, and I know like Senator Borah, I, too, have a profound regard for religion. Mine may be broader than Brother Hawley's or even Mr. Richardson's. I don't want to say to these twelve men that I think the Christian religion is the only religion that the world has ever known. I don't believe it for a moment. I have the greatest respect for any

religion or any code of ethics that would do anything to help man, whatever that religion may be. And for the poor black man who looks into the black face of a wooden idol, and he prays to that wooden idol to make him a better man and a stronger man, I have the profoundest respect. I know that there is in him when he addresses his prayers to his wooden idol the same holy sentiment and the same feeling that there is in the breast of a Christian when he raises his prayer to the Christian God. It is all one.

This was, perhaps, the most liberal theology that the Haywood jurors had ever heard. But there was nothing in it that was incompatible with a tolerant, golden-rule type of Christianity. When Darrow went on, however, to an attack on the concepts of repentance and salvation, his views must have been offensive to at least some of the jurors. Again managing to include Hawley, he said:

Gentlemen, Hawley doesn't know half as much about religion as I do. If he knew anything whatever about religion he would never tell twelve men that something could be sprinkled upon the head of Harry Orchard and his nature would change in the twinkling of an eye. He is as crazy on religion as he is on other things. You can't do it. He might get a glimpse, he might get an insight, and he may struggle on and on for something higher and better and fall while he reaches, and reach while he falls, and in this way men get religion like they get other things that are good. Let us see what he has got, and then we will see whether it is religion. There are certain qualities which are primal with religion. I undertake to say, gentlemen, that if Harry Orchard has religion now, that I hope I never get it. I want to say to this jury that before Harry Orchard got religion he was bad enough, but it remained to religion to make him totally depraved.

He went on to argue that if Harry Orchard had really gotten religion he would have felt kindness and charity toward his friends of the Western Federation of Miners instead of implicating them in his long career of foul deeds. It was a novel plea, one that could be forthcoming only from a man of Darrow's unconventional philosophy.

Another recurrent theme in Darrow's summation speech considers an alleged capitalist plot to kill Bill Haywood, and with him, the labor movement. Early in the speech Darrow alluded to the people who were after Haywood:

He has fought many a fight, many a fight with the persecutors who

> are hounding him into this court. He has met them in many a battle in the open field, and he is not a coward. If he is to die, he will die as he has lived, with his face to the foe.

Even though Judge Wood had been disturbed when Darrow had argued during the pleas on admissibility of evidence that the mineowners had been linked to the Independence depot explosion, and even though Judge Wood at that time had specifically ruled out such a line of argument, Darrow again brought up this allegation. He dwelt on it for some time. Finally, Borah interrupted politely to inquire if such material had not been ruled out. The judge replied that it would be called to the jury's attention in the instructions. Darrow replied curtly, "If counsel cannot answer their criminality except by an instruction of this court, let them answer it that way. I will argue this case as far as I can and take my chances on the instructions of the court." Darrow had reason not to fear the judge's instructions. He later observed, "Judges seem to be quite unaware that it is a hard task to put anything into the average mind, and, once in, an impossible one to take it out."[10] It is interesting to note, however, that at the end of the Haywood trial Darrow viewed the judge's instructions as the key to the verdict.

In addition to the allusion to the MOA plot in Colorado, there are several references in the speech to McParland and the Pinkertons as the engineers behind the prosecution. In fact, Darrow made this reference as frequently as did Richardson, but the newsmen chose to consider the Pinkerton plot as primarily Richardson's theory, and personal grudge as Darrow's explanation of the case.

At the end of the first morning session of court, Clarance Darrow, still pursuing the same theme, put what was obviously a peroration at the end of his argument. Whether he intended to to do this at each of the four sessions, we do not know. But the most eloquent portion of his first day's argument—and the first day's argument was generally considered superior to that of the second day—was in the final moment when he said:

[10] Clarence Darrow, *The Story of My Life* (New York: Charles Scribner's Sons, 1934), p. 145.

> To kill him, gentlemen? I want to speak to you plainly. Mr. Haywood is not my greatest concern. Other men have died before him, other men have been martyrs to a holy cause since the world began. Wherever men have looked upward and onward, forgotten their selfishness, struggled for humanity, worked for the poor and the weak, they have been sacrificed. They have been sacrificed in the prison, on the scaffold, in the flame. They have met their death, and he can meet his if you twelve men say he must. Gentlemen, you short-sighted men of the prosecution, you men of the Mine Owners' Association, you people who would cure hatred with hate, you who think you can crush out the feelings and the hopes and the aspirations of men by tying a noose around his neck, you who are seeking to kill him not because it is Haywood but because he represents a class, don't be so blind, don't be so foolish as to believe you can strangle the Western Federation of Miners when you tie a rope around his neck. Don't be so blind in your madness as to believe that if you make three fresh new graves you will kill the labor movement of the world. I want to say to you, gentlemen, Bill Haywood can't die unless you kill him. You have got to tie the rope. You twelve men of Idaho, the burden will be on you. If at the behest of this mob you should kill Bill Haywood, he is mortal. He will die. But I want to say that a hundred will grab up the banner of labor at the open grave where Haywood lays it down, and in spite of prisons, or scaffolds, or fire, in spite of prosecution or jury, these men of willing hands will carry it on to victory in the end.

This passage makes it quite clear that Darrow was talking to society in general, not just to the Haywood jury. In a similar vein, Darrow avowed:

> Let me tell you, gentlemen, if you destroy the labor unions in this country, you destroy liberty when you strike the blow, and you would leave the poor bound and shackled and helpless to do the bidding of the rich . . . It would take this country back . . . to the time when there were masters and slaves.

This theme is given its fullest treatment in the actual peroration of the speech which will be considered shortly. A variation on this theme, one which was startling and disturbing to a number of trial observers, was the idea that law was an instrument by which middle and upper classes oppressed the lower classes. Along these lines, Darrow announced, "What is the constitution for except to use for the rich, to destroy the laws that are made for the poor? That is its main purpose in these latter days . . ."

Another of Darrow's themes must have been even more startling to the courtroom audience, if not the national audience.

This was Darrow's insistence that violence done in behalf of the labor movement was justified. Said Darrow, "If for any reason a thousand men deliberately determined to go up and blow up the Bunker Hill mill then it needed blowing up." If this reference was too fleeting for the jurors to catch its significance, they could not fail to get Darrow's meaning when he discussed, at some length, why unions could do no wrong.

> I am here to say that in a great cause these labor organizations, despised and weak and outlawed as they generally are, have stood for the poor, they have stoood for the weak, they have stood for every human law that was ever placed upon the statute books. They stood for human life, they stood for the father who was bound down by his task, they stood for the wife, threatened to be taken from the home to work by his side, and they have stood for the little child who was also taken to work in their places—that the rich could grow richer still, and they have fought for the right of the little one, to give him a little of life, a little comfort while he is young. I don't care how many wrongs they committed, I don't care how many crimes these weak, rough, rugged, unlettered men who often know no other power but the brute force of their strong right arm, who find themselves bound and confined and impaired whichever way they turn, who look up and worship the god of might as the only god that they know—I don't care how often they fail, how many brutalities they are guilty of. I know their cause is just. I hope that the trouble and the strife and the contention has been endured. Through brutality and bloodshed and crime has come the progress of the human race. I know they may be wrong in this battle or that, but in the great, long struggle they are right and they are eternally right, and that they are working for the poor and the weak. They are working to give more liberty to the man, and I want to say to you, gentlemen of the jury, you Idaho farmers removed from the trade unions, removed from the men who work in industrial affairs, I want to say that if it had not been for the trade unions of the world, for the trade unions of England, for the trade unions of Europe, the trade unions of America, you today would be serfs instead of free men sitting upon a jury to try one of your peers. The cause of these men is right.

Darrow must have realized how dangerous his position was on this matter. Several months after the trial he denied that he had made any "violent utterance" in the speech, and cited the text reprinted in the *Appeal to Reason* in which, he said, ". . . not one word has been cut . . ."[11] But the editors of *Collier's* were sus-

[11] Letter, Clarence Darrow to Editor of *Collier's,* September 23, 1907, in *Collier's,* October 26, 1907, p. 9.

picious; the notes of their correspondent, C. P. Connolly, as well as many newspaper accounts mentioned several remarks about violence not found in the *Appeal to Reason* version. Another Socialist journal, *Wayland's Monthly,* inadvertently supplied the evidence which discredited Darrow. It ran the full text of his speech, complete with all the passages defending violence whose existence Darrow had denied.[12]

One of the most interesting themes in Darrow's summation was that which treated Orchard's disclosure of his family background as his greatest crime. Richardson had also developed this idea, but not to the degree that Darrow did. Darrow led into his dramatic denunciation of Orchard with a discussion of the images of the trial that would remain in the minds of the participants. Each person may have a different image of Orchard, said Darrow, as a result of his testimony.

> Hawley will picture him as a cherubim with wings growing out from his shoulders and with a halo just above his head, and singing songs with a detective on one side of him and McParland on the other. I don't know yet how Borah will picture him, but everybody will picture him according to how they see him. My picture is not these, none of these. I see what to me is the crowning act of infamy in Harry Orchard's life, an act which throws into darkness every other deed that he ever committed as long as he has lived. And he didn't do this until he had got Christianity or McParlandism, whatever that is. Until he had confessed and been forgiven by Father McParland, he had some spark of manhood still in his breast.

The *New York Times* described how Darrow went on to castigate Orchard for bringing grief and infamy to his family by disclosing who they were:

> Darrow then demonstrated his skill in oratory by picking up his audience again and moving them as nothing he had said before had done. He was at his very best. The tears filled up in his eyes and rolled across his cheeks, and all through the courtroom handkerchiefs were busy concealing weeping faces. He was making his own picture of Orchard.[13]

It is interesting to observe, as Borah was soon to do in his closing argument, that it was not the prosecution but the defense

---

[12] Editorial, *Collier's,* November 30, 1907, p. 7.
[13] *New York Times,* July 25, 1907, p. 5.

that brought out all the information about Orchard's wife, child, and other relatives in Ontario. Hawley's direct examination had drawn out Orchard's correct name of Horsley, and little else. Had Orchard denied his family on cross-examination, it would have been a simple thing for the defense to have located the family and then impeached Orchard as a perjurer. Darrow's maneuver put him in the odd position of maintaining on one hand that Harry Orchard was the greatest liar of his era, and on the other that his greatest crime was in telling the truth. Perhaps the fact that Darrow forgot who was responsible for Orchard's disclosures would not matter if it had been just a strategic device in the trial. But Darrow has kept the fiction alive by saying in his own autobiography that Hawley handed him a good issue by getting Orchard to admit at the end of his examination that he had a wife and child in Ontario.[14]

The Darrow that biographer Charles Harrison admires had "a dignity and sincerity about his appeals that other lawyers fail to achieve," and a "vast, abiding humanity." But this same Darrow used the physical appearance of prosecution witnesses as an object of derision, as he developed the theme that defense witnesses were more honest looking than those of the prosecution. In taking up the testimony of Dewey, the man who had testified to riding the dynamite train, Darrow recalled an experience as a youth on a farm (during what he admitted was the only week of manual labor in his entire life) when he had once seen a sheep-killing dog.

> Now, whenever I think of Dewey, I will know exactly how to classify him, exactly. You remember him; didn't anyone, didn't anybody see his eyes. He didn't look up. He didn't speak. He held his head down, and I suppose for the first time in thirty odd years I remembered my walk on the farm away back in Ohio and that sheep-killing dog. You remember Hawley told him to take the toothpick out of his mouth. He ought to have taken a crowbar and pried it out.

Darrow then went on to compare the face of Dewey with that of Thomas Wood, the defense witness on whom Darrow and Richardson had built the accident theory to explain the Vindicator

---

[14] Darrow, *op. cit.*, p. 150.

explosion. There was an effective maneuver here to establish that the jurors were good judges of character—something every man likes to think he is.

> Now gentlemen, we have got one witness in this case outside of it. I never saw this man until he came to Boise. I don't want you to think that I know anything about him, whether he is honest or dishonest. I never saw Thomas Wood until I saw him here. I don't know any more about him than you twelve men know. But I have spent some time studying human nature. I've been doing that while these poor chumps have been digging in the mines and you people have been plowing corn, and it is not so clean a job but it is pleasanter and more profitable. And I think you gentlemen in your journey through the world, have learned something about human nature, and somehow or other, not always, the Lord stamps upon the face of a man His stamp if he is genuine, just as much as the minter puts the stamp upon the coin. And if he is a hang-dog fellow like Dewey, the Lord has put that upon his face, or for some other reason which providence has so far withheld from me, and he is bound to carry it through his life with him, unfortunately. I am sorry that Dewey has got that sort of a face. Maybe he could not help it, but it is not a face to hang a man on, unless that man should be Dewey. Now, you saw Thomas Wood. To me, Thomas Wood's face shows that he is an honest man. I believe if none of you ever saw him before in your lives, when you looked upon him you thought you looked into the face of an honest man, a man whom you could trust and depend on and believe in. And I believe that when you heard the story you thought you were hearing the story of an honest man. And for anybody to say that the story should be set aside for a moment to give credit to Orchard is a thing too monstrous for me to consider or to talk about.

Other similar references to the appearance of prosecution witnesses were made by Darrow with respect to Bynum and the Denver roominghouse keeper.

Although it was not always explained in the same way, Orchard's reason for killing Steunenberg was another recurring theme in Darrow's argument. Darrow flirted with several explanations of the killing during the speech. Early in the speech he asserted that Orchard thought he could redeem his interest in the mine when he sold it. At several points the attorney reviewed Orchard's threats against Steunenberg as the man who caused him to lose the property, laying the groundwork for the personal revenge theory. But on one occasion Darrow rather recklessly indicated that he believed Orchard was a soldier of fortune who was ready to work for anyone, including the mineowners and the Western Federation of Miners. He also placed considerable emphasis on the possibility that Orchard was a tool of the mine owners, as indicated by his relationship with Sterling. He even touched upon Richardson's "bubble-theory" that the fact that Orchard's victims were still alive was proof that he was not working for the WFM. But he saved for the last session of court his explicit statement of what motivated Orchard.

"Now, let us see about his motive," said Darrow, "and why he did it, gentlemen. Let us see who has the best of this side of the argument." At this moment the *Statesman* writer made an observation that adds insight into the relationship between Darrow and Richardson, albeit no real explanation of why each man ended up with the theory that he did. H. L. Crane noted:

> It was with wicked delight seemingly that Darrow took up and argued the personal grudge motive on Orchard's part for killing Steunenberg. He did not start on that argument without first casting a glance toward Mr. Richardson, who, it will be remembered, while he was arguing the case, suddenly threw overboard the personal motive theory, and in thundering language builded up a theory before the jury that the murder was all a result of a diabolical plot on the part of the Pinkertons . . . When Darrow sent that challenging look toward Richardson he was met by a glance from Richardson which seemed to telegraph: "You take that course at your own risk! I wash my hands of responsibility!" But Darrow shook his head savagely, and began his argument along the line indicated.[15]

In the final analysis, no theory of Orchard's motive was particularly important to Darrow. In a sense, even Haywood himself was not important to Darrow, except as he represented the broader cause that Darrow was advocating. In the peroration Darrow threw all the ethical appeal he could muster into identifying himself, too, with that broader cause of the lower classes in the class struggle.

> Gentlemen, Mr. Hawley has told you that he believes in this case, that he would not ask you to convict unless he believes Haywood was guilty. I tell you, I believe in my case. I believe in it as I believe in my very life, and my belief does not amount, nor his belief does

[15] *Idaho Statesman,* July 26, 1907, p. 1.

not amount to anything or count. I am not an unprejudiced witness in this case. Nobody knows it better than I. My mind is not unbiased in this great struggle. I am a partisan and a strong partisan at that. For thirty years I have been working to the best of my ability in the cause in which these men have given their toil and risked their lives. For thirty years I have given the best ability that the God has given me. I have given my time, my reputation, my chances—all this to the cause which is the cause of the poor. I may have been unwise, I may have been extravagant in my statements, but this cause has been the strongest devotion of my life, and I want to say to you that never in my life did I feel about a case as I feel about this. Never in my life did I wish anything as I wish the verdict of this jury. And if I live to be a hundred years old, never again in my life will I feel that I am pleading a case like this.

At this point, Darrow unleashed his most emotional eloquence. His voice by now was harsh and pathetic, and his eyes were full of tears. Women were openly crying in the courtroom; Haywood's wife sobbed audibly and his mother shed silent tears. Haywood himself sat with head erect, his mouth tightly set, apparently trying to control his emotions. He was visibly affected by Darrow's plea; his face seemed pale to the *Statesman* reporter but flushed to the *Times* correspondent.

I have known Haywood. I have known him well and I believe in him. I do believe in him. God knows it would be a sore day to me if he should ascend the scaffold; the sun would not shine or the birds would not sing on that day for me. It would be a sad day indeed if any calamity could befall him. I would think of him, I would think of his mother, I would think of his babes, I would think of the great cause that he represents. It would be a sore day for me. But, gentlemen, he and his mother, his wife and his children are not my chief concern in this case. If you should decree that he must die, ten thousand men will work down in the mines to send a portion of the proceeds of their labor to take care of that widow and those orphan children, and a million people throughout the length and the breadth of the civilized would will send their messages of kindness and good cheer to comfort them in their bereavement. It is not for them I plead. Other men have died, other men have died in the same cause in which Bill Haywood has risked his life, men strong with devotion, men who love liberty, men who love their fellow men have raised their voices in defense of the poor, in defense of justice, have made their good fight and have met death on the scaffold, on the rack, in the flame. They will meet it again until the world grows old and gray. Bill Haywood is no better than the rest. He can die if die he needs, he can die if this jury decrees it; but, oh, gentlemen, don't think for a moment that if you hang him

> you will crucify the labor movement of the world. Don't think that you will kill the hopes and the aspirations and the desires of the weak and the poor, you men, unless you people who are anxious for this blood—are you so blind as to believe that liberty will die when he is dead? Do you think there are no brave hearts and no other strong arms, no other devoted souls who will risk their life in that great cause which has demanded martyrs in every age of this world? There are others, and these others will come to take his place, will come to carry the banner where he could not carry it. Gentlemen, it is not for him alone that I speak. I speak for the poor, for the weak, for the weary, for that long line of men who in darkness and despair have borne the labors of the human race. The eyes of the world are upon you, upon you twelve men of Idaho tonight. Wherever the English language is spoken, or wherever any foreign tongue known to the civilized world is spoken, men are talking and wondering and dreaming about the verdict of this twelve men that I see before me now. If you kill him your act will be applauded by many. If you should decree Bill Haywood's death, in the great railroad offices of our great cities men will sing your praises. If you decree his death, amongst the spiders of Wall Street will go up paeans of praise for those twelve good men and true who killed Bill Haywood. . . .
>
> There are still those who will reverently bow their heads and thank these twelve men for the life and the character they have saved. Out on the broad prairies where men toil with their hands, out on the wide ocean where men are sailing the ships, through our mills and factories, down deep under the earth, thousands of men and of women and children, men who labor, men who suffer, women and children weary with care and toil, these men and these women and these children will kneel tonight and ask their God to guide your judgment. These men and these women and these little children, the poor, the weak, and the suffering of the world will stretch out their hands to this jury, and implore you to save Haywood's life.

As one might expect, opinions varied considerably on the effect that Darrow achieved with this kind of speaking. The contemporary Socialist press acclaimed the speech enthusiastically, of course, but the more moderate segment of society was divided in its appraisal. The *New York Sun* called it "a vicious appeal to class prejudice."[16] The *Anaconda Standard* considered it a "bitter and intemperate speech,"[17] while the *New York Tribune,* referring to Darrow's "vehement and frothy insinuations," called it "untenable and ridiculous."[18] The strongest language came from the

[16] Quoted in *Capital News,* July 30, 1907, p. 2.
[17] Quoted in *Idaho Statesman,* August 1, 1907, p. 4.
[18] Quoted in *Capital News,* July 30, 1907, p. 2.

Chicago Tribune: ". . . the most unseemly, abusive, inflammatory speech ever delivered in an American courtroom . . . the mud brawling of an anarchist."[19] But the *Idaho Statesman* was surprisingly complimentary to Darrow:

> After listening spellbound to the eloquence of Clarence Darrow yesterday there were many who expressed the belief that if the jury brings in a verdict of acquittal for William D. Haywood, that the Chicago attorney may be the one who won the victory.[20]

"Masterful" was the term the *Statesman* used in editorially characterizing Darrow after the first day of the address:

> [Darrow] has summoned all his powers in the cause in which he is enlisted and will no doubt continue to the end of his argument on the same plane upon which it has been cast and round out an address that will be recognized as one of the great ones in the records of the western courts.
>
> There were many points in his address to which exception could be taken, but throughout he showed great discrimination and tact in pursuing the varying branches of his subject . . . There were times when he dropped somewhat below the general plane of his effort, but in few instances, excepting in his attack on the Christian religion, did he fall into gross error necessarily prejudicing his case. While one thoroughly familiar with the conspirators of whom the man on trial has been one can have no sympathy with the cause Mr. Darrow represents, few will be willing to withhold praise from the advocate for the skillful and eloquent manner in which he is handling a case that is so desperate for the defendant.[21]

This editorial, presumably by Calvin Cobb, showed no indignation at the treatment James Hawley received from Darrow. But another brief item on the same editorial page commented:

> Why did Mr. Darrow mar a fine address by such a villainous attack on J. H. Hawley, counsel for the state? Was it because Mr. Hawley, in his address to the jury, opening all the doors and raising all the shades, let in such a flood of light upon the awful, hideous, satanic murder conspiracy through which Frank Steunenberg was done to death that all the perjury of numerous witnesses for the defense and all the ingenuity and sophistry of counsel cannot blot out the truth from the gaze of the world?[22]

Although he could forgive Darrow's attacks on Christianity and

---

[19] Quoted in *Idaho Statesman,* August 2, 1907, p. 4.
[20] *Idaho Statesman,* July 25, 1907, p. 1.
[21] *Idaho Statesman,* July 25, 1907, p. 4.
[22] *Ibid.*

upon James Hawley, the *Statesman* publisher found after the second day of the address, however, that he could no longer overlook Darrow's antisocial attitude. The lead editorial observed:

> There was never a greater descent than Clarence Darrow made on Thursday. He started out in the morning on a plane that led his hearers to believe he was going to make a great speech, but in the evening he dropped into the depths of socialistic horrors, advocating doctrines that are so abominable that no honest man—not a single honest person on the face of the earth—can tolerate for a moment.[23]

The *New York Times* was similarly impressed with the first day of Darrow's address, but not with the second. It referred to the opening session as a "most brilliant oratorical exhibition." It described Darrow as "a master of invective, vituperation, denunciation, humor, pathos, and all the other arts of the orator, except argument." It observed that in reality Darrow's plea was not addressed to the twelve jurors but to "his Socialist clientele throughout the country."

> Darrow was at his very best as a rhetorician, a special pleader. He was delivering his masterpiece, on which he has worked and studied for eleven weeks or more, ever since this trial began. Whatever the effect upon the jury, he satisfied the crowd in the stifling court room with conspicuous ease. He moved himself to tears and half the court room with him. He made himself the subject of jest, and the bailiffs were obliged to restrain the demonstration of the audience....
>
> . . . Darrow was not making an argument upon the facts that have been presented in the evidence to the jury. He was expressing with passionate eloquence his views on certain phases of life. He was doing the thing which certain friends of the defense had hoped against hope, he would not do, before a jury unused to discussions of the great social problem of responsibility for crime, and unsympathetic to his view of that question, and he was mingling with it a vituperative denunciation of Mr. Orchard, and a sneer at religion, attacking Hawley in the home of his friends, some of whom are jurors, and revealing his contempt for all religion under the guise of a profusion [*sic*] of respect for it.
>
> It was the work of a man grown desperate because of his situation, and striving with all his might for a disagreement of the jury as his utmost hope. But he had the fortitude, while doing that, to make the great bluff, and demand a verdict either of acquittal or of murder in the first degree. The effect that it produced was the

---

[23] *Idaho Statesman,* July 26, 1907, p. 8.

> inevitable result of his masterly skill as an orator, the complete submission of a great part of his audience to his mood. . . . Most of it was at the very stretch of the orator's art, but there were occasional lapses into flippancy and irrelevancy in the beginning, a few references to the jury and the State not calculated to produce a good result. But whatever else it may have been, it certainly was a speech of extraordinary interest from first to last, and there were few of those lucky enough to get into the courtroom who did not endure to the end the discomfort of the midsummer day in order to lose no word of it.[24]

But, by the end of the second day the *Times,* too, was disenchanted. It noted that the jurors were getting quite restless.

> They were tired of Darrow's talk. Perhaps they were tired of all the talk, but whether it was that they don't want to hear any more argument at all, or only that they had heard enough of Darrow's, they certainly took no pains to conceal the fact that they were bored almost to the limits of endurance. They twisted about in their chairs, looked everywhere but at the speaker, shut their eyes, yawned, and in all sorts of ways showed how they felt. Grandfather Russell, who has been the least fidgety and most attentive man of the twelve up to today, suddenly found that the spring in his revolving chair would squeak if properly encouraged, and put in the greater part of the afternoon giving it encouragement, but Darrow kept at it regardless, and would not have quit when he did if the Judge had not interfered.[25]

Another interesting reaction from the jury occurred when one of the men in the second row interrupted Darrow to ask that he stand back farther from the jury box because his speaking at such close range gave the juror a headache.

Darrow attracted a large audience to the courtroom for each session of his speech. During the first day it was predominantly an audience of what Darrow called "working men, socialists and radicals, with idealists and dreamers from every section of America."[26] This kind of audience was very responsive to Darrow's sarcastic humor, and Judge Wood found it necessary to stop the presentation and warn against outbursts of laughter or other demonstrations in the courtroom. During the evening session the audience was somewhat more genteel, due to the fact that

---

[24] *New York Times,* July 25, 1907, p. 5.
[25] *New York Times,* July 26, 1907, p. 2.
[26] Darrow, *op. cit.,* p. 153.

fifty young women who were attending a summer teachers' institute were present. But during the following day it was again predominantly an audience sympathetic to Darrow's cause.

Some interesting observations on Darrow's techniques of delivery have been recorded by eye-witnesses to the trial. Bill Haywood is given credit for this widely quoted observation:

> He had spoken eleven hours. While he spoke he was sometimes intense, his great voice rumbling, his left hand shoved deep in his coat pocket, his right arm unlifted. Again he would take a pleading attitude, his voice would become gentle and very quiet. At times he would approach the jury almost on tiptoe. This speech was, I think, one of Clarence Darrow's greatest.[27]

The *Statesman* described the strenuous physical activity of Darrow's speaking:

> He continually walks up and down before the jury box. He leans forward and talks to the jurors individually, one at a time. He looks them squarely in the eyes. When warmed up to his subject—and he warmed up every minute of his time yesterday—he brings into action every muscle of his body in emphasizing his sentences. He waves his hands. He shrugs his shoulders; he wags and nods and tosses his head about. He bends his knees and he twists his body. And his contortions, if he were not so serious about them, would be almost as interesting as what he says.[28]

These contortions, noted the *Statesman* a day later, took so much out of Darrow that he was worn out on the second day of his speech.

The casual, almost sloppy, appearance of Darrow in courtrooms became in time almost a legend, and the Haywood trial was no exception. The *Capital News* noted with an air of mild disapproval that Darrow wore no vest in the courtroom. To Martin

---

[27] William D. Haywood, *Bill Haywood's Book* (New York: International Publishers, 1929), p. 216. The authenticity of this book has frequently been questioned. According to Benjamin Gitlow, *I Confess, The Truth about American Communism* (New York: E. P. Dutton & Co., 1940), pp. 466-467, Bill Haywood did write the book but with much Communist supervision. It was written in Moscow with the assistance of Lydia Gibson, a Communist Party member. Gitlow approved it for the Comintern, and Alexander Trachtenberg of International Publishers edited it. How much the book reflects Haywood's thinking is a matter of conjecture.

[28] *Idaho Statesman*, July 25, 1907, p. 3.

Maloney this casual appearance was a part of Darrow's "Lincolnesque personality," and of his ability to look and act more like a juror than an attorney.[29] This appearance was, perhaps, a part of the studied theatricality in Darrow's courtroom technique. Ethel Barrymore, after seeing Darrow in action in the Haywood trial, described another of these techniques:

> That was the first I had heard of the flowery Mr. Darrow. He had all the props, an old mother in a wheelchair and a little girl with curls draped around Haywood. I don't know whether she was his daughter or just one of Mr. Darrow's props.[30]

In truth, she was both. Darrow certainly recognized the powerful emotional appeal in having Haywood's young daughter, his invalid wife, and his invalid mother in the courtroom throughout the trial.

Making use of such techniques Clarence Darrow, quite obviously, made an impressive appearance during the two days of his closing argument. But the final word belonged to the prosecution staff, and they, too, could offer an impressive appearance—that of William E. Borah.

---

[29] Maloney, *op. cit.*, p. 300.

[30] Ethel Barrymore, *Memories, An Autobiography of Ethel Barrymore* (New York: Harper and Brothers, 1955), p. 158.

15

WILLIAM E. BORAH for the PROSECUTION

TO WILLIAM E. BORAH went the privilege of closing the argument in the Haywood case. With this privilege went the task of overcoming the inertia established by four straight days of defense argument by two extremely able opponents. The situation was replete with challenge for Borah, particularly since this was to be the last argument of his legal career.

The several-sided career of William Edgar Borah began on June 29, 1865, in a farm house near Fairfield, Illinois. The future senator was one of ten children born to William Nathan Borah and Elizabeth West Borah. The elder Borah was a leader in the Presbyterian Church, and was considered a fine speaker by his friends and neighbors. He enjoyed debating various interpretations of the Bible, especially with Judge Silas D. Bryan who lived some seventy-five miles away but visited the Borah farm often. Apparently on these visits Judge Bryan never brought his son, William Jennings, for there is no record of the soon-to-be-famous sons of farmer Borah and Judge Bryan ever meeting at this time.[1]

[1] Claudius Johnson, *Borah of Idaho* (New York: Longmans, Green and Co., 1936), p. 4. Much of the biographical material in this chapter is from this definitive biography.

The Bible was a strong influence on young Borah's life, as were his father's Presbyterian convictions on the evils of alcohol and the values of the traditional virtues of good character and hard work. But William E. Borah soon displayed the individualism for which he was later famous, and after belonging to the church as a boy he was never again more than a nominal church member. With politics it was different. Lincoln was a saint in the Borah household, and Will followed his father's political philosophy without question.

Education, too, became a strong influence on the boy at an early age. At the Tom's Prairie public school Will was fortunate enough to have as his teacher an ex-college professor, an alcoholic who was an inspirational teacher in his more sober moments. Will developed his speaking ability while he was still at the Tom's Prairie school, and was often called upon on special occasions. Later he enrolled in an institution which has been variously described as Enfield College, Southern Illinois Academy, and Cumberland Presbyterian Academy. Borah remained at Enfield for only one year and did not complete the college preparatory course. During this time he became interested in political speaking, most of which was generated by the Garfield-Hancock election of 1880.

Financial reasons kept Borah from returning to Enfield the next year. He considered joining a road show as an actor—some accounts actually credit him with a six-week career[2]—but when the show folded he gave up this idea. He maintained an interest in the theater, however, and some of his friends continued to see in Borah and his speaking something of the actor he once wanted to be.

Biographers do not account accurately for Borah's activities in the early 1880's, but it must have been a time of decision for him. Eventually he left Fairfield to go to Lyons, Kansas, where one of his older sisters lived. Here he managed to finish another year of public school and then taught a country school briefly. During this time he thought seriously of studying law, influenced

[2] Walter Davenport, "The Man Who Grew Up," *Collier's,* September 10, 1932, p. 11.

largely in this direction by his sister's husband who was a lawyer. In 1885 Borah entered the University of Kansas as a sub-freshman.

At Kansas, William E. Borah scarcely distinguished himself as a typical collegian or as a speaker. He took only one course in elocution. He was most interested in reading and serious study, although he permitted himself the luxury of joining a fraternity. One of his acquaintances of college days, later to become a great friend, was William Allen White of Emporia, the first of the "press corps" to be attracted to the future senator.

Before finishing his freshman year Borah was forced to leave the university because of poor health. He returned to Lyons where he soon regained his health. During this period of convalescence Borah read law books. With the help of his brother-in-law, he passed the relatively easy bar examination in 1887, and launched his legal career in the western Kansas town. Since a young lawyer in this community in the 1880's had more time than business, Borah used his leisure to good advantage by reading extensively. He was particularly interested in histories of the American Revolution, as well as the works of the great essayists such as Emerson. He also read the orations of Cicero, Demosthenes, Sheridan, Fox, Pitt, Burke, Lincoln, Douglas, and Phillips. He practiced his speaking on every occasion, and reportedly wrote a Fourth-of-July oration without having had an invitation to deliver one.

But young Will Borah wanted to do more than rehearse speeches and write practice orations. Seeking greater opportunity than Lyons, Kansas, offered, in 1890 he left the Great Plains, bound for the Pacific Northwest. He intended to investigate Seattle, Washington, as a place to locate. He also planned to check Boise, Idaho, recommended to him by the mayor of Lyons, who had relatives living there.

On the train he met a gambler from Nampa, the mainline junction point for the Boise branch of the railroad. The gambler thought that Boise would indeed have possibilities for a young lawyer. He even offered to throw some business Borah's way to help him get started. With this inducement, William E. Borah arrived in Boise with $15.75 in his pocket.

His career began inauspiciously with cases involving the sporting element of the town, the kind of business the gambler on the train must have envisaged. But soon the young attorney became established and began to develop a sizeable practice. By 1896 he had "arrived" to the degree that he was chosen to represent the sheepmen in the Diamondfield Jack case, and in 1899 he joined with James Hawley in the state's prosecution of Paul Corcoran. After 1900 he represented great mining, livestock, and timber interests.

Borah had wasted no time getting into public life in Idaho. Less than a year after arriving in Boise, he delivered the Fourth-of-July oration, perhaps the same one written in his long hours of leisure in Lyons. He ran for city attorney that same summer, losing by only three votes in what was later admitted to be a rigged election.[3] In 1892 be became chairman of the Republican State Central Committtee, pushing for such liberal planks in the platform as woman suffrage and direct election of senators, measures designed to keep in the Republican party voters who otherwise might be attracted to the reform program of the Populists. By the mid-nineties the Idaho political situation was thoroughly confused, however. A wave of Populism was sweeping the West, and at the same time the national Democratic platform called for free coinage of silver, an issue dear to the hearts of most Idahoans. Borah recognized the impossibility of the position of the old-line Republican organization in Idaho. Along with many others he became a Silver Republican and even ran unsuccessfully for Congress as such in 1896.

In 1900 Borah returned to the regular Republican organization, and by 1902 the Populist movement was dead and Idaho was safely back in the Republican camp. In 1902 Borah contested the nomination for the U. S. Senate in the legislative caucus with W. B. Heyburn, the state's prosecutor in the 1892 Coeur d'Alene cases. Borah lost the nomination, reportedly when Heyburn

[3] Johnson, *op. cit.*, p. 40.

secured the votes of six or seven men for $750 each.[4] Four years later Borah successfully led a campaign to provide for senatorial nominations to originate in state party conventions. Taken out of the legislative caucus, the nomination was easily Borah's, and in the year of "law and order" the Republicans swept Idaho, and the legislature sent Borah to the Senate. Borah missed the satisfaction of defeating Heyburn, but he must have found pleasure in defeating Fred DuBois, the Democrat incumbent who had left the Republican party on the silver issue and had never returned. DuBois represented anti-Mormonism as a political philosophy, an attitude rejected equally by Borah and most Republicans and by the Hawley wing of the Democratic party.

With his election to the Senate, William E. Borah demonstrated that he was a man to be reckoned with. Not only was he an accomplished orator, but he was a man who knew what he wanted and how to get it. He had already used the Haywood case to great personal advantage, and there are those who maintain that he used his closing argument in the trial for the same purpose. In any event, it was a summation speech delivered by an uncommon man under uncommon conditions: Borah was ending his legal career, and he was under a federal indictment for land fraud.

Borah's speech was equal to the occasion. Although it was not the masterpiece that some critics described it to be, it was nevertheless a well planned and executed closing argument. Clarence Darrow, who became famous for his own lack of preparation in jury pleas, later called Borah's presentation ". . . forcible and scholarly. It was worked out with care and understanding. Few men that I ever met in a court room contribute so much industry, learning, and natural ability to a cause as Mr. Borah."[5] There is, however, some question as to the type of "industry" involved in Borah's speech preparation. Several speech scholars have identified Borah primarily as an extemporaneous speaker, while several legal colleagues and friends insist he memorized his speeches almost completely.

---

[4] Johnson, *ibid.*, p. 56.

[5] Clarence Darrow, *The Story of My Life* (New York: Charles Scribner's Sons, 1934), p. 153.

For example, Waldo W. Braden points out that Borah spoke almost entirely from notes after preparation of speech outlines. Braden says, ". . . in speech preparation Borah insisted upon thorough preparation and a complete understanding of his subject. Nevertheless, he preferred to speak extemporaneously, adjusting his presentation to the changing demands of the audience and of the occasion."[6]

A. E. Whitehead agrees that "Borah believed in extemporaneous speaking . . ."[7] But in another analysis Whitehead modifies this view, saying, "Borah outlined his speeches in advance, and it is not likely that many of his beautiful periods were spontaneous. He had the natural gifts and talents of the orator, but in spite of his abilities he knew that cultivation of them was necessary."[8]

Claudius Johnson is careful to qualify chronologically his conclusions regarding Borah's speech preparation. In his later Senate and public speaking, says Johnson, Borah carefully prepared for speeches but delivered them extemporaneously. In his younger days, however, Borah wrote out his speeches in full. With respect to Borah's amount of practice, Johnson makes an interesting observation:

> Because he has often been heard reading aloud, the report has gone abroad that he rehearses his speeches. The Senator denies that he ever rehearsed a speech aloud or before a mirror. On the other hand, several of his companions of the early Boise-lawyer days smile at this denial, admit that perhaps he was just reading, but say that to them he sounded more like a man speaking to empty chairs. But one may easily imagine that when Borah read aloud a selection from some great parliamentary debate or an impassioned plea by some popular tribune, he read with care to reproduce the effect. It may well be, therefore, that eavesdroppers, not so familiar with the masters of oratory as was Borah, were convinced that he was rehearsing a speech.[9]

---

[6] Waldo Braden, "The Bases of William E. Borah's Speech Preparation," *Quarterly Journal of Speech,* February, 1947, p. 30.

[7] A. E. Whitehead, "William E. Borah," in Marie Hochmuth, editor, *A History and Criticism of American Public Address,* Vol. III (New York: Longmans, Green and Co., 1955), p. 397.

[8] A. E. Whitehead, "The Oratory of William Edgar Borah," *Quarterly Journal of Speech,* October, 1946, p. 295.

[9] Johnson, *op. cit.,* p. 26.

There are several men who, indeed, would "smile at this denial." The Boise men who knew Borah intimately—if this was possible with such an enigmatic person—have expressed themselves unequivocally on this question. John MacLane said, "He never made, so far as I know, an impromptu address, but prepared it in advance with the greatest care and detail, memorizing it and delivering it like Mark Antony over the corpse of Caesar."[10] Charles Koelsch agrees that Borah committed his speeches to memory, and regards hard work rather than brilliance as the secret of his success.[11] James Hawley also reports that Borah wrote his speeches out and memorized them, and that Borah would honestly admit this. Hawley illustrates the point with an anecdote. Once, at a bar association banquet at the Natatorium, a famous Boise resort, the speakers had been assigned topics in advance. Most of the lawyers prepared a few ideas, but Borah had memorized his speech. The toastmaster had had a few drinks and was in a playful mood; he deliberately mixed the topics, forcing Borah to speak on another subject. Borah hemmed and hawed briefly, then went ahead with the memorized speech on the original topic. But, later in life, Borah was more adaptable. Young James Hawley once heard Borah speak in the U. S. Senate and congratulated him on his speech. Borah replied that he had not given a speech, but merely a "few remarks."[12]

With this background of Borah's concept of speech preparation, and with the realization that Borah had a full week to prepare his closing argument in the Haywood case, it is easy to conclude that a great amount of preparation went in to the summation speech. This conclusion, however, should be tempered with the fact that Borah in the summer of 1907 was unusually preoccupied with his own legal difficulties.

But it is not the question of preparation that makes Borah's closing argument unique. It is, instead, the question of textual authenticity. For, almost all of the authors who have dealt with Borah's summation, and all the anthologies that have abridged

---

[10] John F. MacLane, *A Sagebrush Lawyer* (New York: Pandick Press, 1953), pp. 166-167.

[11] Conversation with Charles Koelsch, Boise, Idaho, August 1, 1960.

[12] Conversation with James Hawley, Boise, Idaho, August 1, 1960.

the text of the speech, have used as their source a pamphlet entitled *Haywood Trial—Closing Arguments of W. E. Borah,* a text which differs markedly in places from the trial transcript. This pamphlet was published, undated, by the Statesman Shop in Boise, and contains a highly refined and edited speech that is stylistically superior to the one actually given in the courtroom.[13]

This polished speech was abridged in *Classics of the Bar,* a 1909 anthology of forensic speaking, edited by Alvin V. Sellers.[14] It was in this, or perhaps another, collection of forensic speeches that the judge of the United States District Court for the Territory of Hawaii saw the speech, which prompted him to write to Borah:

> A short time ago by sheer accident I became possessed of a book of public speeches in which is included your argument to the jury, years ago in the Haywood trial. It deserves a place among the world's forensic orations, equalling, in my opinion, anything given to us by Henry or Webster or the great English orators. I passed it on to the young assistants to the United States Attorney as a model of the attitude and argument of the prosecutor in cases of highest concern.[15]

Obviously, such praise, based on a corrupt text, could unduly affect an analysis of the speech, unless the critic knew the circumstances surrounding the edited text, and kept his wits accordingly.

In the Borah collection of the Idaho Historical Society are three different versions of the speech. The first is a typewritten carbon copy on legal size paper, apparently a copy of the actual transcript. Corrections are handwritten on this copy in what appears to be Borah's handwriting (by comparison with the handwritten *Brief Book of W. E. Borah* in the same collection). Corrections do not occur throughout the text, but are concentrated in relatively few spots that seem to mark emotional climaxes in the speech. A second copy is in ditto, and incorporates the changes

---

[13] W. E. Borah, *Haywood Trial—Closing Arguments of W. E. Borah* (Boise, Idaho: The Statesman Shop, n. d.).

[14] Alvin V. Sellers, *Classics of the Bar* (Baxley, Georgia: Classics Publishing Co., 1909).

[15] Quoted in Whitehead, *Q. J. S.*, p. 292.

on the original. A third copy is the printed pamphlet which differs in only a few minor respects from the dittoed version.[16]

To illustrate the extent of the changes between the true and the edited speech text, compare the style of the transcript and pamphlet version as Borah spoke of Darrow's intimation that the state was trading in lives, with respect to Orchard and Haywood:

Transcript	*Pamphlet*
We are not asking for vicarious atonements. Fighting Haywood for Harry Orchard? Trading in blood? You may turn him loose, but you will never get twelve men in the state of Idaho that will turn Harry Orchard loose, and you can never get a man in this state who will turn him loose afterwards as governor. And I hope if the man who planted that bomb is ever compromised by me or with my connivance, I hope the great God will wither my right arm in its socket. We are only using him for the very purpose which we are entitled to, but there is no compromise, and there won't be . . . And I want to say to you that the man who intimates that I would compromise with Harry Orchard does not understand a single drop of blood that circulates in my body.	We are not asking for vicarious atonements. Fighting Haywood for Harry Orchard? Trading in blood? You may turn *him* loose, but you will never get twelve men in the State of Idaho who will turn Harry Orchard loose and you will never find a man in this State who will, as Governor, turn him loose. And I trust that if ever I compromise with the man who planted that bomb at Steunenberg's gate that the great God will wither my right arm until it falls from its socket. We are only using him for the very purpose which we are entitled to use him, to bring other guilty men to punishment. But there is no compromise, and there will not be; no immunity, and there will not be . . . And I want to say to you that the man who intimates that I would compromise with Harry Orchard does not understand the kind of blood that circulates in my body. He does not know the love I bore the dead.

The differences in text are even more pronounced at the conclusion of the speech which will soon be considered.

[16] Copies of the speech were received and acknowledged as early as September 12, 1907, by individuals who had requested them in letters and telegrams immediately following the speech. There is no indication whether these copies were dittoed copies or printed pamphlets. It is interesting to speculate on the possibility that Borah's pending trial in the land fraud case might have prompted the rapid distribution of copies of the Haywood speech, to build public support for the Senator.

The rhetorical invention of the edited text does not depart from that of the actual speech. Borah's closing argument, as delivered, was a 5½-hour review of the conspiracy case that the state had built against Haywood. It inferred the existence of the conspiracy throught the acts of its members, together with certain documentation. Unlike the other attorneys, Borah did not attempt to deal with all of the evidence in depth and with any events other than the Steunenberg murder and the Bradley affair. Although the speech was relatively brief, it was delivered over three sessions of court. About one quarter of the total speech was given during an evening session of court on Thursday, July 25, 1907, after Clarence Darrow had occupied a morning and afternoon session the same day. On Friday, July 26, Borah reached about the three-quarter mark in his speech during a morning session, and concluded during an evening session. His general approach varied with the session; with one exception, Borah used his most dramatic and emotional appeals in the evening sessions and a more subdued legal logic in the daytime.

Conditions in the courtroom remained oppressive. On both days the temperature reached 89°. On Thursday, after the long day in the courtroom, Borah announced after speaking only an hour, "I would like to close this evening for it is too hot here to proceed." On Friday evening it was just as hot, and the room was jammed full of spectators; at least one thousand people were turned away from this session. As might be expected, Borah's overflow audience was drawn largely from the local citizenry, and included such prominent people as Governor Gooding and Mrs. Frank Steunenberg. As Darrow observed:

> There was a marked contrast between the audience during his argument and mine . . . Mr. Borah finished his argument in an evening session on a Saturday [*sic*] night. The courtroom was packed with the elite of Boise and all the State. All of them were dressed as though attending a social event, which indeed it was. The common people had been given their opportunity in the afternoon. The courtroom had been thoroughly aired, if not fumigated, during the recess. The elect now had their turn.[17]

It was Thursday, of course, when the "common people" prevailed

---

[17] Darrow, *op. cit.*, p. 154.

in the afternoon and the "elite" in the evening, but the interesting comparison of audiences is not weakened by Darrow's misrecollection of details.

Borahs began on Thursday evening with a number of random impressions of and reactions to the trial and the preceding arguments. He first paid the traditional compliments to the jury for their service. Acknowledging that he was in the case as a special prosecutor, he defended the much maligned Canyon County prosecutor, Owen Van Duyn. He went on to defend another colleague, James Hawley, but it was hardly a spirited or vigorous defense:

> I know of no reason why a man who has lived in this community for forty years and whose loyalty to his clients has never been questioned should be attacked apparently upon the theory even of corruption. The burden of this case has been upon him. He has been the man who has had charge of it in large measure, and you saw the condition to which his health had arrived at the time that he appeared before you. Perhaps he was more irritable at times than he should have been with Mr. Darrow. Perhaps he was not as pleasant upon all occasions as counsel for the defense would have him be. But you must be satisfied with one proposition, and that is that he simply, fairly and earnestly presented such evidence as the state had here and asked at your hands a verdict, and nothing more.

Borah told the jurors that one thing had been indisputably established by the trial: that terrible conditions had existed in the Rocky Mountain area during the preceding five years. Then he began a refutation of some of Darrow's major themes. In rather abstract terms, he denied that the trial represented more than a murder trial:

> There is here no fight on organized labor. This is simply a trial for murder. Frank Steunenberg has been murdered, and we want to know. A crime has been committed, and the integrity and the manhood of Idaho wants to know. An offense which shocked the civilized world has taken place within our borders, and unless we went about it earnestly and determinedly to know, we would [be] unfit to be called a commonwealth in the sisterhood of commonwealths of the Union.

For a moment he put himself in Darrow's place, in an effort to discredit Darrow's persuasive techniques:

> But if I were fighting for the cause of labor, and there are possibly some friends of labor aside from those who flaunt it to the four

> winds—if I were fighting for the cause of labor I wouldn't seek to engender hatred and ill will, faction against faction, or class against class; I would not inveigh against law; I wouldn't inveigh against society; I wouldn't inveigh against every man who owned his farm or his home; I wouldn't inveigh against Christianity, because without those things the laboring man goes down into slavery and dirt. You had an account of it in the French Revolution. You had a history of in the fall of the Roman Empire. The moment that one class is arrayed against the other, that faction is against faction, the man who goes to the bottom first is the man who toils; and his only protection, his only safety is in the flag; the integrity of the state, the integrity of the law, the integrity of the union. The only protection which he has is in the integrity of this fabric under which we have lived and under which he has prospered more than any other place upon the face of the earth.

It is interesting to contrast the abstract words that Borah used in this passage to the more concrete words used by Darrow in a similar passage. Where Darrow had spoken of "human life . . . the father . . . the wife . . . the little child . . . rugged, unlettered men . . . strong right arm . . . the poor and the weak . . . serfs . . . free men," Borah talked about "faction . . . class . . . society . . . history . . . flag . . . integrity of the state . . . the law . . . the union . . . the integrity of this fabric." With this theme Borah did not achieve the same degree of personification or identification that Darrow obtained; Borah socialized, but Darrow humanized the problem.

But the psychological advantage belonged to Borah throughout the speech, since he and the jurors were fellow Idahoans while Darrow was an outsider from far off Chicago. Referring to Darrow's justification of violence, Borah reminded the jurors what the defense attorney had said:

> Why, he says, if you can get a thousand men together to go and do that thing it is proof positive that it ought to be done. That may be so in Chicago but it isn't so in Idaho. There is only one rule here, and that is whether you are a mine owner, a scab or a union man, you are entitled to the protection of the law and to the preservation of your property and the protection of your life.

Woven between Borah's denials of Darrow's assertions were references to the law of conspiracy, the criminal record of the Western Federation of Miners, and the inconsistency of the defense position. In a neat bit of double-barrelled sarcasm, Borah declared that if Harry Orchard had not implicated the WFM officials, Darrow would now be defending Orchard. "And instead of hearing him argue upon the leader of the Western Federation of Miners you would have had a chance to hear him upon Harry Orchard, the man of unblemished character, as was said by the firm of Richardson & Hawkins in November of 1904."

Borah then turned to what Darrow had described as Orchard's worst crime.

> But another thing, perhaps the most awful thing that occurred in this case, and the one which Mr. Darrow pointed out with all the pathos and eloquence of an Ingersoll,—the fact that this man who had killed fifteen or twenty men came on the witness stand and told you what his true name was.

When he pointed out that the defense had drawn out this information, Borah was interrupted by Richardson and Darrow denying that they had done so. An exchange took place, but Borah's keen memory proved correct and the judge told him to continue.

Borah then argued that no man could maintain a lie as complicated and involved as the story of Orchard's movements from 1899 through 1905, particularly when cross-examined repeatedly on the essential details. This point of view, interestingly enough, was the position that Judge Wood took one year later in passing judgment on Harry Orchard. Had Borah been able to get Judge Wood to include this observation in his instructions to the jury, the Haywood trial might have had a different outcome.

When Borah took up the question of religion, he borrowed a page from Clarence Darrow and used the same technique of personal illustration which the defense attorney had utilized. In a long passage containing insight into his boyhood, Borah said:

> Now, gentlemen of the jury, Mr. Darrow testified to some extent with reference to his religious views, and as he is not an expert, nor neither am I on that subject, I desire to testify just a little. In the first place, his statement reminded me of an experience which I had when I was a small boy, raised up in family of Cumberland Presbyterian parents. About the time I had arrived at an age when I knew precisely how the world had been created and that it was made by some force other than divine power, I got hold of a book

> written by Colonel Ingersoll on the mistakes of Moses, and I was perfectly fascinated with the story. I learned that this man whom my father had been reading about in family prayers for a number of years was a worse man [than] Darrow's Orchard. He had killed an Egyptian and hid him in the sand, and had done a great many other things which are unnecessary to mention here, and I was perfectly fascinated with the story. One day while I was sitting out under a tree reading the book, when I ought to have been pulling weeds out of the corn, father came along and asked me what I was reading; I closed up the book and like Pettibone, concluded I would keep still, so I said nothing. Father thinking my silence, under such circumstances, was an admission of guilt, reached over and took the book and I did not read any more out of that volume. Some other things happened which are unnecessary to mention also. I went my way, disconsolate. I did not have any Ingersoll, and I did not know what to do. Finally one day I got hold of the life of Napoleon Bonaparte, and I read it until I came to the conclusion that Napoleon Bonaparte was a greater man than Ingersoll—the greatest genius in war or statesmanship that ever lived, and I came to this story of his Egyptian campaign; I read of how when he started from Paris he took with him a lot of philosophers from Paris, a lot of savants from the French salons, learned men, wise men, philosophers, men who were teaching in that day that there was no difference between the barbarian who kneeled with unmeaning words at the foot of a blackened idol, an Egyptian, and still those who look up to God upon Calvary and ask direction; he took with him the philosophers who had been raised up in an atmosphere of that character, and they were riding out upon the boat one night and discussing the question of no God, no religion, that it was all a matter of manhood—nothing higher than the man, and they turned to Napoleon and asked him for an opinion, and Napoleon said to them, "Tell me who made that firmament and I will discuss this question with you;" and the philosopher was at the end of his journey. And I say to you that while I am not a religionist and not a hypocrite, that it is too late in this the morning of the twentieth century, too late to write upon the brow of Him upon Calvary "Imposter;" too late to write upon the brow, "False Prophet," of Him who said, "This day shalt thou be with Me in paradise."

The reference to "men who were teaching in that day that there was no difference between the barbarian who kneeled with unmeaning words at the foot of a blackened idol . . ." made it clear that Borah was taking a direct stand against Darrow's liberal theology. Under other circumstances, Borah himself might have championed this liberal theology, but he was this day the spokesman for a rather doctrinal faith. Defending the validity of Orchard's conversion, he said:

> In our strength and pride we are given over to mockery and derision; in the hour of success we are all of us more or less blasphemous and inclined to declare as the fool did, that there is no God; but when we are cast down, things are altogether different,— in the night of [despair] every sinner of us turns at last to the old book which our mothers love.

This must have been a powerful passage to an audience conditioned to the homiletic style of fundamentalist America in 1907.

After this wave of eloquence on the question of Orchard's atonement, Borah then subsided into a quieter discussion of the requirements of corroboration. A few minutes later he announced his intention of ending for the evening.

On Friday morning, July 26, 1907, the Senator resumed his argument. He announced for the first time his organizational plan for the speech on which he was already embarked; it would involve grouping the evidence under four points.

> I want to call your attention to the first point, and that is whether or not a conspiracy existed; whether there was an agreement upon the part of four or five certain men whom I shall name, to commit a crime and to do violence to those whom they believed to be antagonistic and unfriendly to the Western Federation of Miners. Second, was the defendant a member of that conspiracy,—did he know that it existed,—did he aid, abet, assist and encourage any one in the commission of that crime; third, is Harry Orchard telling the truth in this case; and fourth is there sufficient corroborative evidence of itself to tend to connect the defendant Haywood with the crime, aside from Orchard's testimony. I want you to keep these four propositions in mind and be patient with me while I go through some of this evidence, and of course I will have to travel over territory that has been covered and much of it more successfully than I can do.

Borah further explained that he intended to work backwards from the Steunenberg murder, rather than in the chronological pattern followed in the other summation speeches, and that he did not plan to deal with any of the events of the labor war in Colorado. He explained that these events of 1903-04 were irrelevant in the case, but nevertheless disturbing:

> I am not here to defend the mine owners,—I don't care anything about them. I am not here to defend the militia—I don't care anything about that. I am not here to criticize them farther than

> to say that I apprehend that the time will come when Colorado will awaken to the fact that there ought to be something in Colorado better than militia, better than the question of union men or non-union men, and that is the manhood, the integrity and the patriotism of the state.

After discussing Steunenberg's death, Borah took up Orchard's close relationships with the men of the "Inner Circle" during the summer of 1905 as he was preparing to go to Caldwell to kill the governor. Borah argued that it was difficult to find any explanation of Orchard's leaving Denver bound for Caldwell, except that the "Inner Circle" was responsible. He went on to assert that all the documentary evidence in the case supported Orchard's story—such things as telegrams, registered letters, deeds, etc., the things that cannot be tampered with as witnesses can.

Reviewing the testimony of some of the witnesses who tended to discredit Orchard, Borah in turn sought to discredit these witnesses. He noted that Dave Coates, onetime lieutenant-governor of Colorado, did nothing to alert Paulson to the kidnapping attempt, but actually helped Orchard get money from Paulson to go to Caldwell. Eugene Engley, once Colorado's attorney general, knew of Orchard's threats, yet failed to go to the authorities in January of 1906 with this information before Orchard turned against the Western Federation of Miners. John O'Neill, who wrote the vicious obituary on Steunenberg in the *Miner's Magazine,* was capable of murder, and had actually turned out to be a murderer. Any feelings that Orchard might have had toward Steunenberg, said Borah, were insignificant alongside the sentiments expressed in this official Western Federation magazine.

Then Borah described the coming and going of various men in the Federation: Simpkins, Orchard, Haywood, Moyer, and Pettibone. "This," said the *Oregonian,* "was done carefully and almost monotonously—the quiet before the storm. Then Mr. Borah's voice and manner changed. He sprang into action. His voice quivering and hand upraised, fingers outstretched, he shouted:"[18]

> Watch these five men. In a little over thirty days Frank Steunen-

[18] *Portland Oregonian,* July 27, 1907, p. 1.

> berg is going to die. What are their actions? They are going to and fro, their association, their connection—you will find out whether there is evidence here or not to show a conspiracy outside of any testimony of Harry Orchard.

"The dramatic utterance and tense figure of the pleader sent a thrill through the court room. For a space of ten seconds there was silence. Then relaxing, Mr. Borah continued with his merciless logic."[19] This bit of drama, the only emotional climax of the daytime session of Borah's argument, occurred about midway through the session.

The balance of the session was taken up in a lackluster review of the incriminating features of Simpkins' movements, the letter transactions, the arrangements for Hogan's lawyers, and other features of the alleged conspiracy. Borah concluded with a discussion of the Bradley affair in which he tried, rather unsuccessfully, to explain the flat roof that had consistently damaged Orchard's story. Using logic that could hardly be called "merciless," Borah minimized the importance of the exact details of the roof, noting that Orchard had said only that he got on a flat roof somewhere around the back porch. The fact that this information was brought out in cross-examination, argued Borah, proved that the story was not built on manufactured evidence.

Senator Borah opened the final evening session of court with a bit of humor designed to answer Darrow's challenge to the final prosecution pleader to deal with the question of whether defense witnesses had perjured themselves.

> Mr. Darrow wanted to know if I would say that Dr. McGee was a liar, and I will say to Mr. Darrow that I will not say that Dr. McGee is a liar or was a liar, because I am not in the habit of saying that in the court room any more times [than] I can help, and I never say it to a man as large as Doctor McGee outside of the court room.

He went on to say that he thought McGee was honestly mistaken, because McGee had first said the events took place in 1905, which would have been consistent with the rest of the evidence, before insisting it was 1904. Borah's position here was in direct contrast to Hawley's; the senior prosecuting attorney had said McGee

[19] *Ibid.*

deliberately perjured himself. (McGee, incidentally, had been released for lack of evidence on the perjury charge earlier in the week, but had been rearrested on the day that Borah concluded his argument.) Borah might have given Hawley better support at this point, but apparently he did not wish to weaken his own reasonableness by backing up any of Hawley's weaker assertions. Darrow's challenge to confirm or deny perjury on the part of the Cripple Creek roominghouse keepers went unanswered.

Moving rapidly to clear up numerous details that remained to be covered, Borah next answered the defense inference that Harry Orchard was a Pinkerton detective by arguing that if this were true, Orchard would have gone to great lengths to get and preserve documentation of all of the transactions in which he had been involved, since this evidence would have been extremely damaging. The Senator also read again to the jury the no-violence contract signed by the Western Federation of Miners in Telluride, to show the jurors that the union had unwittingly left behind damaging documentation of its purposes and methods. He digressed into a rambling discussion of the Colorado events he had told the jury he would not consider. He chided Darrow for not putting Steve Adams on the witness stand, although he admitted that most lawyers, under the circumstances also would have prevented Adams from testifying. Rather briefly, he took Darrow to task for his doctrine that laws and constitutions were for the rich alone.

Somewhat abruptly, Borah arrived at his peroration. Now he began his emotional appeal particularly addressed to the jurors' sense of honor and duty. The old virtues that William Nathan Borah had taught his son were given heavy stress; such words as *duty, faithful, humanity, manhood, brave, courage* punctuated the closing moments of the speech.

> You have been patient and considerate in this case in the extreme. The great task imposed upon you, the great trust reposed in you, has stimulated and sustained you throughout this long and tedious trial and you have watched and listened and been faithful. You are carrying with you tonight the solicitude of an entire people. There is no home in Idaho tonight but that a thought of you and your final duty will mingle with the sentiment which made that home possible. Very soon the court and the faithful officers and the attorneys will

> pass into the background and all thoughts and all considerations will be with you, the twelve men selected and sworn and solemnly charged to perform the most important and solemn task ever given to twelve men in the state of Idaho. You will never again occupy a position so important in all its bearings as you occupy now. On the one hand there is the defendant; upon the other the State. If he has not been proven guilty under the measure of the law, he must be released and given his freedom. On the other hand, if this case has pointed you to the man or the men who conceived and caused to be carried into execution this dire and awful crime, then in the name of the humanity of the state and of the manhood of the state you will do your duty without dread of men or the fear of men.

In a final wave of emotion, Borah fashioned an unforgettable image for the jurors. In quiet, almost pleading, tones he concluded:

> After this trial has been finished, after the work is over, after the excitement has died away the thing which will remain with us is that sleepless mentor of the soul asking over and over again as the years go by were you brave and faithful in the discharge of the most solemn duty of [your] life? You have no doubt often in this case been moved by the eloquence of counsel for the defense. They are men of wonderful powers. They have been brought here because of their power to sway the minds of men. It has been their part and duty and in loyalty to their clients, as it seems to be, to sometimes draw you away from the consideration of the real facts in this case; to beguile you from a consideration of your real and only duty. But as I listened to the voice of counsel and felt for a time their great influence there came to me after the spell was broken another scene. There came to me in more moving tones than of voices—I remembered again the awful thing of December 30th, 1905, a night which has added ten years to the life of some who are in this court room now. I felt again its cold and icy chill, faced the drifting snow and peered at last into the darkness for the sacred spot where last lay the body of my dead friend, and saw true, only too true, the stain of his life's blood upon the whitened earth. I saw Idaho dishonored and disgraced. I saw murder—no, not murder, a thousand times worse than murder; I saw anarchy wave its first bloody triumph in Idaho. And as I thought again I said "Thou living God, can the talents or the arts of counsel unteach the lesson of that hour?" No, no. Let us be brave, let us be faithful in this supreme test of trial and duty. If the defendant is entitled to his liberty, let him have it. But, on the other hand, if the evidence in this case discloses the author of this crime, then there is no higher duty to be imposed upon citizens than the faithful discharge of that particular duty. Some of you men have stood the test and trial in the protection of the American flag. But you

> never had a duty imposed upon you which required more intelligence, more manhood, more courage than that which the people of Idaho assign to you this night in the final discharge of your duty.

The passage just cited is what Borah said, according to the transcript, in closing his argument in the Haywood case. The pamphlet version of the speech not only has perfected this paragraph, but it contains three additional paragraphs containing those passages most frequently quoted by the writers who have described Borah's speaking in the trial:

> *Soon these men will be gone, their homes are elsewhere, and as brothers of the bar I wish them well. They look for protection to other States, to other laws. But we remain and with us remains the solemn duty of protecting life and property, of standing by the State you have helped to build and within whose borders you have planted the reign of law. Gentlemen, I do not want innocent men convicted, heaven knows I do not thirst for innocent blood. Counsel for the defense have tried to make you believe that we would have professional distinction at the cost of human liberty or life. There has been something in this case to make a man forget all professional pride. I only want what you want—murder stopped in Idaho. I only want what you want—human life made safe—assassination put out of business. I only want what you want—the gate which leads to our homes, the yard gate whose inward swing tells of the returning husband and father, shielded and guarded by the courage and manhood of Idaho juries.*
>
> *But they say it is a solemn thing to take life. True, very true. But the fearless performance of duty by courts and juries protects society and prevents the spread of murder and anarchy. In the older days when man walked closer to his God and heard more clearly the admonitions of the moral teachings under which we must thrive or perish, it was said, "By man's blood shall man's blood be shed." He who takes life in the malice of the heart forfeits his right to live—for the sake of society, for the sake of all men who love their fellow men and want to live with them in peace—he forfeits his right to live. It has been so from the beginning, so by the sanction of Him who provides all things for the good of the children of men. If this be true where individual man slays but another, ten thousand times more true it be where men in hatred and malice, in stealth and in secrecy combine, confederate and agree to carry on and commit indiscriminate murder, where men defy law, denounce society, trample upon all rights, human and divine, and thirst for the blood of all who chance to thwart or oppose their criminal purposes. Anarchy, pale, bloodless, restless, hungry demon from the crypts of hell—fighting for a foothold in Idaho! What shall we do? This is the question. Shall we crush it, shall we make it unsafe for the*

> *disciples of this creed to do business here, or shall we palter and trim and compromise and invite it to choose other victims? These are the questions to be settled by you and you alone. It is up to you. In the court of your own conscience the verdict must be worked out and I must leave it all with you. Yet I hesitate to close. This matter lies nearer my heart than anything in my whole life. Nevertheless I can but turn the matter over to you for your final action. Thanking you for the State for your long and devoted service and bidding you have courage for your final great duty, I leave the State's interests with you.*[20]

These extra paragraphs, particularly the references to anarchy and to the yard gate on which the Steunenberg bomb had been planted, have been quoted in numerous accounts. Charles Harrison cites passages from them in his biography of Darrow. In Charles Koelsch's pamphlet on the Haywood trial and in a biographical sketch of Borah by C. P. Connolly[21] the edited text is not only quoted, but given an air of authenticity since Koelsch and Connolly were both in the courtroom during the trial. Even in two recent books, *The Good Years* by Walter Lord and *Borah* by Marian McKenna,[22] the fiction of Borah's polished eloquence is kept alive. The research for these latter books was done at the Idaho Historical Society in Boise *after* this organization came into possession of the original transcript text of the speech and a dittoed preliminary draft of the pamphlet version.

But perhaps the thing that has made the analysis of Borah's closing speech difficult is not the wide distribution of the edited text, but rather the wide dependence upon Oscar King Davis' overly enthusiastic report of the speech in the *New York Times*. One phrase in Davis's story—a reference to Borah's "marshaling of the evidence"—has been repeated in the writing of Lord, Holbrook, Johnson, Koelsch, and MacLane, all of whom have drawn conclusions favorable to Borah. Claudius Johnson in his biography of Borah specifically cites the *Times* account,[23] as does A. E.

---

[20] Borah, *op. cit.*, pp. 128-130.

[21] C. P. Connolly, "Presidential Possibilities: Borah of Idaho," *Collier's*, July 31, 1915, p. 28.

[22] Marian C. McKenna, *Borah* (Ann Arbor: University of Michigan Press, 1961), pp. 57-61.

[23] Johnson, *op. cit.*, p. 82.

Whitehead in his rhetorical analysis of Borah's speaking.[24] When one considers that Davis and Borah were warm personal friends, and that at the time of the summation speech Davis had already written to President Roosevelt asking that the land fraud indictment against Borah be dropped,[25] it seems necessary to discount some of Davis' glowing statements, even though there is no discounting the influence of his coverage of the trial on later writers.

This is what Davis wrote, after hearing the Friday sessions of Borah's speech:

> It has been many a day since anything like the speech which Senator Borah made this morning in his closing argument in the trial of W. D. Haywood, charged with the murder of ex-Gov. Steunenberg, was delivered in any courtroom in this country. With wonderful lucidity, with deadly precision, he gathered up the vital facts of the whole case, and, brushing away all the mass of sophistry and immateriality, presented a vivid living picture of the conspiracy and showed the conspiracy at their work.
>
> It was a display of intellectual power that amounted almost to revelation. The personal effect of it was overwhelming, terrific. It carried the crowded courtroom breathless and spellbound before it, and when it came to an end, with the noon adjournment, it left the audience oppressed with the feeling that they had seen the flashing sword of justice.
>
> It was not a personal arraignment of Haywood. There was nothing of invective or denunciation or vituperation or hate in it. It was simply an overpowering marshaling of the evidence presented by the prosecution. And Haywood understood. He sat with face held steady, fronting his accuser, but a dull flush covering it that told in a manner no words could deny of the thumping heart beneath. The wife and mother knew it, too, and on their faces there was a revelation of pain no power of pride could prevent, and the lawyers also knew. Darrow and Richardson strove in vain to hide their feelings.
>
> Even Pete Breen, the dynamiter from Butte, for once lost the sneer of contempt from his expression and sat with white face and downcast eyes. There is little ease in trying to convey an adequate picture of it all. The dingy courtroom was lighted up by a flame of living fire as this man stood there pleading the cause of outraged law, crying in the name of manhood and the integrity of the State,

[24] Whitehead, in Hochmuth, *op. cit.*, pp. 401-402.

[25] Acknowledged in letter, Theodore Roosevelt to Oscar King Davis, July 20, 1907, in Elting E. Morison, editor, *The Letters of Theodore Roosevelt,* Vol. V (Cambridge: Harvard University Press, 1952), pp. 722-723.

not for the blood of any man, but for justice to the murderers of Frank Steunenberg.

The charm in the magnetism about the personality of Borah lent emphasis to the force of his speech. His is a mental engine of amazing power. It runs at terrific speed and at every revolution it throws out a fact, an argument, an assertion, an inference, the logical connection of which is instantly apparent.

Terrific, crushing, destroying, these are the words that come nearest to describing the tremendous power of the man in argument and the tremendous effect of his speech. He is not a large man physically, of medium height, with a big barrel of a body, surmounted by a big head, and there is nothing about him as he goes along the street to attract attention or differentiate him from his fellows. But in action he is a different being. His face lights up, his eyes gleam, he radiates power. His gift of speech is wonderful. His words flow with astonishing rapidity, but they always go straight to the mark. There never is any hesitation, never any uncertainty. Endowed with the highest dramatic power, he seizes unerringly the telling point, rushes along with tremendous energy and deadly precision the climax, and with a burst of eloquence drives home and clinches his conclusion.

That is perhaps the most distinguishing feature of his performance, its absolute lucidity. It is not merely that he never deviates from the line of his argument, but that every word he utters as he goes along is absolutely necessary to the clear presentation of his thought. There is no superfluity, and there is no repetition. What he says simply had to be said, and when it is said he turns to something else.[26]

Lavish as it is, this report by Davis is the most complete extant criticism of Borah's summation by an eye-witness. It is difficult today, in reading the transcript, to share Davis' enthusiasm for the superlative logic and lucidity he describes, but it is nevertheless clear that in the hands of a dramatic pleader—and Borah was indeed an actor—there are portions of the argument that could be as powerful and convincing as Davis thought they were.

Other contemporary critics had similar reactions. Newsmen quoted Clarence Darrow as saying that Borah's argument was the fairest and ablest he had ever heard in a criminal court. "There were several things he might have said and remained within his

---

[26] *New York Times,* July 27, 1907, p. 3.

rights, but he did not touch them. His conduct of the case throughout has been eminently fair."[27] Even Bill Haywood conceded, "I have heard the best of them all over the country, but Borah beats them all."[28]

It remained to be seen whether Borah could beat Bill Haywood.

---

[27] *Ibid.*

[28] *Portland Oregonian,* July 27, 1907, p. 3.

16

THE JURY DECISION

On July 27, 1907, Judge Fremont Wood instructed the jury in the Haywood case. The importance of the Judge's instructions in a case of this type has been characterized by Justice Felix Frankfurter of the United States Supreme Court:

> Charging a jury is not a matter of abracadabra. No part of the conduct of a criminal trial lays a heavier task upon the presiding judge. The charge is that part of the whole trial which probably exercises the weightiest influence upon jurors. It should guide their understanding after jurors have been subjected to confusion and deflection from the relevant by the stiff partisanship of counsel.[1]

Judge Wood's instructions were for the most part concerned with the law regarding presumption of innocence, burden of proof, reasonable doubt, conspiracy, corroboration, and circumstantial evidence. They have generally been regarded as favoring the defense. As MacLane recalled,

> After the addresses to the jury Judge Wood instructed them as to the law, emphasizing throughout the necessity of corroboration of Orchard's testimony and confession by witnesses not parties to the alleged conspiracy. As I recall, one of his frequent expressions in one form or another was that even if they believed Orchard's testi-

[1] Felix Frankfurter, concurring in *Andres v. United States,* 333 U. S. 765.

> mony and though they did not believe that Haywood was innocent, they should not convict unless they were convinced beyond a reasonable doubt from independent testimony corroborative of Orchard that Haywood was guilty.[2]

Charles Koelsch, who, like MacLane and Wood, was also district judge for Ada County, agrees that Wood repeated certain features of the instructions unnecessarily. Koelsch, in his 21 years on the bench, gave each point of the instructions but once.[3]

Judge Wood presented sixty-five instructions to the jury. The defense had offered about the same number of their own, but the Court accepted only five in modified form and rejected all the others. It is worth noting that the jury was in the courtroom during the presentation of the defense's set of instructions, so the jurors heard a number of statements of law that they might have confused with the actual instructions. Some of the defense instructions were remarkably similar to the final set promulgated by Judge Wood, but some had no basis in law, e.g., one that said that detectives should be given less credence than other witnesses.

Of these sixty-five instructions, at least ten dealt with reasonable doubt and a comparable number with the legal requirements of corroboration. It is this repetition to which Judge Koelsch referred. The instructions, says MacLane,

> . . . were strongly criticized in high quarters, particularly by Governor Gooding who went around the state denouncing Wood on every occasion with all the billingsgate of which he was capable. Personally I think Wood leaned over backwards because he was so convinced himself that Orchard had told the truth and thought that the jury would convict, he wanted to protect the reputation of a fair trial which he had helped to establish, and secure general approval of the conviction. In any event, my subsequent experience as Wood's successor on the bench, during which I presided over many criminal trials including several for murder, convinced me that Wood's instructions were generally sound and calculated to protect the prosecution from liability to reversal by a higher court. The mass of tripe imposed on State trial judges, by decisions of Supreme Courts of various western States operating under the California Code, by way of instructions to the jury in the criminal cases is

---

[2] John F. MacLane, *A Sagebrush Lawyer* (New York: Pandick Press, 1953), p. 168.

[3] Conversation with Charles Koelsch, Boise, Idaho, August 1, 1960.

> calculated only to so completely befuddle and confuse the mind of the juror that he can only conclude that any process of reasoning which he may follow is justified so long as it results in a verdict of acquittal.[4]

Justice Frankfurter seems to agree with this point of view. "To avoid reversal on appeal," he points out, "trial judges err, as they should, on the side of caution. But caution often seeks shelter in meaningless abstractions devoid of guiding concreteness."[5]

Another observer felt that Judge Wood had erred on the side of caution. O. K. Davis, nearly twenty years later, reported a conversation he had had with Judge Wood while the two men were on a weekend fishing trip during the trial. Wood had said, "Haywood is guilty and has been convicted. I believe he will be hanged, for I don't see how it can be upset." After hearing this opinion, Davis could not understand why the judge stressed reasonable doubt so constantly in his charge to the jury, nor why Wood failed to use only the definition of reasonable doubt in a then-recent decision of the Idaho Supreme Court, the court which would have heard any appeals from the Haywood verdict.[6]

All accounts of the actual jury decision in the Haywood trial point up the influence that the instructions had in the jury room. The most complete account of the twenty hours of deliberation was reported in an interview given to the *Idaho Statesman* by Samuel D. Gilman. Gilman's first impression was that most of the jurors announced as soon as they reached the jury room that they could not find Haywood guilty under the instructions.[7]

After electing Thomas Gess as foreman, the jurors took their first ballot about half an hour after reaching the room. Eight voted for acquittal, two (Gilman and Powell) for conviction, and two (Burns and Gess) did not vote. The second ballot was taken

---

[4] MacLane, *op. cit.,* pp. 168-169.

[5] Frankfurter, *op. cit.*

[6] Oscar King Davis, *Released for Publication* (Boston: Houghton Mifflin Company, 1925), pp. 42-44.

[7] The following account of the jury vote is from the Gilman interview, *Idaho Statesman,* July 29, 1907, p. 1.

after lunch. On this ballot Gess voted for acquittal, which resulted in nine votes for acquittal, two for conviction, and one undecided.

Considerable discussion took place before the next ballot. There was some talk of a second-degree verdict, but agreement was reached that the decision should be either first degree or acquittal. After looking at the exhibits in the jury room, Burns voted on the third ballot with the minority. The vote was 9-3 in favor of acquittal at this point, the nearest to conviction that the vote ever stood. After supper a fourth vote was taken. Burns joined the majority on this ballot, making it ten for acquittal and two for conviction.

The vote stood this way all night. At about three thirty in the morning a fifth ballot brought no changes. Some of the jurors apparently napped from time to time. At six o'clock, a sixth ballot was taken, and Powell, who had favored conviction from the beginning, voted with the majority. This change left Gilman as the only holdout. As he described the experience to reporters,

> That left me all alone. Then they worked on me. Finally I told them to let me think it over. I finally concluded it would not be right for me to hold out any longer. I think it was close around 6:30 when I finally gave in.

In the same interview Gilman described how he felt about giving in:

> It was hard for me to cast that last vote, but I knew that the others would never change. I stood out as long as I could and would have stood until doom's day had another staid [*sic*] by me, but on the sixth ballot Mr. Powell went over to the majority. I thought an hour about it, trying hard to determine my duty and I finally decided it was right that I should give in. When they shook me and said they wanted to take another ballot, I said: "Boys, I'll not hang out any longer; I know how all you will vote, put me down for not guilty."[8]

At about seven thirty on Sunday morning Judge Wood, who had been hastily summoned by bailiffs, reconvened court to hear the jury's decision. Foreman Thomas Gess handed the verdict to the judge in a sealed envelope. Judge Wood opened the envelope,

---

[8] *Ibid.*

looked at the piece of paper inside, and passed it to the court clerk. When the clerk read aloud the words "Not guilty" a happy demonstration broke out among the defendants, their attorneys, and the small group of loyal supporters who had kept an all night vigil.

The newspaper men were surprised. After getting the first report of the jury deliberations from Gilman they were still not satisfied. They tried to poll the jurors informally. In a second interview Gilman said that neither he nor Powell nor Burns thought Haywood innocent. The latter two voted for acquittal, reported the juror, because they thought the instructions called for such action.[9]

Powell spoke for himself in an interview in the *Capital News*. He said that he thought Haywood was guilty, but the instructions were long and not clear to the jurors ". . . which helped those opposed to a conviction." He complained that in trying to argue for conviction he was confronted constantly with the statement that "that testimony has been thrown out." Said Powell:

> The jurors all thought Haywood guilty but some of them said the state under the instructions had not made out a case against the prisoner. We argued all night, except for an hour at midnight when we ate lunch and rested for awhile.
>
> We took just 10 ballots. When I saw there was no show for a conviction—the trial having cost $125,000, I did not feel that it would be right to hang the jury when a majority was for acquittal. Gilman, myself, Burns and Gess were for conviction. Gess weakened at midnight and went over to the other side, Burns followed soon after. That left Gilman and I to argue against 10 men. It was hard work in the face of the instructions and the cutting out of so much testimony.[10]

Since the only testimony that was ruled out was testimony that the defense had entered,[11] it is difficult to understand how the jurors thought they could not use certain testimony in convicting Haywood—unless they regarded Orchard's testimony in general as

---

9 *Idaho Statesman*, July 30, 1907, p. 1.

10 *Capital News*, July 29, 1907, p. 1.

11 There was very little testimony ruled out. Judge Wood even neglected to rule out the allegations concerning a counter-conspiracy in Colorado which he had promised to cover in his instructions.

uncorroborated. But the same idea was expressed by other jurors. O. V. Sebern thought the verdict was

> . . . a grave miscarriage of justice—and many of the jurors concurred in this opinion. There was little or no doubt of the guilt of the defendant, but skillful lawyers presented facts in such manner, and the final instructions of the presiding Judge to the jury were such that much of the testimony was stricken and could not be considered. Consequently, the resulting verdict was the only one that could be rendered.[12]

Another of the Haywood jurors, J. A. Robertson, defended the decision of the jury as the only possible outcome of the instructions:

> To those who would criticize the actions of the jurors in rendering their verdict of acquittal, let me say, for myself, that no one can appreciate the hard position in which I was placed. There was the strong feeling and suspicion naturally entertained from the fact that the murdered man was a dear friend, and my solemn oath that these feelings must be put aside and my verdict be governed entirely by the law and evidence.
>
> Mr. Hawley's masterful presentation of the case could not have been better and Senator Borah's wonderful and convincing plea increased my admiration for him more than ever. It was my constant hope that if the defendant was guilty that the state would prove it beyond all doubt, and the evidence would be so strong that no doubt could be entertained. Now, then, no matter what we may have thought when the case was closed, our opinion must conform to the instructions of the court. These repeatedly said that outside of Orchard's testimony "the circumstantial evidence must be sufficiently conclusive to convince the jury to a moral certainty and beyond a reasonable doubt of the guilt of the defendant."
>
> Take, for instance, the letter which was supposed to have been sent from Pettibone to Orchard. We had only the copy. We needed the original letter with some corroboration as to the handwriting in order to consider this the most important and material link in the chain of evidence offered by the state. Hence it is my honest opinion that there was little left of the state's case after applying this great mass of instructions.[13]

Most of these comments indicate that the jurors believed that they were voting as the evidence and instructions would warrant. However, it may be naive to assume that these men actually voted in the idealistic fashion envisaged by the law. Articulate and

---

[12] Letter, Mrs. Oral Sebern Coleman to the author, August 19, 1960.

[13] *Capital News,* July 30, 1907, p. 5.

discriminating men of the legal profession have expressed serious doubts concerning the ability of juries to perform their fact-finding function or to apply the law intelligently. Aristotle in his *Rhetoric* admitted, "They will often have allowed themselves to be so much influenced by feelings of friendship or hatred or self-interest that they lose any clear vision of the truth and have their judgments obscured by considerations of personal pleasure or pain."[14] In a more contemporary era, George B. Clementson said, "It is a matter of common knowledge that the general verdict may be the result of anything but the calm deliberation, exchange of impressions and opinions, resolution of doubts, and final intelligent concurrence which, theoretically, produced it. It comes into court unexplained and unpenetrable."[15] The Haywood verdict was not entirely unexplained; some of the jury, as we have seen, offered explanations of the verdict, but these may have been rationalizations to an aroused community in which the jurors would continue to live, rather than honest explanations of what took place. The judge's instructions could be used as a convenient target of these rationalizations.

But in the case of several jurors, about whom more information is available than for the others, it is extremely difficult to offer any consistent explanation of their vote. Consider the case of juror number six, O. V. Sebern. At the start of the trial he seemed to be an unfavorable juror to the defense because of his vote in the Tom Horn case. Richardson had been forced to accept Sebern inasmuch as the defense's last peremptory challenge had been used. The judge had not permitted an extensive examination of Sebern on his previous jury experience, but it was general knowledge that he had been on the jury which voted to convict the Wyoming murderer. Thus, his presence on the Haywood jury was reason for the defense to worry; even the delegates to the Western Federation of Miners convention in Denver in June of 1907 expressed concern over this juror.

---

[14] Aristotle, *Rhetoric,* Book I, c. 1, translator, W. Rhys Roberts (Oxford: The Clarendon Press, n. d.).

[15] George B. Clementson, *Special Verdicts and Special Findings by Juries* (St. Paul: West Publishing Co., 1905) quoted in Jerome Frank, *Courts on Trial* (Princeton, N. J.: Princeton University Press, 1949), p. 111.

But, ultimately, as we have seen, Sebern voted to acquit Haywood, citing the instructions and the "stricken" evidence as the reason he could not vote to convict, even though he believed the defendant guilty. It may seem difficult to reconcile Sebern's vote to acquit in 1907 with his vote to convict in 1902, particularly when the circumstances of the earlier case are known. With respect to proof of Horn's guilt, John Charles Thompson, who was a Cheyenne newspaperman in 1902, observed:

> He was hanged not because the murder of the boy was fastened upon him "beyond peradventure of a reasonable doubt," but on "general principle" that he "had it coming."
> . . . Before a shred of testimony was offered he was a doomed man; public opinion had convicted him and intended to have him hanged. . . . On October 24, the jury returned the verdict, "Guilty of murder in the first degree," despite the testimony of a physician who performed an autopsy on the Nickell boy that the bullet which killed him was of much greater calibre than those of Horn's gun, a .30-.30.[16]

Sebern's vote in 1902 is made more difficult to explain by the fact that the juror knew Horn quite well; the stock detective had been a guest at the Sebern ranch house on many occasions. Thus, it would seem that in 1902 in the aroused community of Cheyenne, Sebern voted to convict a friend on the basis of rather questionable and inconclusive evidence, but in the aroused community of Boise in 1907 Sebern voted to acquit a man he did not know—but a man he thought guilty—on evidence which was also somewhat inconclusive.

An explanation of this paradox may lie in an observation by Mrs. Oral Sebern Coleman, daughter of the juror. As she describes the Tom Horn verdict, "The crucial fact was that this *boy* was an innocent victim in a war between *men*." (Italics are by Mrs. Coleman.) Thus, she asserts, "It is possible—the laws of the West being what they were regarding western justice,—that Horn may not have been tried or convicted, had his victim been the man he had intended to kill. But when his gun mowed down, instead, an innocent *boy*, public feeling rose rampant."[17]

[16] John Charles Thompson, "The Hanging of Tom Horn," in Herbert C. Brayer, editor, *1945 Brand Book* (Denver: Westerners Denver Posse, 1946), quoted in B. A. Botkin, *A Treasury of Western Folklore* (New York: Crown Publishers, Inc., 1951), pp. 336-338.

[17] Letter, Mrs. Oral Sebern Coleman to the author, April 10, 1961.

In fairness to Sebern and the Horn jury, it should be noted that the judge's instructions in that case favored the prosecution, whereas the instructions in the Haywood case favored the defense. For example, Judge Fremont Wood charged the jury that in order to convict from circumstantial evidence, the facts must be absolutely incompatible with any rational theory of innocence; Judge Richard H. Scott in Cheyenne in 1902 specifically denied such an instruction requested by the Horn defense.[18]

Regardless of the instructions, two conclusions are suggested by Sebern's vote in the Tom Horn case: that Sebern was willing to convict on rather inconclusive circumstantial evidence, and/or he was willing to use the "Code of the West" in certain legal judgments.[19] For either reason the Haywood defense would have feared him and the state of Idaho seemingly would have valued him as a juror. Thus, in the end, Sebern may have been one of the men to whom James Hawley referred in commenting on the verdict: ". . . two or three that we depended upon absolutely and had the best reasons that we could absolutely depend upon them, stood for the defense at the final outcome."[20]

Another man who must have been a disappointment to the prosecution was J. A. Robertson, the old man of the jury, in seat nine. Robertson, like Sebern, had been the object of concern at the WFM convention. In his case it was his friendship with Steunenberg that caused the union men to fear his presence on the jury. Again, like Sebern, he was the object of unsuccessful attempts by Richardson to keep him off the jury. And, like Sebern, he voted consistently for the defense.

Robertson, in previously cited passages, also seems to have credited the instructions with being all-important in the verdict. But certain post-trial reactions of Robertson suggest that there were other influences on this juror. For example, he told Charles Koelsch that he got the impression from the audiences in the court-

[18] *Horn v. State,* 73 Pacific 724-725.

[19] It is no discredit to Sebern to have used such a code, rather than legally prescribed justice, on occasion. James Hawley, a staunch believer in law, nevertheless had a strong sense of extra-legal equity.

[20] Letter, James Hawley to Jacob Fillius, July 28, 1907.

room each day that the people of Boise did not want the labor leaders convicted.[21] Koelsch regards Robertson's observation as significant; the courtroom *was* frequently loaded with Western Federation men, and the audience reactions were more favorable to Darrow, Richardson, and the WFM witnesses than to the prosecution staff and witnesses. This situation could influence the jury—through intimidation or through more subtle persuasion—into believing they should not convict.

Robertson also had an interesting reaction to Darrow. He liked the defense attorney's religious appeals, certainly an odd response for a man of reportedly strong Calvinist beliefs. Koelsch, who had known Robertson well and even roomed at his house at one time, has no explanation to offer for this unexpected bit of religious tolerance.[22] Nevertheless, on this basis, J. A. Robertson does not sound like the kind of man who decided the case solely on its legal merits, and on the instructions of the judge.

Perhaps the jury, as Powell maintained, did not understand the instructions. Jerome Frank, discussing what he calls the "realistic" theory of jury decisions, offers what may be the most accurate appraisal of the role of the instructions:

> . . . often the jury are neither able to, nor do they attempt to, apply the instructions of the court. . . . It is inconceivable that a body of twelve ordinary men, casually gathered together for a few days, could merely from listening to the instructions of the judge, gain the knowledge necessary to grasp the true import of the judge's words. For these words have often acquired their meaning as a result of hundreds of years of professional disputation in the courts. The jurors usually are as unlikely to get the meaning of those words as if they were spoken in Chinese, Sanskrit, or Choctaw.[23]

Thus, it would seem that the instructions may not have been as directly responsible for the verdict as the jurors reported them to be. Further examination may be required at this point to determine just what factors were responsible for the verdict.

If the facts and the law, as represented by the judge's instruc-

---

[21] Conversation with Charles Koelsch, Boise, Idaho, August 1, 1960.
[22] *Ibid.*
[23] Frank, *op. cit.*, p. 24.

tions, were not the key to the verdict, perhaps considerable credit should then go to the persuasive powers and forensic strategies of the attorneys. With lawyers as talented as Hawley, Richardson, Darrow, and Borah, one must expect that the advocate himself, rather than the merits of his case, would be largely responsible for the outcome of a trial. It is now necessary to determine to what degree this was true in the Haywood trial, and in what way each of the four men affected the final outcome, particularly by their closing arguments.

Hawley

In the case of James H. Hawley, contemporary press comments did an excellent job of evaluating the prosecutor's immediate effectiveness on the courtroom audience and on the jury. At this point, however, the jury and the newsmen had heard only the *one* argument, and they had no idea of what the verdict would be. The latter-day critic, fully aware of the verdict and faced with the task of determining Hawley's ultimate effectiveness as one of *four* speakers heard by the jury, must make a more complex evaluation than that offered by the journalists of 1907. Furthermore, the very nature of team effort makes it difficult to measure the contribution of an individual member of a team.

Nevertheless, there is no justification for the approach taken by some writers in trying to simplify the analysis by dropping Hawley and Richardson out of the case, turning it instead into a personal struggle between Darrow and Borah. It would be wiser to conclude that each of the four attorneys had a somewhat different purpose in the trial; on this basis, long-range judgments can at least be made on whether these goals were realized, and the responsibility for success or failure can be assigned accordingly, albeit subjectively.

Hawley, as we have seen, was Idaho's spokesman of righteous indignation in the Haywood trial. He was anxious to see the criminal element of the Western Federation of Miners "obliterated." Perhaps the most unusual testimony to his effectiveness in the trial came from an unexpected source, the men of the labor movement, who would seemingly be hostile to Hawley for this position. James Hawley was actually asked to represent the defense in the 1910-11 McNamara brothers case growing out of the bombing of the *Los Angeles Times.* But Hawley declined the call, and his old adversary Clarence Darrow became the defense attorney in the case that was to end his career as a labor pleader.[24]

There is another measure of a speaker's effectiveness: the esteem in which he is held by his fellow men. Although he lost the Haywood case, James Hawley did not lose the favor of the people of Idaho. A few years later in 1910 they indicated their regard for him by electing him their governor. No one has ever recorded an unkind word said of James Hawley, except the things that Clarence Darrow said during the trial. Another unusual tribute to the Sagebrush Lawyer took place in 1921 when the Supreme Court of Idaho passed a resolution commemorating James H. Hawley's fifty years of practicing law in Idaho. This, says McLane, is unique in the annals of any state.[25]

But the real measure of Hawley's effectiveness must be expressed in terms of the course of future events. The goal that Hawley sought, "obliteration" of the criminal element of the Western Federation of Miners, was actually accomplished within the next few years as a result of the disclosures of the trial. Without attempting to measure the total effect of that trial, we might consider Hawley's own reflections on the Haywood case, written in the same pragmatic spirit as his views of the Paul Corcoran case:

> While most of the people of Idaho believed that the acquittal of Haywood and Pettibone was a miscarriage of justice and while the trials of these persons cost the State of Idaho a large amount of money and no convictions were had, still the results of the trials were seemingly worth the effort that had been made. At the next election of the Western Federation of Miners following his acquittal, Haywood was retired as secretary-treasurer of the federation and the members of the executive committee who had assisted him in his attempts to terrorize the mining sections of the West were supplanted by others who believed in law enforcement and since that time there have been no labor troubles in the mining states of the West. The miners' unions composing the Western Federation have as a general thing been under the management of law abiding men

[24] Conversation with Hawley's son James, Boise, Idaho, July 26, 1960.
[25] MacLane, *op. cit.*, p. 176.

> and have assisted in the various communities where they existed in upholding the law.[26]

Thus, the "plain, blunt" man of the Haywood prosecution lived to see his efforts bear fruit. The hanging of Bill Haywood was the avowed forensic goal of both Borah and Hawley, but the broad social goal of rehabilitating the Western Federation of Miners was exclusively Hawley's goal. The goal of conviction was not attained, but the larger goal of social change was. In this sense, James H. Hawley spoke to his first national audience with great success.

Richardson

Where Hawley's ultimate effectiveness in the Haywood trial was long range, that of Edmund F. Richardson was immediate. If one assumes that the jury decision in the Haywood trial was a verdict fairly arrived at, through consideration of the law and the evidence, then Richardson should be credited with calling these things to the jury's attention in his argument, more so than Clarence Darrow. In spite of the scatter-shot nature of Richardson's defense he did make clear the legal weaknesses of the state's case. As MacLane described his contribution, he was

> . . . lawyerlike in his discussion of the evidence from his viewpoint, and its defects, apparently directed to the demonstration of a sufficient doubt as to the adequacy of the State's testimony in its attempted corroboration of Orchard's story.[27]

MacLane, incidentally, was well qualified to pass judgment on the "lawyerlike" qualities and effectiveness of criminal lawyers. Several years later he occupied the bench in this same courtroom; he also served to revise the Idaho statutes collected since territorial days into a new law code. In MacLane's judgment, Richardson was a "most capable trial lawyer, especially skilled in the tactics of criminal defense." Other figures of the Haywood trial made similar observations of Richardson. Charles Koelsch, the Ada County prosecuting attorney at the time, spoke of him later as "an eminent lawyer from Denver and, in my judgment, one of the ablest criminal lawyers it has been my pleasure to see or

---

[26] James H. Hawley, *History of Idaho* (Chicago: S. J. Clarke Publishing Co., 1920), p. 274 of Vol. I.

[27] MacLane, *op. cit.*, p. 165.

meet."[28] James Hawley called Richardson "one of the most skillful men in court that I ever practiced with."[29] Significantly, none of these men made a similar endorsement of Clarence Darrow.

The clue to this admiration of Richardson by conservative Idaho lawyers perhaps lies in the fact that Richardson was in many ways much like James Hawley. His background was similar; he was self-educated, something of a pioneer, a successful and highly regarded lawyer with a substantial practice, a devoted family man. There were also similarities in physique and character between the two men. Both were big, vigorous, outgoing men. Both had a strong sense of social justice tempered with a respect for the law. Each had a strong code of ethics, stronger than that of their respective principal colleagues in this case.

Even Vernon Jensen, who has generally been pro-Darrow in his analysis of the trial, concedes that Richardson's conduct of the trial was more ethical than Darrow's. Drawing on a conversation with Horace Hawkins, Sr., Richardson's one-time law partner, Jensen describes how Richardson almost quit the case when, after Darrow joined the defense staff, Haywood decided not to take the stand. Months before, Richardson had promised publicly that Haywood would testify. Now, when Haywood wanted to avoid testifying, Richardson threatened to go before the jury with his reason for quitting the case. This threat was enough to keep the defense forces together. Jensen also suggests that Richardson was not convinced of Haywood's innocence,[30] and this view is supported by Koelsch who, many years later, was told by friends and relatives of Richardson that the lawyer thought Haywood guilty.[31]

Richardson's purpose in the trial was to gain an acquittal for

---

[28] Charles F. Koelsch, *The Haywood Case* (Boise: Idaho Mining Association, 1946), p. 19.

[29] James H. Hawley, pamphlet, *Arguments Presented in Favor of Commutation at the Hearing Before the Pardon Board of the State of Idaho in the Matter of the Application of Harry Orchard, Held in the Governor's Office, Nov. 13, 1922,* p. 10.

[30] Vernon H. Jensen, *Heritage of Conflict* (Ithaca, New York: Cornell University Press, 1950), pp. 215-216.

[31] Conversation with Charles Koelsch, Boise, Idaho. August 1, 1960.

Haywood, a purpose considerably narrower than that of Clarence Darrow. By citing the law and the evidence, even though he burdened his argument with some contradictory and ineffective appeals, Richardson saw his purpose realized. But, since his argument lacked the lucidity and simplicity normally associated with a jury plea, it is quite possible that Richardson did not have his greatest effect on the jurors, but rather on the court. Judge Wood, as a man trained in the techniques and responsibilities of the law, could recognize through the confusion of Richardson's scatter-gun argument that the questions of corroboration and reasonable doubt raised by the defense attorney were valid issues, although other portions of the argument were not. In time, Judge Wood wrote a set of instructions for the jury that would be widely acclaimed as favoring the defense. These instructions must have been influenced by the persuasion of Edmund F. Richardson. The trial had once almost ended after Richardson's convincing legal argument for a directed verdict of acquittal. Later, after a less convincing summation speech, the legal questions of corroboration and reasonable doubt raised by Richardson still commanded the attention given to them by Judge Wood in his instructions to the jury.

Perhaps the most noteworthy effect of Richardson's participation in the trial was the effect on Richardson himself. When the trial ended he quit the defense staff immediately, leaving Darrow to conduct the second Steve Adams trial and the Pettibone trial. Richardson had had enough. He told reporters, "I will not work with Mr. Darrow under any consideration."[32] He returned to his lucrative Denver law practice, and there is no record of his having again defended the labor movement in a courtroom. Ironically, when Richardson met his death in an automobile accident in 1911, the other victim of the crash was Richardson's houseguest, a millionaire mineowner from the Cripple Creek district.[33]

Darrow

Clarence Darrow's contribution toward the verdict of the Haywood trial has been more widely evaluated—and perhaps

[32] *Capital News,* August 6, 1907, p. 2.
[33] *Denver News,* May 8, 1911, p. 5.

overvalued—than that of the other attorneys. A number of authors have commented on his summation speech. Fairly typical in its praise is the statement several years later by the Pinkerton detective, Charley Siringo, that ". . . Haywood owes his liberty to the masterful plea to the jury by Clarence Darrow of Chicago."[34]

For an extempore address from a man not noted for extensive preparation, it was indeed a remarkable oratorical effort. The use of series, the rhetorical question, the periodic sentence, the imagery—all combined to produce a moving and lyrical conclusion. Because of the perfection of its key passages, the speech has gone into anthologies of great speeches with but little editing.

Measuring the true effect of Darrow's speech upon the outcome of the trial and upon subsequent events is complicated, however, by the fact that so many writers have assumed that Darrow was the only persuasive force for the defense. This has led them to reason, from effect to cause, that Darrow alone achieved the verdict. When Richardson is restored to his proper role, this conclusion is untenable. The analysis of effectiveness must then consider the relative contribution of each man, a task more difficult than simply identifying the appeals of one man. However, it is still possible to measure the achievement of purposes that were unique to Darrow. He wanted to reach a wide audience beyond the courtroom with his ideas, and because of the excellent press coverage of the trial he was eminently successful. As Darrow observed in his autobiography, "In all my experience I never had a better opportunity, and when I had finished I felt satisfied with the effort I had made."[35] But, no clear conclusion can be drawn relative to achieving the purpose common to both lawyers, the acquittal of Haywood.

This common purpose did not imply a mutuality of method, however. E. F. Richardson was disgusted with Darrow's techniques and quit the defense staff immediately following the trial.

---

[34] Charles A. Siringo, *Two Evil Isms: Pinkertonism and Anarchism* (Chicago: Charles A. Siringo, Publisher, 1916), p. 96.

[35] Clarence Darrow, *The Story of My Life* (New York: Charles Scribner's Sons, 1934), p. 153.

It is necessary to discount his opinion somewhat because of the obvious jealousy between the two attorneys, but Richardson made this comment:

> Preaching socialism and trying a law case are entirely different matters. If you don't believe it, look at Darrow's closing speech before the jury. It was rank. It was enough to hang any man regardless of the fact of his innocence or guilt.[36]

James H. Hawley, the subject of Darrow's anathema throughout the speech, had a similar reaction to the effect of the speech on the jury, as well as a personal reaction:

> Darrow's blackguard address hurt his case instead of helping. I was at home sick at the time he made his talk upon me, and my first impression upon hearing about it was to teach him a proper lesson by means of a personal chastisement, but believing that he is trying to make a martyr of himself, I concluded after advising with my friends to let the matter pass for the time being.[37]

Whether the speech hurt or helped Darrow's cause with the jurors cannot, of course, be directly ascertained. It should be noted, however, that Darrow did several things in the address that would seem to be ill-conceived in terms of the kind of men to whom he was talking. These questionable techniques would include the attack on Hawley, the attack on the Christian doctrine of repentance and salvation, his justification of labor violence, even the sheer length of his speech. Another would be his admitted distaste for physical work, and his contempt for the "chumps" who engaged in hard work. Darrow's persuasion was tactless. Marie Hochmuth describes the strategy of a persuader practicing rhetoric as Kenneth Burke has redefined it: " 'I was once a farm boy myself,' he will say to his adversary in order to establish a bond or to bring about identification or to make two separate identities substantially one."[38] But Clarence Darrow in effect told the Haywood jury of farmers, "I was once a farm boy myself, but I'm not so dumb that I remained one."

To give Darrow primary credit for influencing the jury vote is to assume both that the jurors were not concerned with the

---

[36] *Capital News,* August 6, 1907, p. 2.

[37] Letter, James H. Hawley to C. D. Goodwin, July 28, 1907.

[38] Marie Hochmuth, "Burkeian Criticism," *Western Speech,* Spring, 1957, p. 95.

application of evidence and law—for Darrow had little argument along these lines—and that Darrow was able to overcome the negative effect that his strategy seemingly would have had on the jurors. Furthermore, as a jury plea the speech made its emotional appeal through an attempt to identify the defendant with the cause of the lower classes, in a class struggle with which the jurors themselves were not closely identified. Thus, Darrow's rhetoric was too unconventional to suggest the effect-to-cause generalization that the acquittal came about through Darrow's argument.

On the other hand, as a speech of social propaganda Darrow's argument is perhaps too conventional to have made many converts outside the Boise courtroom. Stone has enthusiastically proclaimed that,

> Read today in the back files of newspapers and magazines, it sounds as though a truly great writer had sat at his desk for many months to pour out this magnificent appeal, so beautiful is the language, so richly lyrical and cadenced, so varied in mood, so pungent the sarcasm juxtaposed to tenderness and pity for man's struggle, so stirring in its passion for life and justice to the poor, the people.[39]

Perhaps, but much of the eloquence in Darrow's summation—and the speech has long passages of prosaic prose between its moments of genuine eloquence—is expressed in a plain style heavy with cliches and tired slang. Darrow has been compared with Lincoln, but there is little of the warm simplicity of Lincoln in Darrow's wordy style. Even as a classic emotional statement of the Socialist position, the summation is inferior to the "Cross is Bending" courtroom speech of Eugene Debs in its rhythm, imagery, alliteration, and climax[40]—and Debs was generally regarded as a platitudinous speaker.

But style is not the ultimate consideration in evaluating the social propaganda of Darrow or of any other "movement" speaker. *Ideas* are more important. And in Darrow's Haywood

---

[39] Irving Stone, *Clarence Darrow for the Defense* (Garden City, N. Y.: Doubleday & Company, Inc., 1941), pp. 238-239.

[40] Eugene Debs, Statement to the Court, Columbus, Ohio, September 14, 1918, reproduced in *Writings and Speeches of Eugene V. Debs* (New York: Hermitage Press, Inc., 1948), pp. 437-439.

summation there is nothing new, nothing said better than before, nothing designed to close the gap between wage earner and employer. Darrow was in the strategic position of having served corporations, government, and labor in the courts; out of this background he might have used his persuasive powers in the cause of moderation and understanding. Instead, he chose to keep alive the class hatreds that had prevented each side from recognizing the legitimate rights of the other.

Most significantly, those Americans who were sympathetic to Darrow's speech were faced with a cruel dilemma. Either Clarence Darrow and the Socialist party line were right and Bill Haywood would be hanged by the capitalist plot, or—as they discovered three days later—Clarence Darrow and the Socialists were wrong, and Bill Haywood would go free. In other words, as social propaganda the speech's validity depended upon Haywood's being hanged. A number of American newspapers, commenting on the verdict, pointed out that the Socialists had actually hoped for a martyr but now had an unexpected—and almost unwanted—acquittal. The organized Socialists had behaved indiscreetly enough, but Darrow's identification of Haywood with the cause of Socialism in the closing argument did nothing to create a better public image of Socialism. On the contrary, Darrow may have hurt the Socialist cause. As the *New York World* observed, "If Socialism was really on trial with Haywood, then Socialism is convicted of being an ass."[41] Thus, as a broad social message, as well as a legal appeal, Darrow's closing argument militated against its own purposes.

Borah

As the man who made the final argument before the Haywood case went to the jury, William E. Borah received considerable attention from contemporary writers and from later writers who have parroted what the observers of 1907 reported. But relatively little genuine analysis of Borah's persuasion has taken place since that time.

One of the most interesting reactions to the summation speech

[41] Quoted in *Capital News,* July 30, 1907, p. 2.

appears in the later reflections of Jess Hawley who, as a young lawyer, assisted his father in the Haywood case.

> In the closing argument of the Haywood case Senator Borah made an argument that has found its place in the legal literature of this country. It was really a magnificent effort. But it was written to be read, and it was not particularly addressed to the jury men. His address received highest of praise from the newspaper men, particularly those who had much literary talent. On the other hand, my father's address did not meet with the approval of these men. They criticized his language, and they did not like the familiar way in which he acted. He sat on the edge of the table and conversed with them, and while they admitted that he got their interest and warmed up to him, nevertheless his speech wasn't a literary gem. It had so many errors in it that it wouldn't make good copy, or rather it couldn't be inserted in a book of great legal orations. It has always been my notion that if Borah had talked to the jury instead of to the intelligentsia, and with an eye to getting the jury convinced rather than getting a speech which would go into the best legal orations, there would have been a different result in the Haywood case.[42]

This observation, together with O. K. Davis' rapturous report of the speech, might suggest that there was something of Cicero in Borah. The classic comparison of Cicero and Demosthenes has Cicero's hearers exclaiming, "My, how well he speaks today!" while those of Demosthenes cry out, "Let us march against Philip!" Darrow once called Boise "the Athens of the sagebrush;" it is, perhaps, carrying the analogy too far to assert that Borah talked to these sagebrush Athenians as a Roman Cicero, rather than a Demosthenes. But there may well have been too much mastery of technique in Borah's oratory, and too little communication with the jury. Quite possibly the appeals were directed too often toward the loftier emotions of honor and social responsibility, and too infrequently toward the simpler sentiments of self-preservation and humanity. Conceivably, Borah, the advocate, may have momentarily yielded to Borah, the actor, for this last great Idaho audience. If this were so, the memory of the performance may have been impressionistic, rather than realistic, hours later when the jury began to grapple with the testimony, the arguments, and the instructions. Thus, Borah's ideas may

[42] Typewritten manuscript of Jess Hawley, "Notes on Haywood," 1947, in possession of James H. Hawley, the younger.

have been no more dominant in the jury room than those of Hawley, Richardson, and Darrow.

While it is clear that Borah's closing argument did not wrest the victory away from the defense, there is no way to know how close he came to this goal. Nevertheless, certain conclusions are suggested by the evidence that has been reviewed. First, the argument that Borah delivered, read today from the transcript, is likely to disappoint the reader who has read Oscar King Davis' account, or the pamphlet version of the speech. The logic is no more effective than the logic of the other attorneys, but it may seem more consistent because it was applied to a narrower study of the case than that made by the other lawyers. The speech is lucid, but not singularly so. Borah, like Darrow, used two styles: a plain one for reviewing the evidence, and a more elaborate one for drawing conclusions and refuting key ideas. In the plainer passages are some not-so-lucid moments:

> The court, in my judgment, will instruct you that when important testimony is within the control of the defendant, or when important testimony is to be important to the defendant,—and it is to the defendant in this case—if Mr. Pettibone was a member of this conspiracy Haywood knew of it and his act was Haywood's act and his act requires explanation as much as Mr. Haywood's; and if they were associated together they cannot say it was the act of Pettibone and not the act of Haywood, because it was the act of Haywood, and when he remains off the witness stand, charged with the fact that he had done a certain thing associated with Mr. Orchard which is vital and controlling in this case, that of itself is strong evidence of itself and corroborates Mr. Orchard in this case.

Second, it is necessary to discount much of the praise showered upon Borah's summation speech, because of the close personal relationship between the Senator and his journalist friends. Unquestionably, Borah received great credit—some of which belonged rightfully to James Hawley—for his role in the Haywood trial, thanks to his "press corps." C. P. Connolly of *Collier's,* on his way east to represent Borah before President Roosevelt in the land fraud matter, wrote to the Senator: "The verdict was one of the greatest surprises I have ever run up against . . . You, at least, came out of the whole affair with honor, and with a fame which it is given to few men to achieve in so short a while."[43] This fame, or at least that portion for which Connolly was responsible, was tarnished, however, by the $300 that Borah paid Connolly to intercede in his behalf with Roosevelt (see page 122). O. K. Davis' share of Borah's fame was also sullied by direct repayment. Davis capitalized on Borah's gratitude for his intervention with Roosevelt and his favorable comments during the Haywood trial by asking the Senator for a particularly important news beat. Borah repaid the newsman by "leaking" to him the highly secret Taft platform at the opening of the 1908 Republican convention in Chicago. This must have squared the debt; Davis, who in 1907 had called Borah's speech "an overpowering marshaling of the evidence," in later years admitted that he had always had reservations about the speech. ". . . It has always seemed very strange to me," said Davis, "that none of the lawyers in the Haywood case spent any time in arguing Orchard's credibility to the jury . . . Borah argued ably and powerfully, but it never seemed to me that any of the argument was as convincing to the jury as it might have been if there had been a painstaking examination of Orchard's story from the sole point of its reliability and truth."[44]

Third, Borah's activity throughout the trial in lining up support for his impending defense in the land fraud case made demands on his time and loyalty, and possibly injected a personal motive into his speaking. The resourceful Borah of 1899 rode a boxcar down a canyon to prove his case, but the Borah of 1907, sufficiently worried to consider resigning his new Senate seat, had little time for such imaginative advocacy.

And finally, Borah's consubstantiality with the jury was not through conventional *ethos,* but rather through a mutual identification of lawyer and juror with law and order, and with civic pride in Idaho and its institutions. (In addition, some of the strongest *ethos* occurred in the spurious passages.) It was the same appeal that Borah had successfully used in the Paul Corcoran case eight years earlier. But in the 1899 trial the conspiracy to be proved was no bigger than Shoshone County, Idaho. In 1907 the con-

[43] Letter, C. P. Connolly to William E. Borah, August 1, 1907.
[44] Davis, *op. cit.,* pp. 73-80, p. 40.

spiracy to be proved was a broad one, in time and in geography. When Borah chose to rule out the Colorado events, perhaps he narrowed the conspiracy to Idaho—but left Haywood out.

Like Darrow, Borah talked to a broader audience than the jury and the court. But, unlike Darrow, Borah had a burden of proof. This proof had to be demonstrated to the satisfaction of twelve jurors for whom the "manhood and integrity of the state" was a harder principle to understand than was "reasonable doubt."

Thus, the four lawyers—their strategies and techniques—must be reckoned a part of the final outcome of the Haywood trial. It may be premature, however, to conclude that those aspects of the trial which have been examined in the previous pages—the instructions and the rhetoric of the courtroom—were the only, or even the most important, influences on the jury.

Inevitably, the question of fear arises. Were the jurors in the Haywood case afraid for their own safety, and the safety of their families? Enough attention has been given to this theory by contemporary journalists and subsequent writers to justify further examination of the evidence. Among prominent men voicing such a view was President Roosevelt, who said:

> There has been a gross miscarriage of justice, to my mind, out in Idaho, in the acquittal of Haywood. I suppose the jury was terrorized, but it is not a pleasant matter from my standpoint.[45]

Governor Hawley also expressed the same view, in testifying before the commutation hearing for Harry Orchard in 1922. Said he:

> The jury thought—as, of course, they had a right to think—I always believed they were terrified to a certain extent—that the evidence was not sufficient to finally convict Haywood.[46]

Claudius Johnson discusses the same theory and even cites an example of a juror so intimidated, but he admits he cannot document the incident:

> It has been said that the jurors returned such a verdict in fear

[45] Letter, Theodore Roosevelt to Whitelaw Reid, July 29, 1907, in Elting E. Morison, editor, *The Letters of Theodore Roosevelt*, Vol. V. (Cambridge: Harvard University Press, 1952), p. 733.

[46] James Hawley, *Commutation Hearing* pamphlet, *op. cit.*, p. 10.

of their lives. Possibly this is true. . . . One juror, whom Borah had fought to keep on the list because he knew him for a man of courage, told the Senator a few months later that he 'had the guts' to risk his own life in voting for a conviction but that he had a wife and children to think of.[47]

Charles Koelsch remembers talking, after the trial, to several of the jurors who indicated that they were afraid of retaliation to their families if they voted for conviction, but he cannot recall which men he talked to.[48] During the trial the *Oregonian* reported that several of the jurors' wives had expressed similar fears. Mrs. Thomas Gess went to Judge Wood's home to see the judge because she was worried about her husband. Two bailiffs physically restrained the distraught woman when she threatened to invade the courtroom to see her husband.[49] Mrs. Levi Smith was reported to be nearly hysterical, fearing her house would be blown up if her husband voted the wrong way. In an interview with the *Oregonian,* Mrs. Smith said:

Yes, I have been very apprehensive lest harm come to us if my husband should vote for conviction. I would have tried to see him if I had thought it possible. But maybe everything will come out for the best, and I shall try to content myself and wait and see.[50]

The wife of another juror was said to have wept freely while discussing the case with friends. The *Oregonian* concluded:

Word from various places in rural districts where wives of jurymen reside is to the effect that several are very apprehensive of what may follow to themselves and property in case Haywood is found guilty.[51]

---

[47] Claudius Johnson, *Borah of Idaho* (New York: Longmans, Green and Co., 1936), p. 83.

[48] Conversation with Charles Koelsch, Boise, Idaho, August 1, 1960.

[49] If the Gess family had any fear of Haywood it was well concealed at the end of the trial. Haywood, in his autobiography, indicated that immediately after the verdict was read, Gess, the jury foreman, invited Haywood to visit his home before he left town. On the next day Haywood accepted the invitation. Gess then told the labor leader that he had cast a blank ballot only to find out who was voting for conviction. (There is no explanation of how this procedure would work.) Haywood seemed satisfied that Gess was one of his real friends on the jury, but at least one account of the deliberations—that of Powell—reported Gess voting for conviction until midnight. Incidentally, two months later in the Borah trial Thomas Gess was again a juror.

[50] *Portland Oregonian,* June 19, 1907, p. 5.

[51] *Ibid.*

It would be easy, many years later, to write off these fears of jurors and the families of jurors as completely unfounded, and to discount any possibility that fear was a factor in the verdict. However, two events of 1907-08 proved that their fears were justified. The Western Federation of Miners retaliated against two men who had been responsible for aiding the prosecution get evidence during the trial. On September 30, 1907, during the Borah land fraud trial, Sheriff Harvey K. Brown of Baker County, Oregon, was killed by a gatepost bomb at his home in Baker.[52] This bombing has generally been regarded as WFM retaliation for Brown's role in implicating Orchard and Adams. Then, in the spring of 1908, a bomb attempt was made on Adjutant General Bulkeley Wells of the Colorado militia in Telluride, Colorado. Wells was not hurt, but his house was wrecked[53]—the same house in which his predecessor, Arthur Collins, had been assassinated in 1902. These two bombings provide reason to believe that the Haywood jurors *were* justifiably fearful. Hence, a reasonable and plausible explanation of the jury's vote could be built on these fears.

However, it would be unrealistic to think that the state had made a good case against Haywood, a case that would otherwise have influenced the jurors to convict the defendant. Robertson had talked about needing the actual letter to Orchard in the Caldwell jail, rather than a copy, in order to have convincing proof; but he was nevertheless talking about a letter from Pettibone, not Haywood. The state had not connected Haywood directly with the Steunenberg murder, although the existence of a general conspiracy had probably been effectively demonstrated. It would have taken only common sense and a reasonable determination to follow the instructions for a juror to have voted to acquit.

James Hawley in later years admitted that the corroborating proof of Orchard's story of the crime was "comparatively slight." In dedicating the Steunenberg Memorial in Boise—a striking statue of the ex-governor, authentic down to the missing necktie—Hawley offered his own explanation of the jury vote:

---

[52] *Portland Oregonian,* October 1, 1907, p. 1.
[53] *Engineering and Mining Journal,* April 11, 1908, p. 775.

> I have sometimes thought in considering the reasons for this conclusion of the jury, that perhaps the overwhelming confirmation of Orchard's testimony in regard to other crimes of itself tended to lessen the convincing quality of the small amount of corroborating proof connecting Haywood with the Steunenberg murder, and was partly responsible for the disappointing verdict.[54]

It has been suggested by jurors—Powell and Sebern at least —and by many contemporary newspaper editorial writers that Haywood was guilty, but could not be proven so in the narrow and rigid form prescribed by law. Seven months after the Haywood trial, in passing sentence on Harry Orchard, Judge Fremont Wood revealed how he felt about Orchard's disclosures in the Haywood was guilty, but could not be proven so in the narrow the fall of 1907:

> I am more than satisfied that the defendant now at the bar of this court awaiting final sentence has not only acted in good faith in making the disclosures that he did, but that he also testified fully and fairly to the whole truth, withholding nothing that was material, and declaring nothing which had not actually taken place. During the two trials to which I have referred the testimony of the defendant covered a long series of transactions, involving personal relations between himself and many others. In the first trial he was subjected to the most critical cross-examination by very able counsel for at least six days, and I do not now recall that at any point he contradicted himself in any material manner, but on the other hand, disclosed his connection with the commission of many other crimes not known to the attorneys for the state, at least not brought out by them on the direct examination of witnesses . . . It was the particular province of the court to observe and follow this witness upon former trials, and I am of the opinion that no man living could conceive the stories of crime told by the witness and maintain himself under the merciless fire of the leading cross-examining attorneys of the country, unless upon the theory that he was testifying to facts and circumstances which had an actual existence within his own experience. A child can testify truly and maintain itself on cross-examination. A man may be able to frame his story and testify falsely to a brief statement of facts involving a short and single transaction and maintain himself on cross-examination.
>
> But I cannot conceive of a case where even the greatest intellect can conceive a story of crime covering years of duration, with con-

---

[54] James H. Hawley, typewritten mss. of speech dedicating the Steunenberg Memorial, December 11, 1927, in Hawley papers, Idaho Historical Society.

> stantly shifting scenes and changing characters, and maintain that story with circumstantial detail as to times, places, persons and particular circumstances, and under as merciless a cross-examination as was ever given a witness in an American court, unless the witness thus testifying was speaking truthfully and without any attempt either to misrepresent or conceal.[55]

On the day before Fremont Wood made this statement, Harry Orchard had told Jess Hawley, "I do feel rather bitter toward Judge Wood for his instructions, because I think these caused the Haywood jury to agree on a verdict of acquittal. He emphasized reasonable doubt so often that the jury evidently thought he had a reasonable doubt." Orchard told the prosecutor's son that he planned to make these criticisms to the judge on the following day if Judge Wood lectured to him in passing sentence.[56] But when Wood endorsed Orchard's truthfulness, Orchard stood silently choking back tears. When the judge commuted Orchard's hanging sentence to life imprisonment, the prisoner thanked the judge and said no more.

In another interesting sidelight to the trial, the opinion—widely held by writers covering the trial—that Orchard was telling the truth was supported by the observations of a highly qualified spectator. Dr. Hugo Munsterberg, professor of psychology at Harvard University, visited Boise to conduct psychological examinations of Harry Orchard. Before the trial was over, eastern newspapers were reporting that Munsterberg believed that Orchard was telling the truth. In an article in *McClure's*, after the trial was over, the psychologist reported how he gave Orchard "nearly 100 tests." Apparently the word-association test was the key to Munsterberg's conclusion that Orchard told the truth; very short response times reportedly indicated there was no attempt at fabrication. The psychologist offered one comment which would have interested Clarence Darrow:

> . . . Orchard's emotional life is simply dead—the small figures of his association-times would otherwise be quite impossible. And it may be added that even if his religious conversion is genuine, his so-called religion lacks also every sound and deep feeling; it is

[55] *Idaho Statesman,* March 19, 1908, p. 1 of 2nd section.
[56] Jess Hawley, "Notes on Haywood," *op. cit.,* p 20.

> thoroughly utilitarian; he serves God because He will reward him after death.[57]

While Munsterberg's explanation of Orchard's truthfulness and his explanation of Orchard's religion were consistent with prosecution assertions, Borah and Hawley cannot be blamed for not using Munsterberg as an expert witness during the trial. In 1907 popular audiences were not yet conditioned to regard psychology as anything like a science, or college professors as men who knew human behavior better than the average man did.[58]

Subsequent events also tend to prove that Orchard's confession was true and his conversion genuine. Orchard lived the remainder of his life as a model prisoner at the Idaho State Penitentiary in Boise, without ever changing his story. When he died in 1954 he was genuinely mourned as a man who had acted as a stabilizing influence on many prisoners at the penitentiary. On the other hand Bill Haywood died unmourned in Russia in 1928, a fugitive from the American justice which he and the Socialists continued to denounce.

In spite of what the courts of other states did to radicals—Illinois to the Haymarket rioters, Utah to Joe Hill, California to Tom Mooney, and Massachusetts to Sacco and Vanzetti—Bill Haywood had received justice in Idaho. Considering all the evidence of the trial, the statements of Wood and Munsterberg, and Orchard's forty-seven repentant years in prison with no change in his story, it is reasonable to conclude that Orchard had told the truth—that he *was* the tool of Haywood in the Steunenberg affair. But the state did not prove within the narrowly prescribed procedures of law that a conspiracy existed, so Haywood went free. Under more normal, quieter circumstances, the jury might still have accepted the state's case as conclusive, but in the excitement, the notoriety, and the explosiveness of the Haywood case, few prudent men would have voted for conviction.

---

[57] Hugo Munsterberg, "The Third Degree," *McClure's Magazine,* October, 1907, p. 620.

[58] "Alienists"—forensic psychiatrists who testified as experts on sanity—were just appearing on the American legal scene in the early 1900's. By the time Darrow defended Loeb and Leopold in 1924 alienists were a common feature of murder trials. But in the Loeb-Leopold trial, as in a number of similar cases, the net effect of the testimony of these experts was small since each side had competent alienists to support its position. See the *Encyclopedia of the Social Sciences.*

17

THE HAYWOOD VERDICT:

Effects and Causes

THE VERDICT OF JULY 28, 1907, freed Bill Haywood. It was also responsible for a series of aftereffects. As one might expect from a trial of great national interest and consequence, a number of men and events were affected by the outcome. In this final chapter the broad effects of the trial will be considered, and an attempt made to sum up, briefly but definitively, the role of communication in bringing about the verdict.

One of the most direct effects of the Haywood trial was that produced upon the labor movement in the West. Haywood's imprisonment from February of 1906 until July of 1907 coincided with a critical period in the relationship of two great unions, the Western Federation of Miners and the Industrial Workers of the World. By the time the trial ended, the relationship of the two unions had ended in estrangement.

The IWW, or the Wobblies as they were commonly known, came into existence in 1905. Bill Haywood presided at the convention which established the organization, and the support of the Western Federation of Miners was a key factor in the formation of the union. But from its beginning the IWW was plagued with the problem of dualism that had crippled the Knights of

Labor, the Western Labor Union, and other attempts at industrial unionism. By 1906 a serious factional fight erupted in the IWW between "conservatives" and "radicals." Significantly, most of the Western Federation delegates to the IWW were conservative; the exceptions were Haywood and Vincent St. John, both of whom were arrested in 1906 for their "Inner Circle" crimes. As an official publication of the Wobblies later explained,

> Haywood's imprisonment gave the right wing in the Federation control of its offices and a deal was worked out between these right wing forces, commonly called the "Denver Triumvirate," and Charles Sherman, President of the IWW, aiming to make the second convention, in Sherman's phrase, "the Waterloo of the revolutionists."[1]

But at the 1906 IWW convention the revolutionists or radicals countered the Western Federation move by unseating the conservative, President Sherman, and by abolishing the office of president. Sherman and William E. Troutman, leader of the radical group, then engaged in a court battle for leadership of the union, a curious procedure for men who were noisily attacking the courts for their role in the Haywood case. Eventually, two separate IWW organizations emerged, Troutman's group the stronger of the two.[2]

With Haywood imprisoned, the Western Federation leadership in Denver (the "Denver Triumvirate" of Acting President Mahoney, Acting Secretary-Treasurer Kirwan, and Editor O'Neill of the *Miner's Magazine*) reacted to the IWW's swing to the left. After first refusing to pay dues to either the Sherman or the Troutman faction of the IWW, the Western Federation, led by its conservative second-rank officers, then withdrew from the IWW completely in 1907.[3]

A number of writers have commented on the cause and effect of this split. Brissenden observes:

---

[1] Fred Thompson, editor, *The I. W. W., Its First Fifty Years* (Chicago: Industrial Workers of the World, 1955), p. 25.

[2] Selig Perlman and Philip Taft, *History of Labor in the United States*, Vol. IV (New York: The Macmillan Co., 1935), pp. 232-233.

[3] Paul F. Brissenden, *The I. W. W., A Study of American Syndicalism* (New York: Columbia University, 1920), p. 175.

> The Moyer-Haywood-Pettibone deportation was unquestionably one of the causes operating to split off the Western Federation of Miners. The imprisonment of Haywood certainly weakened that element in the Western Federation which backed the I. W. W. and strengthened the hands of those who were opposed to continued incorporation with it. This, combined with the deposition of President Sherman, which yet further weakened the forces of the Miners who supported the I. W. W., finally gave the I. W. W. knockers in the Western Federation the upper hand.[4]

Ray Ginger expresses a similar view that Haywood's imprisonment was responsible for the Western Federation's secession:

> The imprisonment of Haywood for fifteen months, and the involvement of his supporters in his defense campaign, permitted his enemies to capture the Western Federation of Miners. They promptly withdrew it from the IWW.[5]

But G. D. H. Cole argues that the disclosures of the trial were behind the WFM-IWW split:

> This sensational trial focused attention throughout the United States on the affairs and policy of the I. W. W.; but it also gave rise to deep dissensions inside the Western Federation of Miners, and was largely responsible for the secession of that Union from the I. W. W. while its principal left-wing leaders were out of the way.[6]

Brissenden, generally considered the foremost scholar on the early days of the IWW, had previously expressed an opinion which would tend to contradict Cole's view that the trial focused attention on the IWW:

> Although the Moyer-Haywood trial and the final acquittal of the accused men made the I. W. W. somewhat more commonly known and understood among the working class throughout the country, it was on the whole nothing less than a calamity for that organization. The I. W. W. did not even get publicity out of the Moyer-Haywood case. The Western Federation got all the advertising. It was a well-established labor organization with an eventful—almost a lurid—history. Its early activities were more or less related to the Moyer-Haywood-Pettibone affair and the general public very naturally thought of the Western Federation when they thought of the Haywood deportation. The I. W. W. was not popularly associ-

[4] *Ibid.*

[5] Ray Ginger, *The Bending Cross* (New Brunswick, N. J.: Rutgers University Press, 1949), p. 255.

[6] G. D. H. Cole, *A History of Socialist Thought*, Vol. III (London: Macmillan & Co., Ltd., 1956), p. 792.

> ated with the Boise trial at all. The organization was obliged almost completely to suspend its vital work of organizing to raise funds for the defense.[7]

In any event, the Haywood trial, with its resultant long imprisonment of the union leaders and public disclosures of WFM methods, served to alienate the conservative and radical elements in the western labor movement at a time when the need for labor solidarity was recognizable. The IWW was free to expand in the direction of radical industrial unionism. But the Western Federation of Miners swung to the right, only two years after that union had been instrumental in setting up the more radical industrial union. Later in 1907, the Goldfield strike helped convince the WFM leaders that their decision to withdraw from the IWW was a sound one, and that the IWW approach created more antilabor hostility than the miners had ever created even in the violent days in Cripple Creek and the Coeur d'Alenes.

While the miners were swinging to the right, Haywood had grown more radical during his imprisonment. His old friend, John Murphy, the long-time WFM attorney, told him on the day of his acquittal to be humble in his hour of triumph. Darrow, too, advised him to stay out of the public eye.[8] But, instead, Haywood toured the country giving victory speeches that were too rabid, and running up expenses that were too exorbitant, for the Western Federation of Miners. In the spring of 1908 the Executive Board of the union terminated his services as secretary-treasurer. Cut loose from the increasingly conservative miners' union, Haywood could now pursue the kind of radical socialism and syndicalism he believed in. He and Vincent St. John could carry the old militancy of the Western Federation into the IWW and the Socialist party.

On the other hand, Charles H. Moyer, who had not gotten along well with Haywood, became more conservative during his imprisonment. He had spent more of his life in prison than had Haywood, including his burglary conviction and his imprisonment

---

[7] Brissenden, *loc. cit.*

[8] William D. Haywood, *Bill Haywood's Book* (New York: International Publishers, 1929), pp. 217-218.

in Telluride during the labor trouble there. He was tired of being a radical. When the Idaho charges against him were dropped, he resumed the presidency of the Western Federation and shaped it more and more into a conventional trade union. A few years later James Hawley at the Orchard commutation hearing publicly praised Moyer for his courageous leadership of the Western Federation through its period of internal violence in Butte in 1914, and noted that the Western Federation mining camps had become peaceful and orderly communities.[9] Recognizing that it had acquired a new character, the union in 1916 changed its name to the International Union of Mine, Mill, and Smelter Workers. While the new union continued to be somewhat to the left of most unions, it was a far cry from the old WFM which had often been called in Cripple Creek "The Western Federation of Murderers."

Another example of a conservative reaction to the Haywood trial from the labor movement can be found in the McNamara brothers case in Los Angeles. James Hawley, who spoke for law and order in the Haywood trial, was the original choice of the AF of L McNamara defense committee rather than Clarence Darrow who had justified violence in 1907. This choice suggests an attempt by the committee to identify the AF of L with Hawley's concept of unionism, rather than with Darrow's. At this stage of the preliminary negotiations for an attorney, the committee must have believed in the innocence of the McNamaras, or they would have had no reason to seek out Hawley who was opposed to violence in labor relations. Thus, it must have come as a shock to this committee—and to the entire membership of the American Federation of Labor—when Clarence Darrow eventually had the McNamara brothers plead guilty to the dynamiting charge as a part of an agreement worked out with the prosecution.

Not only was the American labor movement directly affected by the outcome of the Haywood trial, but society in general felt the influence of the trial and the verdict. Dozens of newspapers commented editorially that the Socialists had been proved wrong.

---

[9] James H. Hawley, pamphlet, *Arguments Presented in Favor of Commutation at the Hearing Before the Pardon Board of the State of Idaho in the Matter of the Application of Harry Orchard, Held in the Governor's Office, Nov. 13, 1922,* p. 12.

In spite of the radicals' cry that the courts were "corporation courts" and the judge and jury "puppets of plutocracy," the Idaho trial had been a fair trial, and the verdict reached by the jury was the same verdict reached by the unofficial Socialist jury which sat in the courtroom. The Haywood verdict was a repudiation of the charge that a man of the laboring class could not get justice in the American judicial system.

A few Socialist journals admitted that these charges had been proved false. But others, in the peculiar rhetoric of Marxism, said that the verdict proved that the capitalist courts were corrupt. *The People* of New York City said, "The jury's verdict, 'Not Guilty,' translates itself into a thundering verdict of: 'Guilty! Guilty!! Guilty!!!' hurled at the whole capitalist class."[10] Eugene Debs, interviewed in *The Worker,* said that powerful interests behind the prosecution realized that a conviction would have a decided bearing on the approaching national election, and brought influence to bear on the court in favor of acquittal. Said Debs, "This in my judgment accounts for the instructions of the court, which amounted to a plea in favor of the defendant for the verdict resulting in his acquittal."[11] This kind of observation prompted a number of papers to comment on the ungracious way the Socialists had received the verdict; some newspapers suggested that what the Socialists really wanted was a martyr, not an acquittal.

John W. Carberry, who had covered the trial for the *Boston Globe,* told the *Capital News* a few hours after the trial,

> . . . the county of Ada delivered the most telling blow to radical socialism that the doctrine of class warfare has ever received in this country when William D. Haywood was acquitted. Had he been convicted he would have been a martyr, innocent he contradicts the aspersions of the socialist propaganda cast upon the state of Idaho and to their confusion the justice and honor of the courts have been established.[12]

Other magazines and papers editorialized that the great value of the trial came from the public exposure of the methods of the Western Federation of Miners. *Nation,* in an editorial which also

[10] Quoted in *Current Literature,* September, 1907, p. 248.
[11] *Ibid.*
[12] *Capital News,* July 29, 1907, p. 5.

appeared in much the same form in the New York *Evening Post*, observed: "The Haywood acquittal has been called a 'triumph for labor.' Perhaps, but it is certain that the evidence brought out in the Haywood trial has affixed the blackest stigma to one branch of organized labor. To say Western Federation of Miners is to-day very much like saying the Camorra, or the Black Hundred."[13]

Still other newspapers likened the verdict to the old Scotch verdict of "not proven." Perhaps the best short evaluation of the effect of the Haywood verdict on American society was written by a newspaperman, Mark Sullivan, in his five-volume history of the United States in the first quarter of the twentieth century. After agreeing that "not proven" expressed the "general feeling of the country," Sullivan went on to say:

> Important, and also amusing, was the effect of the outcome of the trial on the noisy element among the Socialists and radicals who for months had been charging that the scales of American justice were loaded against Haywood. The trial had been conducted with dignity and decorum by serious men. The Judge had instructed the jury in the law. The jury had considered the facts and the law bearing on the case and had reached the decision indicated by these factors. As a result those who had decried American justice, who had alleged the impossibility of a fair trial for Haywood, found themselves discredited with persons of common sense. Up to that time there had been a country-wide trend toward Socialism as a cure for various of the ills of democratic government; the hysteria and excesses of Debs and the other extremists among the Socialists, during and before the Haywood trial, had the effect of a brake applied to this trend, indeed brought it almost to a halt, at a time when in France, Germany, and England it was going forward strongly.[14]

Although one might take exception to Sullivan's assertion that the Haywood trial acted as a brake on the trend to socialism —since the highwater mark of Socialist presidential vote did not come until 1912—it is clear, nevertheless, that socialism, like the labor movement, became more conservative after the Haywood trial. The 1912 Socialist Party constitution provided that "any member of the Party who opposes political action or advocates

---

[13] "Haywood's Acquittal," *Nation*, August 1, 1907, p. 92; New York *Evening Post* quoted in *Idaho Statesman*, August 4, 1907, p. 10.

[14] Mark Sullivan, *Our Times, The United States 1900-1925*, Vol. III (New York: Charles Scribner's Sons, 1930), pp. 495-496.

crime, sabotage, or other methods of violence as a weapon of the working class to aid in its emancipation shall be expelled from membership in the Party."[15] Not only did this clause exclude Haywood's radical followers from the party, but later the same year Haywood himself was ousted from the national executive committee of the party by a recall vote.

Another explanation of the effect of the Haywood trial on society appears in *The Good Years* by Walter Lord.

> Actually, the verdict took the wind out of the radicals' sails, restoring a wavering faith in capitalism. For months the left-wing press had driven home the point that Haywood couldn't get a fair trial under the capitalist system of government—and now he was acquitted. . . .
>
> So the law of the land was the same for everyone. And the law alone was enough to win justice. There were still many thousands who believed in a basic conflict, but surely even the most left-wing political groups included men who now believed that basic change could be won within the law.
>
> Millions more—the vast majority of the labor movement—actually veered to the right. The I. W. W. lost its magic. For the next twenty-five years, the course would be set by Gompers and his 'pure and simple unionism.'[16]

Idaho Yesterdays, the journal of the Idaho Historical Society, in reviewing this book implies that Lord has made a significant contribution "in establishing the national importance of this local event."[17] In reality, Mark Sullivan had said much the same thing as Lord in his book published thirty years earlier, and the national significance of the Haywood trial was recognized by contemporary newsmen, e. g., the *Denver Times* called it a "national crisis,"[18] as well as by later writers. It should also be noted that Lord's generalization about the IWW losing "its magic" may not be as tenable as his other conclusions, inasmuch as the IWW did not begin to expand aggressively until Haywood and St. John were free to lead it.

---

[15] Quoted in Perlman and Taft, *op. cit.,* p. 285.

[16] Walter Lord, *The Good Years* (New York: Harper and Brothers, 1960), pp. 178-179.

[17] *Idaho Yesterdays,* Spring, 1960, p. 31.

[18] Quoted in *Idaho Statesman,* August 1, 1907, p. 4.

If society had a vested interest in the trial, in terms of the stability and responsibility of the labor movement, then the results of the trial must have been, to use James Hawley's words, "worth the effort that had been made" in spite of the fact that large sums of money were spent without obtaining a conviction. A total of $95,000 was spent by the state of Idaho, with the Pinkerton Agency receiving $30,000, Hawley also getting $30,000, and Borah receiving $5,000.[19] This sum created a heavy burden of debt for the state. But as an investment in a better society, the Haywood trial yielded far greater dividends than the much more expensive Colorado labor war of 1903-04.

The Haywood trial also had an effect on the disposition of the other cases related to it, and on the men involved in these other trials. Charles Koelsch, as prosecuting attorney of Ada County, had been engaged in trying several defense witnesses for perjury and several defense agents for embracery, or attempted influence on prospective jurors. After the Haywood trial he dismissed the remaining cases, largely because Judge Wood "nagged" him to.[20] Judge Wood, as previously noted, was not a popular man in Boise or in Idaho after the trial. He faced not only vilification by Governor Gooding, but the slander of widespread rumors that he had been bribed. He remained as district judge to conduct the Pettibone and Orchard trials, but left the bench shortly thereafter with his career virtually ruined.[21] Public opinion in Idaho did not forgive or forget Wood's instructions to the Haywood jury, particularly after it became known that he believed that Orchard was telling the truth and that Haywood was guilty.

The issue of Steve Adams' guilt remained unsettled. He was tried again in North Idaho in the fall of 1907 with Darrow leading

---

[19] *Capital News,* August 2, 1907, p. 1. Comparable figures for the defense are not available, but as of the 1907 Western Federation of Miners convention in June, the defense had spent about $73,000. The firm of Richardson and Hawkins got $17,500, Darrow received $14,500, and Nugent $22,700. The large amount going to Nugent apparently included the money for Wilson, Whitsell, Miller, and perhaps Breen. These figures were reported in the *Statesman,* June 17, 1907, p. 1, and were quoted from the *Denver Post* which had used the WFM annual report as its source.

[20] Conversation with Charles Koelsch, Boise, Idaho, August 1, 1960.

[21] Claudius Johnson, *Borah of Idaho* (New York: Longmans, Green and Co., 1936), p. 83.

the defense and Hawley the prosecution. The trial resulted in another deadlocked jury. Some of the witnesses whom the state had hoped to use in this trial could not be located, and there was some feeling that these people were concerned for their own safety after hearing the disclosures of the Haywood trial. The failure to convict Adams meant that the state had again lost the chance to offer Adams immunity or leniency in return for the use of his confession in the remaining trials. Nevertheless, the state went ahead with the trial of George Pettibone in December of 1907. Hawley, the chief prosecutor, was aided again by Senator Borah who returned from Washington for the trial. Darrow headed the defense, but he was forced to drop out of the trial because of a serious ear infection. With Darrow out of the picture, the local defense attorneys, Wilson, Nugent, and Breen—remembering the incriminating defense case in the Haywood trial—offered no evidence and waived argument. It was a wise strategy; the jury did not believe Orchard, and Pettibone was acquitted. The charges against Moyer were then dropped. Incidentally, Harry Orchard told Jess Hawley that he believed Pettibone would eventually make a death-bed confession, if he could be kept away from the "protection" of the Western Federation of Miners.[22] But Pettibone returned to Denver where he died the next year without ever confessing.

The Haywood trial was, of course, only one of the five Idaho trials against Western Federation men in 1907-08. Chronologically it was the second trial, but in order of importance it was paramount. It captured the public fancy far more completely than the trials of Adams, Pettibone, and Orchard. It seems safe to conclude that no other American trial of that decade or of the Progressive Era approached the Haywood trial in significance and public interest.

It is not difficult to understand the importance of the process of communication during the trial, in making the case significant and interesting to the American public, and in aiding the jurors to reach their decision. The newspapers of 1907 devoted great

[22] Jess Hawley, typewritten manuscript, "Notes on Haywood," 1947, pp. 19-20.

amounts of space to the trial, and their accounts included detailed descriptions of evidence, of testimony, of the personnel of the case, as well as some remarkably good rhetorical criticism. To a degree inconceivable in the second half of the twentieth century, these newspapers captured the flavor of the oral tradition of communication. The original purposes of rhetoric, the various strategies of persuasion, even the classical canons of criticism were incorporated into vivid journalistic descriptions of the trial. The language of the writers was directed toward twentieth-century readers, but the techniques they described were as old as man's system of justice and forensic disputation. In a sense, every report of the trial was a rhetorical analysis. Yet the audience—in the courtroom, or through the pages of newspapers—could make critical judgments of their own. And regardless of which side an auditor or reader favored, he could still enjoy any speech as, what the *Statesman* called, "an oratorical treat," even though he might disagree with the point of view.

The jury, of course, knew nothing of this reporting and criticism, and yet they were the ultimate rhetorical critics, since they were the men who determined what the *effect* of the courtroom communication would be. One key effect of the courtroom speaking was to give to the broad issues of the trial a clear focus and a proper definition. With prosecution and defense both employing highly effective jury pleaders, and with credible testimony and substantial proof going into the record for both sides, something close to the real truth must have emerged in the courtroom. Intelligent jurors and listeners, as well as the larger audience of newspaper readers, must have realized that both sides in the long labor struggle had acted unwisely, that the hopes and aspirations of both sides were legitimate and worthy, that the states of Idaho and Colorado had been driven to harsh action by the inability of the miners and mineowners to bargain peacefully, and that the whole Steunenberg affair was part of a labor disturbance, not a class war. The jury seemed to regard the case as purely an Idaho murder trial, not as a chance to redress all the wrongs committed by or against the Western Federation of Miners in Colorado.

Although each side in the Haywood case made a skillful and effective presentation, there were still significant omissions and weaknesses which are difficult to explain. The state's case generally was as thorough as the circumstantial evidence permitted, but there were key moments of the prosecution presentation that lacked aggressiveness and persistency. Fred Miller, the Spokane attorney who knew better than anyone else the circumstances of Orchard's sustenance in Caldwell by the WFM, returned to Boise during the trial but was never called by the state to testify. Other bits of seemingly useful circumstantial evidence, as we have seen, were overlooked by the state. Furthermore, Haywood and Moyer were treated with dignity on the witness stand; neither Moyer's burglary conviction or Haywood's infidelity to his invalid wife were brought out to weaken the credibility of the two men. The jury found them likable enough, and as Clarence Darrow pointed out, "Jurymen seldom convict a person they like, or acquit one they dislike."[23]

The defense, too, weakened its position neeedlessly. The greatest shortcoming of the defense case was its inconsistency. Darrow and Richardson could not agree on a single approach, and each man had internal inconsistencies within his own argument as well. The defense case varied from a predominantly legal case of insufficient corroboration to a counter-accusation of guilt levied at an alleged mineowner-militia-Pinkerton conspiracy, from impeachment of Harry Orchard as a liar to a plea of admission and justification for Bill Haywood. Neither Richardson's attempts to break down Orchard's story nor Darrow's efforts to introduce the issue of socialism were successful strategies. Under the circumstances, it is remarkable that the defense's case had any integrity whatsoever.

Of the four attorneys, perhaps James Hawley was the most successful in his summation argument, in terms of making the best use of the resources of evidence available to him, in adapting to the immediate audience, and in using rhetorical techniques consistent with his own relationship to the jury. His thorough, dispassionate, chronological review of the events and the evidence

[23] Quoted in Edwin H. Sutherland, *Principles of Criminology* (Philadelphia: J. B. Lippincott Co., 1934), p. 258.

structured the significant issues of the trial in such a way that the three following speakers could pursue specific topics without the jury losing sight of the relationship of these topics to the total mass of evidence. Hawley's homely style, his conversational manner, and his dignity all combined with his obvious sincerity to create effective and empathic communication. Above all, his enormous ethical appeal to the jurors gave Hawley a persuasive advantage not possessed by any of the other attorneys.

Edmund F. Richardson apparently was the most versatile speaker among the four lawyers. In the Haywood trial he was responsible for the best legally documented plea before the court. He also gave to much of his closing argument a homeliness and a reasonableness similar to that of Hawley's argument. In addition, he gave his audience perhaps the most polished forensic oratory of the trial. But, he also had moments of glaring inconsistency, and the final session of his argument must have been some of the least effective persuasion of the four summations. Richardson's greatest difficulty was Darrow; had the Denver attorney been free to utilize his own ideas more fully, his role in the Haywood verdict might have been more successful and more easily recognized today.

Clarence Darrow's speaking in the Haywood trial seems to have violated all of the precepts of rhetoric, plus some of Darrow's own notions of jury pleading. He picked out, as the object of his scorn, one of the most universally loved men the state of Idaho has ever produced. He introduced the extraneous issue of religion into the trial, then proceeded to attack the Christian doctrines of repentance and salvation. He talked class warfare to men who knew little of such questions. He made it clear that he did not think much of farmers, and then asked these farmers to free Bill Haywood because he was a victim of capitalist greed, something he said the farmers knew nothing about. But in spite of his defective strategy, to Darrow must go the laurels for identification with humanity and for the common touch. Although his ideas seemed badly conceived for his audience, his treatment in style and delivery of these ideas was masterful. His use of pathos was particularly effective: Haywood's invalid mother, his invalid wife, his child, plus Darrow's tears made a case that even the most convincing prosecution evidence might have had trouble defeating.

Perhaps William E. Borah was not as enthusiastic about this case as he might have been. Borah was absorbed in his own legal difficulties; in addition, some writers have suggested that Borah thought the Haywood prosecution was a mistake from the beginning. In any event, the Senator did not seem to have his heart in his case. His summation speech was, at its best, a lofty appeal to duty and civic responsibility, but, in its weaker moments, no more than an ordinary re-examination of certain evidence. His attempts at consubstantiality were hampered by abstractness of language and by an exhibitory, rather than a communicative, delivery. Borah had a considerably narrower purpose than had Hawley in arguing the guilt of Haywood. But in leaving out much of the Colorado testimony, Borah denied himself the very evidence that was needed to show the criminal nature of the alleged conspiracy, which, with only the circumstances of the Steunenberg affair as proof, looked innocent enough.

There were other persuasive forces in the courtroom in addition to the four lawyers and their witnesses. Unquestionably, Judge Wood's charge to the jury was a factor in the verdict, whether that verdict is viewed as one based on the instructions, or as one based on human passions and fears rationalized as conforming to the instructions. It has been suggested by MacLane and Davis that Judge Wood believed the jurors would return a guilty vote, and that he made the instructions so demanding in order to avoid any reversal on appeal. If this is true, Judge Wood's failure to gauge correctly the intentions of his inscrutable jurors should be considered significant in assessing the communications within the courtroom.

The courtroom itself may have communicated much to the jury; the crowded room indicated the importance which the public assigned to the case. Although the jury could not read newspaper accounts of the trial, most of them must have read some of the excited pre-trial acounts which described the explosiveness of the situation. According to Robertson, the jurors were aware that the courtroom spectators were generally pro-Haywood; whether they were aware of the gunmen of both sides in the room is not clear. But the traditional references in the summation speeches to the importance of the case were somewhat unnecessary for this jury; they knew from sitting for ten weeks in such a charged atmosphere that their decision would mean much to many people.

The jury may have been frightened. Some evidence suggests that they were. But there is little evidence to show that they would have otherwise voted to convict Haywood. Only one account of the deliberations—that of Powell—reported that the jurors all thought Haywood guilty. No other account even mentions six of the original eight who voted for acquittal. Only Gilman, Gess, Powell, Sebern, Burns, and Robertson ever expressed—in the jury room or afterward—any doubts about Haywood's innocence. The others apparently were convinced that Haywood was innocent, or at least that he should be acquitted. Therefore, it would appear that even without any possible intimidation as an influence on the jury, a conviction would not have been attained.

There remain in the Haywood case some unanswered—and perhaps unanswerable—questions. This condition probably would be true of any great and controversial jury trial. But there also remains the inescapable feeling that everything turned out for the best, something that cannot be said of all such cases. It is frightening to consider what might have happened if Haywood had been convicted. It is reassuring to note that his acquittal served two social purposes: first, it exposed the violence and brutality of labor-management relations in the West as effectively as a conviction would have done, and second, it repudiated the charge that a laboring man could not get justice before the law, an allegation that Haywood's conviction would have seemed to support. The interests of American society were thus well served by the trial and acquittal of Haywood. In the final analysis, this was true only because the facts and issues of the case were so effectively communicated within and beyond that Boise courtroom in the summer of 1907.

BIBLIOGRAPHY

Unpublished Materials

Cobb, Calvin. Scrapbook. In Idaho Historical Society.

Graduation Program, San Francisco City College, 1867. In Hawley papers, Idaho Historical Society.

Hawley, Jess. "Notes on Haywood." In possession of James H. Hawley (Jr.) (Typewritten mss.)

Hawley, James H. Speech dedicating the Steunenberg Memorial, December 11, 1927. In Hawley papers, Idaho Historical Society. (Typewritten mss.)

Transcript of the Haywood Trial. Idaho Historical Society.

Confessions of Harry Orchard and Steve Adams. Paraphrased version by James H. Hawley. In Hawley papers, Idaho Historical Society. (Duplicated.)

Pinkerton Agency Reports, January 1906 to August 1907. Idaho Historical Society. (Duplicated.)

Rockwell, I. E. "James H. Hawley." In possession of James H. Hawley (Jr.) (Typewritten biographical mss.)

Smith, Robert Wayne. Unpublished research notes. In possession of R. W. Smith.

Correspondence

Borah, William E. Letter to William N. Borah, May 28, 1907.

Borah, William E. Letter to Jonathan Bourne, July 6, 1907.

Borah, William E. Letter to "Grier," June 20, 1907.

Carlin, William P. Letter to Assistant Adjutant-General, Department of the Columbia, July 26, 1892. Quoted in House Report 1999, 56th Congress, 1st Session.

Coleman, Mrs. Oral Sebern. Letters to the author, August 19, 1960, and April 10, 1961.

Connolly, C. P. Letter to William E. Borah, September 12, 1907.
Drake, James F. Letter to William E. Borah, undated [1907].
Hawley, James H. Letter to Jacob Fillius, July 22, 1907.
Hawley, James H. Letter to Frank H. Parker, July 22, 1907.
Hawley, James H. Letter to Jacob Fillius, July 28, 1907.
Hawley, James H. Letter to C. D. Goodwin, July 28, 1907.
Hawley, James H., (Jr.) Letter to the author, June 15, 1960.
Haywood, William D. Letter to *New York World,* June 17, 1904. Quoted in Senate Document 122, 58th Congress, 3rd Session.
Roosevelt, Theodore. Letter to William Henry Moody, March 26, 1906. Letter to James S. Sherman, October 8, 1906. Letter to Honore Jaxon, April 22, 1907. Letter to Whitelaw Reid, July 29, 1907. In Morison, *Letters of Theodore Roosevelt.*
Steunenberg, Frank. Letter to Secretary of War Elihu Root, October 10, 1899. Quoted in House Report 1999, 56th Congress, 1st Session.
Wells, Bulkeley. Letter to Maurice Corbett, May 23, 1907.

Court Cases

Andres v. United States, 333 U. S. 765.

Horn v. State, 73 Pacific 705.

In re Boyle, 57 Pacific 706.

In re Corcoran, 59 Pacific 19.

Pettibone v. Nichols, 203 U. S. 111.

Public Documents

Boyce, Edward. *Crime of the Century, Account of Idaho Infamy.* 56th Congress, 1st Session, Senate Document No. 25.

Coeur d'Alene Labor Troubles. 56th Congress, 1st Session, House Report 1999.

Communication Relative to Reservation of Lands in Fort Sherman Military Reservation in View of Contemplated Use of Such Lands in Connection with Irrigation Works. 58th Congress, 3rd Session, Senate Document No. 91.

Kennedy, J. L. *Paper Relating to Labor Troubles in Idaho, Reply by Kennedy to Charges Made Against Him by Edmund* [Edward] *Boyce.* 56th Congress, 1st Session, Senate Document No. 42.

Labor Disturbances in the State of Colorado from 1880 to 1904, Inclusive. 58th Congress, 3rd Session, Senate Document No. 122.

Mine Owners' and Operators' Association, Cripplecreek [*sic*], *Colo. Statement, Pertaining to Matter Contained in S. R. 50.* 58th Congress, 2nd Session, Senate Document No. 86.

Report of H. C. Merriam on Miners' Riots in Idaho. 56th Congress, 1st Session, Senate Document No. 24.

Report of H. C. Merriam on Miners' Riots in Idaho. 56th Congress, 1st Session, Senate Document No. 142.

Report of the Industrial Commission. Washington: Government Printing Office, 1901.

Western Federation of Miners. Statement of Federation in Answer to Statement of Mine Owners in Colorado Relating to Labor Difficulties in State. 58th Congress, 2nd Session, Senate Document No. 163.

NEWSPAPERS

Boise *Evening Capital News*. 1907.
Boise *Idaho Daily Statesman*. 1906-1908.
Denver News. 1911.
New York Times. 1907.
Portland Oregonian. 1892, 1899, 1906-1907.

PAMPHLETS

Hawley, James H. *Arguments Presented in Favor of Commutation at the Hearing Before the Pardon Board of the State of Idaho in the Matter of the Application of Harry Orchard, Held in the Governor's Office, Nov. 13, 1922.*

Koelsch, Charles F. *The Haywood Case.* Boise: Idaho Mining Association, 1946.

Tamiment Institute Library. Bulletin No. 25, *The State of Idaho vs. William D. Haywood.* New York. January-February, 1960.

Wood, Fremont. *The Introductory Chapter to the History of the Trials of Moyer, Haywood, and Pettibone.* Caldwell, Idaho: The Caxton Printers, 1931.

ARTICLES IN PERIODICALS

Baker, Ray Stannard. "The Reign of Lawlessness," *McClure's Magazine,* May, 1904.

"Border Spirit in the West," *American Magazine,* July, 1907.

Braden, Waldo W. "The Bases of Wm. E. Borah's Speech Preparation," *Quarterly Journal of Speech,* February, 1947.

Braden, Waldo W. "William E. Borah's Senate Speeches on the League of Nations, 1918-1920," *Speech Monographs,* Research Annual, Vol. X, 1943.

"Confession of Harry Orchard," *Current Literature,* July, 1907.

Connolly, C. P. In *Collier's* magazine: "A Little Drama Out in Idaho," December 7, 1907; "Moyer-Haywood Case: The Story of the Idaho Mining Troubles," May 11, 1907; "The Moyer-Haywood Case: The Murder and the Arrest of Orchard," May 18, 1907; "The Moyer-Haywood Case: The Kidnapping," May 25, 1907; "The Moyer-Haywood Case: Harry Orchard and his Story," June 22, 1907; "The Moyer-Haywood Case: The Colorado Labor War," June 29, 1907; "The Moyer-Haywood Case: The Colorado Labor War," July 6, 1907; "The Moyer-Haywood Case: The Colorado Labor War," July 20, 1907; "The Moyer-Haywood Case: What Has Been Brought out in Haywood's Trial," July 27, 1907; "Presidential Possibilities: Borah of Idaho," July 31, 1915.

Davenport, Walter. "The Man Who Grew Up," *Collier's,* September 10, 1932.

"Effects of the Haywood Verdict," *Current Literature,* September, 1907.

French, George E. "The Coeur d'Alene Riots, 1892," *Overland Monthly,* July, 1895.

Grant, Luke. "Haywood Trial: A Review," *Outlook,* August 24, 1907; "Idaho Murder Trial," *Outlook,* April 6, 1907.

Hard, William. "The Western Federation of Miners," *Outlook,* May 19, 1906.

"Haywood's Acquittal," *Nation,* August 1, 1907.

"Haywood's Trial," *Outlook,* June 22, 1907.

"History of the Case," *Current Literature,* June, 1907.

Hochmuth, Marie. "Burkeian Criticism," *Western Speech,* Spring, 1957.

Kissane, Leedice. "Steve Adams, The Speechless Witness," *Idaho Yesterdays,* Fall, 1960.

Johnson, Kendrick. "Trial of 'Big Bill' Haywood," *The Nevada State Bar Journal,* July, 1959.

Maloney, Martin. "Forensic Speaking of Clarence Darrow," *Speech Monographs,* Vol. XIV, 1947.

"Moyer-Haywood Trial," *Outlook,* April 6, 1907.

Orchard, Harry. "Confession and Autobiography of Harry Orchard," *McClure's Magazine,* July, August, September, and November, 1907.

Munsterberg, Hugo. "The Third Degree," *McClure's Magazine,* October, 1907.

"Professional Assassin," *Outlook,* June 15, 1907.

"Roosevelt and the Moyer-Haywood Trial," *Outlook,* May 4, 1907.

Scheinberg, Stephen. "Theodore Roosevelt's 'Undesirable Citizens'," *Idaho Yesterdays,* Fall, 1960.

Turner, George Kibbe. "Actors and Victims in the Tragedies," *McClure's Magazine,* September, 1907.

Warman, Cy. "Story of Cripple Creek," *Review of Reviews,* February, 1896.

White, William Allen. "The Lone Lion of Idaho," *Collier's,* September 12 1925.

Whitehead, A. E. "The Oratory of William Edgar Borah," *Quarterly Journal of Speech,* October, 1946.

ARTICLES IN COLLECTIONS

Borah, William E. Summation Speech in Idaho v. Paul Corcoran, in Hicks, Frederick C., Editor. *Famous American Jury Speeches.* St. Paul: West Publishing Co., 1925.

Braden, Waldo W. "The Political Speaking of William E. Borah," in Reid, Loren, Editor. *American Public Address, Studies in Honor of Albert Craig Baird.* Columbia, Missouri: University of Missouri Press, 1961.

Hawley, James H. "Idaho's Territorial Governors—A Reminiscence," in French, Hiram T. *History of Idaho.* Vol. I. Chicago: Lewis Publishing Co., 1914.

Maloney, Martin. "Clarence Darrow," in Hochmuth, Marie, Editor. *A History and Criticism of American Public Address.* Vol. III. New York: Longmans, Green and Co., 1955.

Rahskopf, Horace G. "The Speaking of Clarence Darrow," in Reid, Loren, Editor. *American Public Address, Studies in Honor of Albert Craig Baird.* Columbia, Missouri: University of Missouri Press, 1961.

Thompson, John Charles. "The Hanging of Tom Horn," in Brayer, Herbert C., Editor. *1945 Brand Book.* Denver: Westerners Denver Posse, 1946. Quoted in Botkin, B. A. *A Treasury of Western Folklore.* New York: Crown Publishers, Inc., 1951.

Whitehead, A. E. "William E. Borah," in Hochmuth, Marie, Editor. *A History and Criticism of American Public Address.* Vol. III. New York: Longmans, Green and Co., 1955.

BOOKS

Adamic, Louis, *Dynamite.* New York: The Viking Press, 1931.

Aristotle. *Rhetoric,* Book I. Translated by W. Rhys Roberts. Oxford: The Clarendon Press, n. d.

Barrymore, Ethel. *Memories, An Autobiography of Ethel Barrymore.* New York: Harper and Brothers, 1955.

Borah, William E. *Haywood Trial—Closing Arguments of W. E. Borah.* Boise: The Statesman Shop, n. d.

Brissenden, Paul F. *The I. W. W., A Study of American Syndicalism.* New York: Columbia University, 1920.

Clement, Travers, and Symes, Lillian. *Rebel American: The Story of Social Revolt in the United States.* New York: Harper and Brothers, 1931.

Clementson, George B. *Special Verdicts and Special Findings by Juries.* St. Paul: West Publishing Co., 1905. Quoted in Frank, Jerome. *Courts on Trial.* Princeton, N. J.: Princeton University Press, 1949.

Cole, G. D. H. *A History of Socialist Thought.* Vol. III. London: Macmillan & Co., Ltd., 1956.

Darrow, Clarence. *The Story of My Life.* New York: Charles Scribner's Sons, 1934.

Davis, Oscar King. *Released for Publication.* Boston: Houghton Mifflin Company, 1925.

Faulkner, Harold Underwood. *American Economic History.* New York: Harper and Brothers, 1943.

Filler, Louis. *Crusaders for American Liberalism.* New York: Harcourt, Brace and Co., 1939.

Fine, Nathan. *Labor and Farmer Parties in the United States 1828-1928.* New York: Rand School of Social Science, 1928.

French, Hiram T. *History of Idaho.* Chicago: Lewis Publishing Co., 1914.

Ginger, Ray. *The Bending Cross.* New Brunswick, N. J.: Rutgers University Press, 1949.

Gitlow, Benjamin. *I Confess, The Truth About American Communism.* New York: E. P. Dutton & Co., 1940.

Hammond, John Hays. *Autobiography.* New York: Farrar & Rinehart, Inc., 1935.

Harrison, Charles Y. *Clarence Darrow.* New York: Jonathon Cape & Harrison Smith, 1931.

Hawley, James H. *History of Idaho.* Chicago: S. J. Clarke Publishing Co., 1920.

Haywood, William D. *Bill Haywood's Book.* New York: International Publishers, 1929.

Hobson, C. C. Editor. *The Idaho Digest and Blue Book.* Caldwell, Idaho: The Caxton Printers, 1935.

Holbrook, Stewart. *The Rocky Mountain Revolution.* New York: Henry Holt & Co., 1956.

Horan, James D., and Swiggett, Howard. *The Pinkerton Story.* New York: G. P. Putnam's Sons, 1951.

Jensen, Vernon H. *Heritage of Conflict.* Ithaca, New York: Cornell University Press, 1950.

Johnson, Claudius. *Borah of Idaho.* New York: Longmans, Green and Co., 1936.

Lord, Walter. *The Good Years.* New York: Harper and Brothers, 1960.

MacLane, John F. *A Sagebrush Lawyer.* New York: Pandick Press, 1953.

McConnell, W. J. *Early History of Idaho.* Caldwell, Idaho: The Caxton Printers, 1913.

McKenna, Martin C. *Borah.* Ann Arbor, Michigan: University of Michigan Press, 1961.

Morison, Elting E. Editor. *The Letters of Theodore Roosevelt.* Vol. V. Cambridge: Harvard University Press, 1952.

National Cyclopedia of American Biography. New York: James T. White & Co., 1904.

Olson, Albert S. *The Problem of Proof.* Newark, New Jersey: The Essex Press, 1926.

Orchard, Harry [Albert E. Horsley]. *The Confession and Autobiography of Harry Orchard.* New York: McClure Co., 1907.

Pelton, A. R. *San Luis Valley.* Denver: Carson Hurst and Harper, 1891.

Perlman, Selig, and Taft, Philip. *History of Labor in the United States.* Vol. IV. New York: The Macmillan Co., 1935.

Press Biographies, Representation Men of America. n. p., March-July, 1906.

Sellers, Alvin V. *Classics of the Bar.* Baxley, Georgia: Classic Publishing Co., 1909.

Siringo, Charles A. *A Cowboy Detective.* New York: J. S. Ogilvie Publishing Company, 1912.

Siringo, Charles A. *Riata and Spurs.* Boston: Houghton Mifflin Co., 1927.

Siringo, Charles A. *Two Evil Isms: Pinkertonism and Anarchism.* Chicago: Charles A. Siringo, Publisher, 1916.

Smith, Robert Wayne. *The Coeur d'Alene Mining War of 1892.* Corvallis, Oregon: Oregon State University Press, 1961.

Sprague, Marshall. *Money Mountain, The Story of Cripple Creek Gold.* Boston: Little, Brown and Co., 1953.

Stoll, William T., as told to Whicker, H. W. *Silver Strike.* Boston: Little, Brown and Co., 1932.

Stone, Irving. *Clarence Darrow for the Defense.* Garden City, N. Y.: Doubleday & Company, Inc., 1941.

Sullivan, Mark. *Our Times, The United States, 1900-1925.* Vol. III. New York: Charles Scribner's Sons, 1930.

Sutherland, Edwin H. *Principles of Criminology.* Philadelphia: J. B. Lippincott Co., 1934.

Thompson, Fred. Compiler. *The I. W. W., Its First Fifty Years.* Chicago: Industrial Workers of the World, 1955.

White, William Allen. *The Autobiography of William Allen White.* New York: The Macmillan Company, 1946.

Who Was Who in America. Vol. I, 1897-1942. Chicago: A. N. Marquis Co., 1942.

W. P. A. Writers Project. *Idaho Lore.* Caldwell, Idaho: The Caxton Printers, 1939.

Writings and Speeches of Eugene V. Debs. New York: Hermitage Press, Inc., 1948.

INDEX

All photographs are from the collections of the Idaho State Historical Society.

Between pages 120 and 121:
Harry Orchard: 72-64.1b
Frank Steunenberg: 13
Fremont Wood: 79-2.116
William D. Haywood: 534
James H. Hawley: 60-108.36
Edmund F. Richardson: 79-2.113
William E. Borah: 2296
Clarence Darrow: 79-2.117

Between pages 136 and 137:
Steunenberg bomb: 79-2.111a
Steunenberg house: 71-84.2
Harry Orchard being transferred: 2006
Trial jury: 71-125
Prosecution staff: 2007
Defense staff: 2298
Courtroom scene, Haywood at left: 79-2.111b
Courtroom scene, Orchard at left: 2005